THE PROVINCETOWN SEAFOOD COOKBOOK

by
Howard Mitcham

Introduction by
Anthony Bourdain

Seven Stories Press / Tim's Books
New York • Oakland • London

The cover design is by Jackson Lambert.
The marginal illustrations are by the author.

Library of Congress Cataloging-in-Publication Data

Names: Mitcham, Howard, author. | Bourdain, Anthony, writer of introduction
Title: Provincetown seafood cookbook / by Howard Mitcham ; introduction by
   Anthony Bourdain.
Description: New York : Seven Stories Press/Tim's Books, [2018] | Includes
   index.
Identifiers: LCCN 2018020509| ISBN 9781609808389 (hardcover) | ISBN
   9781609808396 (pbk.) | ISBN 9781609808402 (ebook)
Subjects: LCSH: Cooking (Seafood)--Massachusetts--Provincetown. | Cooking,
   American--New England style. |
   Fisheries--Massachusetts--Provincetown--History. | Provincetown
   (Mass.)--History. | LCGFT: Cookbooks.
Classification: LCC TX747 .M55 2018 | DDC 641.6/92--dc23
LC record available at https://lccn.loc.gov/2018020509

Printed in the United States of America.

9 8 7 6 5 4 3 2

TABLE OF CONTENTS

New Introduction

by Anthony Bourdain

I was never pals with Howard Mitcham. Howard Mitcham never knew my name. If he knew me by sight, it was because I was always hanging around Spiritus Pizza during the bar rush, waiting for my girlfriend (of whom he was quite fond) to get off work. He'd come in after a few drinks at the Foc'sle or the Old Colony or wherever he was doing his drinking in those days. His face would be flushed and he'd be a little unsteady on his feet, and you could hear him over the crowd, but this was normal. Even then, he was a legend.

I knew Howard through his book. This book. Which was presented to me by a friend pretty much the first day I began working as a cook. In the Flagship restaurant, where I'd only recently started what would turn out to be a long, checkered career in the industry, Howard's word was law: baseline technique, first principles when dealing with fish. His haddock amandine was famous up and down the Cape—people would drive down from Boston to eat it at Pepe's (or later, his own eponymous restaurant). We lifted his recipe shamelessly intact.

More important than his recipes, however, and more enduring, was his prose—his attitude toward the humble quahaug, haddock, mackerel, Wellfleet oysters, striped bass, bluefish—the Portuguese fishing families of P'Town and the Cape. He was not a snob—at a time when most cookbooks sounded as if they'd been written by someone in a smoking jacket, while stroking a pet ocelot.

He put his recipes in context. Told you where they came from, what inspired them, convinced you that he loved them and that you should love them too. He was way, way ahead of his time in his embrace of so-called trash fish. And he understood always that the best place to enjoy seafood was on the beach, among friends, in a pretense-free zone, preferably accompanied by many drinks, or at the beloved Cookie's Tap, whose squid stew he appropriated after much experimentation. That's a recipe I still cook today—one that I've gotten a lot of mileage out of over the years.

Like another great food writer, A. J. Leibling, Mitcham understood there is no difference between the joys of a great meal at a three-star Michelin and at a humble fishermen's bar—as long as it's made with love and with pride.

His love for Provincetown shines through every page of this book. It's a true classic, one of the most influential of my life.

I may never have really known Howard Mitcham, but I miss knowing he was out there.

This book is dedicated to
The Fishermen of Provincetown,
Past, Present and Future

and in memory of
John J. Gaspie
Born on the Island of Pico, Azores, August 8, 1884
Died in Provincetown, July 3, 1961

Acknowledgments

The author wishes to thank all his friends who have contributed recipes, ideas and encouragement in assembling the material in this book; if listed individually their names would cover several pages.

Thanks are due to the old Fish and Wildlife Service, Department of the Interior, for the portrait drawings of various fishes; for information on curing and smoking fishery products; and for valuable information obtained from their bulletin (which has now become a classic) *Fishes of the Gulf of Maine*, by Bigelow and Schroeder.

The photos on pages 6 and 8 were made by John Bell from antique glass negatives in his collection, and for their use we are grateful; they are copyright by John Bell and may not be reproduced without his permission.

For all the other old-time photographs of the Provincetown fishing industry we are indebted to the Provincetown Museum, and its curator Eugene Watson and his assistants, Ernest Irmer, Lewis Watson and Mrs. Margaret Mayo, who aided in assembling the photographs from the Museum's collection.

Other original photos for whose use we are grateful and give credit are as follows: John Gregory for the portrait of John J. Gaspie on page 54; William Berardi for the Gaspie portrait on the dedication page, and for other photos on pages 16, 22, and 239. Paul Koch for his photos on pages 18, 34, 37, 241, 264, 269 and the back cover (none to be reproduced without permission). Thanks to Rachel Giese for her "Skully Joe Factory" on page 187, and to Cookie's Tap for the use of the picture of "Frank Cook and his fish" on page 258.

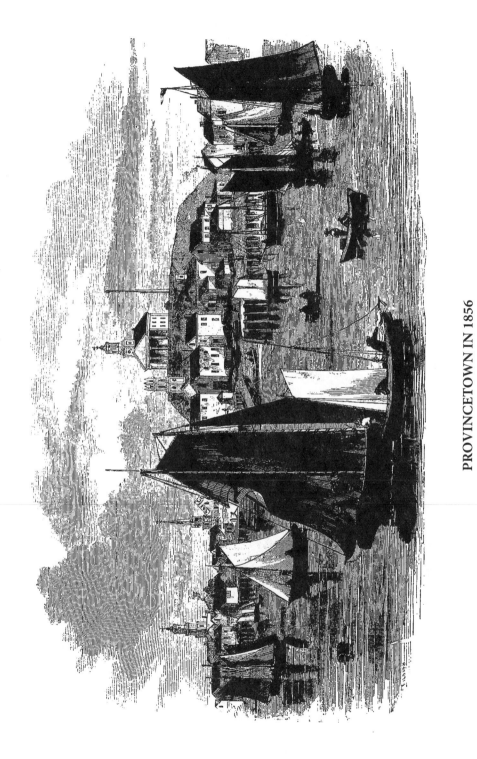

PROVINCETOWN IN 1856

At the height of its fame as a fishing center.

Introduction

P ROVINCETOWN is the birthplace of the commercial fishing industry of the U.S.A. It's the seafood capital of the universe, the fishiest town in the world. Cities like Gloucester, Boston, New Bedford and San Diego may have bigger fleets, but they just feed the canneries; Provincetown supplies fresh fish for the tables of gourmets everywhere. All the fish wholesalers in New York and Boston know that Provincetown fresh fish is the best there is. Our fleet is small but its catch packs a wallop in marketing circles.

From the earliest days of its history Provincetown has been synonymous with fish. Explorers like Champlain and Gosnold in the early 1600's were amazed at the teeming shoals of fish that abounded in our waters. Gosnold described Provincetown Harbor in his journal: "It's a harbour wherein may anchor a thousand ships, and there we tooke great stoare of codfysshes."

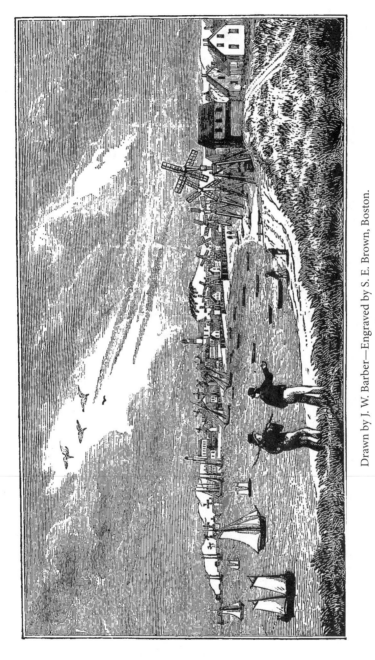

Drawn by J. W. Barber—Engraved by S. E. Brown, Boston.

VIEW OF PROVINCETOWN FROM THE NORTHEAST IN 1840

This is the oldest known print of the town.

He dubbed it forthwith "Cape Cod," and the name stuck. Earlier the Vikings had called it "Wunderstrand" or "Keel Cape," but those names didn't last. Breton, Basque and Portuguese fishermen in the 1500's probably had a summer camp and fish-drying racks on the beach at Provincetown, a convenient spot for curing their catches of cod and haddock harvested both off the Grand Banks of Newfoundland and in local waters. These tough, hardy fishermen were among the best sailors and navigators of the world, and there is a belief that they may have discovered the New World a good many years before Columbus set foot on San Salvador.

No other town was literally spawned by the fishery as was Provincetown. The Cape Tip was one of the first areas in America to be set aside solely as a fishing preserve. The General Court of the Old Massachusetts Bay Colony around 1670 set aside the Province Lands (end of the Cape and the site of Provincetown) to be shared in by all the citizens of the colony who were able to afford the license fees required to participate in the fishery. This was also a protective measure to try to keep out fishermen from the other colonies, and those "furriners"— the French and Portuguese. The first settlement was a bunch of fishermen's shacks on the beach, squatters on the public domain, and even down to today everybody in Provincetown is a squatter of sorts; the only kind of legal deed hereabouts has always been a quitclaim deed.

It was a wild and wooly place, inhabited by a cosmopolitan mob of fishermen, smugglers, outlaws, escaped indentured servants, *filles de joie*, heavy drinkers and roisterers—with no church or law officers; "Helltown" was its general nickname, although this name is more properly applied to a small settlement which was established later out at Herring Cove near Race Point.

These wild goings-on really shocked the solid Christian citizens of neighboring Truro, because from the earliest times they had tried to latch onto the Cape Tip and call it a suburb. Around 1710, they petitioned the General Court in Plymouth to clarify the status of the Cape End "in order that we may know what to do about certain individuals there"; these zealous bigots were all in favor of a Puritanical pogrom to clean the place out. The General Court then established the "Precinct of Cape Cod." This gave Provincetown its independence.

VIEW OF PROVINCETOWN IN 1843

Early artists always showed Provincetowners without any feet. They were buried in the sand.

In those days Provincetown was literally the one and only Cape Cod. The rest of the Cape was Massachusetts Bay Colony. A few years later came incorporation and official christening of the town as Provincetown instead of Helltown, but the roistering was still going on as jolly as ever, and it was the top fishing town of America. The Congregationalists, and later the Methodists, came in and set up churches and partially Christianized the heathen, and when the Portuguese came, they brought the Church of Rome. But no preachers and no credos could completely tame this weird place; down to modern times it has had a wicked, wild streak in it, four hundred years young and half mile wide—and lots of headaches for the forces of law and order and morality.

From the earliest times, cod, haddock and mackerel have been the top fish of Provincetown. Since they are close cousins and look-alikes, the cod and haddock were lumped together as cod in the old days. Provincetown's beaches were once lined with fish drying platforms called "flakes." The curing fish had to be put out each morning at sunrise and taken in at sunset. It was a gruelling chore in which even the women and children had to participate.

These fish flakes were large, flat, horizontal tables, thirty to thirty-six inches high, with tops of triangular wooden slats spaced an inch or so apart to afford drainage and ventilation. The fishing vessels brought in their fares of cod and haddock already split, cleaned and salted down in barrels. These were ferried ashore in dories and carefully washed in the surf on the beach to remove their excess salt. Next they were soaked in new brine pickle in clean barrels for several days. Later they were taken from the brine and dried on the flakes in the sun until they were hard as a bone. This process was called "making fish." And making fish was really the making of Provincetown.

From 1830 to 1850 the town had a thriving saltmaking industry. Windmills lined the beach pumping salt seawater into flat evaporation vats on the shore. Many visitors remarked that the windmills gave the town a Netherlandish look (see the illustration). Most of the salt produced was used locally to cure the fish catch. Almost every square foot of ground in Provincetown which wasn't occupied by a house was covered by the evaporation vats or the fish flakes; they filled back yards, front yards and all the space along the

WASHING FISH IN A DORY AT P.N. WHORF'S WHARF, 1910

The Schooners at the left have just returned from the Grand Banks and are drying out their sails.

beach. Discovery of salt mines in New York State in the 1850's killed Provincetown's saltmaking industry; when the vats were dismantled much of the lumber was used to build new houses. These salt-impregnated timbers were almost impervious to mildew, dry rot and decay. And also to paint; when a man kept slapping paint on his house and it peeled right off he'd eventually give up in disgust and say, "It's a salt works house."

Thoreau eloquently describes the Provincetown waterfront scenes of the 1840's when he paid a visit here.

He said that Provincetown milk had a definitely fishy flavor because the cows hung around on the beach all day eating salt codfish heads. These codfish heads went down in history through a folk song which was popular in those days:

Cape Cod boys, they have no sleds
They slide down dunes on codfish heads.
Cape Cod girls they have no combs
They comb their hair with codfish bones.

WASHING FISH IN THE SURF

Around 1910 the Grand Banks schooner "Lottie Bryant" docked at Matheson's Wharf at the foot of Court Street. The catch was thrown overboard and the crew washed off the excess salt in the surf. They were then transported by wheelbarrow to the flake yards.

This salt cod fishery was well before the days of refrigeration, and most of this product was shipped to Portugal, Spain, South France and Italy, where it was a dietary staple—*bacalhau* to the Portuguese, *bacalao* to the Spanish and *bacala* in Italy. Some of the greatest gourmet dishes ever conceived were constructed by Mediterranean chefs from this early Provincetown product.

Provincetown always maintained a fleet of Grand Bankers, large schooners that sailed on months-long voyages to the Grand Banks of Newfoundland, harvesting the cod and haddock. There was also a fleet of smaller boats that fished on Georges Bank, fifty miles out in the Atlantic from Chatham and stretching northward.

Weather prediction was a primitive thing in those days, and fishing was one of the most hazardous occupations in the world. Fifty-seven natives of Truro were drowned in seven wrecked vessels in the October gale of 1841 (it was probably a tropical hurricane). That wise old seadog Captain Mathias Rich, of Provincetown, was on the way to the fishing grounds, but when he saw the seagulls and other seabirds hightailing it toward shore he turned his boat around and highballed for home. He was off Highland Light when the fury of the tempest struck, and had a hard time making it around Race Point to the safety of Herring Cove. The Truro boats were not so lucky, and they were nearly all swamped.

Provincetown and Truro cemeteries are full of tombstones marked "lost at sea." Shebnah Rich in his great book *Truro, Landmarks and Seamarks* lists the names of hundreds of Truro men who went down to watery graves; this fearful mortality was what led to Truro's becoming a ghost town, almost. Only two families in the whole township today live in the houses built by their ancestors. Provincetown would have gone the same way if the Portuguese hadn't moved in to replace the vanishing Yankees.

The boats used by Cape Cod fishermen were many and varied. At first the Indians, of course, used their canoes. The early colonists were not seafaring people and small shallops, pinnaces, and ketches were sufficient for their close-to-shore fishing enterprises. Thus it went for the first hundred years. But after Provincetown was settled in the eighteenth century and the fishing business began to flourish, larger boats were required. Mellen C. Hatch describes them thus: "After the

THE OLD UNION WHARF

The notch in the center building was for clearance of bowsprits of whaling vessels and large Grand Banks schooners when they were brought up on the marine railway (out of sight behind the building).

Revolution came the pink sterned 'Chebacco boats,' named for the parish of Chebacco (now Essex) in Ipswich, and the square sterned 'Dogbodies,' both with primitive two masted schooner rig without headsails. From these developed the true 'Pinkies,' schooner rigged with bowsprit and jib, and with the characteristic sharp stern and very pronounced sheer of the schooner type. This craft while slow, was burdensome, seaworthy and weatherly; it was inexpensive to build and cheap to run; and until the mid-nineteenth century it was the poor man's fishing boat. There were sloops in the business too, and the schooner was passing through its other early stages of design, such as the roundbottomed high quarterdecked 'Heel Tappers,' to the more conventional types which were almost universally used." These latter swift vessels are described in another paragraph below.

From time immemorial it had been the Provincetown custom to either anchor the boats in the harbor or drag them ashore on the beach, but around 1830 some smart fellow thought up the idea of building a wharf, and when it was finished it worked so well that others followed in rapid succession. For the next fifty years the town went on a wharf-building spree. A bird's-eye view of the town drawn in 1882 shows forty-four wharves, large and small. The largest of these wharves were self-contained communities, beehives of activity; the Central Wharf at the foot of Central Street (behind the present Boatslip Motel) and the Union Wharf (behind Sal Del Deo's Restaurant) were two of the largest. They had marine railways which could haul the largest Grand Bankers and whaling vessels up out of the water for repairs. They each had fish and gear storehouses, a packing shed, a sail loft, a paint shop, a blacksmith shop, grocery, chandler, and hardware stores. The wharf behind Dyer's Hardware Store made a specialty of outfitting whaling vessels, getting them ready for two or three year voyages which would sometimes take them all the way around the world. Many of the wharves, such as Hilliard's Wharf (behind the present Lands End Marine), were covered with fish drying flakes.

A major disaster struck Provincetown on November 26, 1898, the so-called "Portland Gale," the worst storm in the history of the town. The wind reached gale force by 10 o'clock that night, and by 4 A.M. had attained full hurricane force, which lasted for sev-

"MAKING FISH" ON HILLIARD'S WHARF, 1890

eral hours. Nearly all the wharves in town were badly damaged and some of the largest were totally destroyed, including the Central and the Union. The boats in the harbor were either sunk at their moorings or smashed into the beach and piled up like kindling wood. The entire crew of one vessel, five men, froze to death while clinging to the rigging of their sunken craft, only a few feet from the beach; had they only known their location they could have jumped overboard and made it ashore.

TUB of TRAWL

After the Portland Gale, wharf building came to a halt and today there are only four wharves left in Provincetown. But there are plenty of ghosts. As you walk along the beach at low tide and see the rows of rotting stubs of pilings sticking up from the sand and stretching far out into the harbor, it's not very difficult to summon up visions of the old wharves with their multifarious activities in full swing, and somewhere close by, the ghost of some ancient mariner is bound to be singing "Shenandoah."

Provincetown fishermen have used just about every fishing method in the book. In the early days they fished with handlines over the gunwales of their vessels or from dories. Later they fished with long line trawls. A large schooner would have a crew of eighteen to twenty men and about ten dories nesting on the deck. When they reached the fishing grounds, the dories would be launched, two men to the boat, one to fish and one to row. The long line trawls with baited hooks every six feet were coiled in tubes in the bottom of the dory, to be played out as the dory moved along, and later to be hauled in. This trawling was the standard method of fishing for groundfish, cod, haddock, flounder and the like until well into the twentieth century; it was the method used in the Georges Bank and Grand Bank fisheries. It was a dangerous business. The dories had to stay within sight of the mother ship; if a sudden fog or storm came up and they couldn't find their ship, they could be lost forever. Each dory was equipped with a large conch shell horn for the men to blow in case they became lost in the fog. The mother vessel was also equipped with fog horns. The faithful horns saved many lives, but at the end of each year the records would show the names of several fisherman and the brief notation "lost in a fog."

S.O.S.!

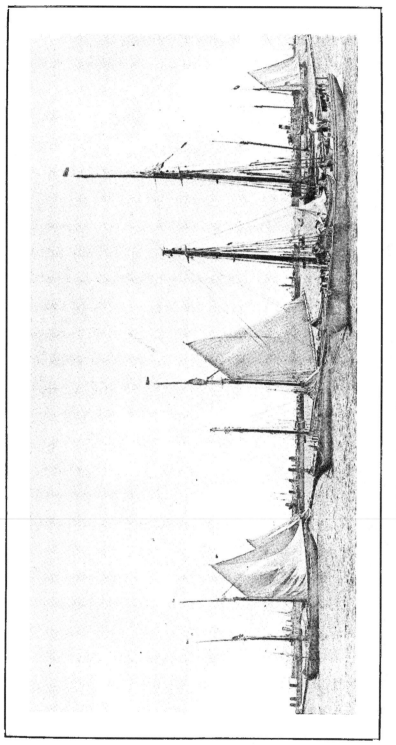

"FRESH FISHING" SCHOONERS AT ANCHOR

Seining was the standard method for catching mackerel and other surface swimming school fish. Gill netting was also popular; when the fish poked his nose through the mesh of the net, it caught him by the gills and he was done for.

When the railroad came to Provincetown in 1873 it created a revolution in the fishing industry; what was called the "fresh fishery" came into being. The boats could sail to Stellwagen Bank north of Race Point, or to Georges Bank, fill their holds with fresh fish, bring it to Town Wharf and ship it out on the train; it would be on sale the next day, sparkling fresh, in the markets of New York and Boston. This was when Provincetown fresh fish came into its great fame. The boats used in this fishery had to be very fast, and as the design of the Provincetown fishing schooner was perfected, they became the swiftest things under sail in America. They could outsail Commodore Vanderbilt's yachts. As they raced with one another on the return from the fishing grounds to Provincetown's Railroad Wharf or to the "T" Wharf in Boston, it produced some of the greatest contests in the history of sailing. But it was just everyday work for them, and none of the details were recorded. The captain whose boat caught the most fish and got them back the fastest was called "The Killer," and there was great competition (and sometimes skullduggery) among crews and boats to achieve and maintain this title. The "Killers of Provincetown" were famous up and down the Atlantic Coast as the best sailors and the best fishermen in the business. I met the last of these "Killers" when I first came to Provincetown, Captain Frank "Vardee" Gaspa, of the schooner *Valerie*. He was over eighty years old, but he had the proud bearing of a prince of the blood; he smoked good Havana cigars and drank the best French brandy. He had dashing handlebar moustaches in his younger days, and it didn't take much stretch of the imagination to see him back in 1915 when he was the high-line "Killer": dressed in a white linen suit and a Panama hat, he would casually stroll into the Parker House in Boston and order a champagne and oyster supper for his crew; hadn't they, by a full twenty minutes, beaten the *Jessie Costa* to the "T" Wharf that very afternoon?

Speaking of these schooners, Mellen C. M. Hatch said: "The Massachusetts fishing schooner was, at the turn of the twentieth century, as fine and able a sailing craft as ever put to sea. Perfec-

GIANT BLUEFIN TUNA IN THE HOLD OF A TRAPBOAT

tion in design, in construction, and in handling made them what they were, and their everyday performance in the usual routine of their work has never been excelled by anything afloat under sail.

They rank on even terms with the clipper ships as the ultimate expression of the maritime genius of America." And Provincetown was the home port of the best of them.

Trap fishing was almost an industry unto itself and the trapboat men were a proud and hardy bunch. Up until a few years ago you could count a dozen large weirs or traps off the shore in Truro, in Provincetown Harbor, and on the outside by Wood End and Herring Cove. These traps were nets on poles so arranged that schools of fish swimming along were directed by a guide net into a central pocket or "bowl" from which they could not escape. The trapboat would move alongside the loaded trap and the crewmen, by pulling on a rope called a "jilson," would close the bottom of the bowl; then nothing whatever could escape. The bowl was raised out of the water and the fish bailed out and dumped into the hold of the boat. There was no sport in it; it was monotonous hard work for the fishermen involved. They would catch enormous quantities of mackerel, herring, striped bass and other school fish. But things would get really exciting when they began to catch schools of giant bluefin tuna, the famous "horse mackerel." Fish of one or two hundred pounds could be gaffed alive and quickly lifted from the net and pitched into the hold of the boat, but fish of 500 pounds or more were very dangerous and could tear

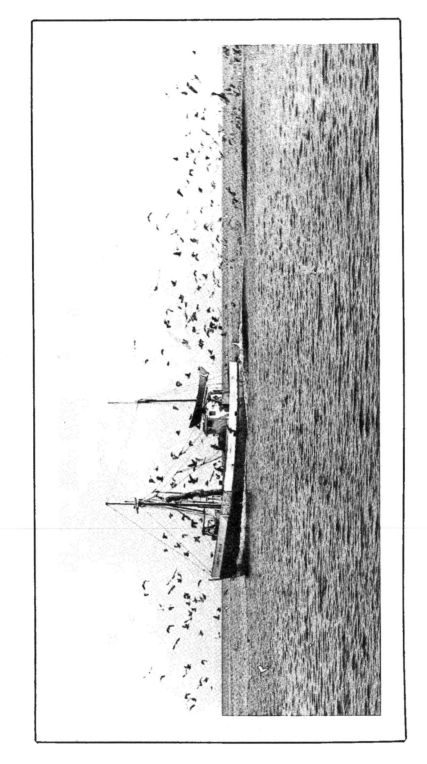

A MODERN DRAGGER

the net to shreds if not handled properly. The accepted method was to shoot them with a shotgun and then haul them aboard.

There were half a dozen large cold storage establishments, or "freezers," in Provincetown in the period 1895 to 1940 to handle the catch of the traps and trapboats. Today the "freezers" are all gone. The trap fishing industry is dying; there are only four traps and one trapboat left, and they will probably disappear soon. The great trapboat captains of the past, such as "Didda" Roderick and "Nonnie" Fields, have all gone to their reward along with most of their crews, and their departure has left a vacuum in the town that will never be filled.

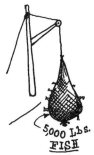

Today's fishing fleet is composed of diesel-powered draggers which pull their bag-like otter trawls across the bottom of the sea. There are about thirty of these vessels in the Provincetown fleet, and when the summer tourists go home the fleet becomes the economic backbone of the town. But economic and ecologic problems have become so acute that no one can say for certain whether the fleet will grow or become extinct; as the catches become smaller and fuel and operating costs rise to astronomic heights, it becomes pretty obvious that the government is going to have to help; it will have to subsidize the fishermen in the same way that it now supports the wheat and cotton farmers.

But as long as the codfish and flounders are with us, things will turn out all right.

Today, codfish still ranks near the top as a money fish for the fleet of Provincetown, but it's a fresh fish market now. A good fresh codfish steak broiled in butter and smothered under a blanket of Portuguese *molho tomate* sauce is treat enough to make any gourmet get excited. Codfish cheeks, tongues and jawbones, when dipped in bread crumbs and fried like chicken, actually look like the leg and thigh of a chicken—and by golly they taste even better (this is also true of haddock cheeks and jawbones). Cod and haddock heads make one of the world's best fish chowders.

One of the saddest chapters of our fouled up modern ecology is the decline and fall of the noble haddock. A few years ago it was the topselling fish in America, and a money maker for Provincetown's fishermen. It is one of the highest gastronomic treats for gourmets. But its numbers have gone into such a tailspin in recent years that

VIEW OF WHARVES IN THE WEST END OF TOWN, 1880

biologists are afraid it will soon be as extinct as the dodo, great auk and passenger pigeon. Overfishing has done it. Foreign factory ships and trawlers and our own beam trawlers (we can't blame the Russians for everything) have swept the Georges Banks so clean that there are not even enough fish left to spawn there, as they did in the past. Man's inhumanity to man is equaled by his inhumanity to nature.

When you eat a haddock in a restaurant today it's a nine out of ten chance that it's a frozen fillet from Norway, but to my tastes even a frozen haddock, if it's cooked right, is more tasty than a lobster. Saute it gently in butter and bury it under a pile of toasted sliced almonds and lemon butter sauce.

The other great fish of the Provincetown trilogy is the mackerel. A fresh-caught Provincetown mackerel split and broiled is one of the best of all seafood treats; its meat is sweet, light and delicate enough to please the most exacting gastronome. As a contrast, brine salt mackerel is strong and high as hell but when you've become initiated to its acridity, it is great fare, especially good for breakfast, with boiled potatoes and Bloody Marys. I could write a whole book about this fish and its title would have to be *Holy Mackerel*. It's a fabulous fish, so plentiful at times that you get tired of it, so scarce at others that you hanker and hunger for it.

In the 1840's and '50's Provincetown was the wealthiest town per capita in New England, and mackerel was one of the cornerstones of this prosperity. In those pre-refrigeration days salt mackerel was the most widely eaten seafood product in America, one of our principal sources of protein, and every small grocery store had its barrel of  salt mackerel standing alongside the cracker barrel (and casting off a reek that you could smell all the way out in the street. Those old-time groceries must have been fragrant things with their medleys of smells: whale oil, mackerel, salt meat, cheeses, hard tack, coffee, kerosene, leather, rope, peppermint, horehound candy and so on. Modern packaging and the supermarket have really murdered the nice smells which gave glamour, mystery and seductiveness to the old-time grocery store).

The plenitude of mackerel was one of nature's greatest bounties for the Cape Tip. Mackerel traveled in enormous schools, so thick you could almost walk across the water on their backs. In the 1840's

CAPTAIN FRANK GASPA
Last of the "Killers."

CAPTAIN "NONNY" FIELDS
Trapboatman

CAPTAIN "DIDDA" RODERICK
Trapboatman

CAPTAIN DAN MORRIS
Truro Shellfish Warden

a school was sighted off the back side of the Cape which stretched all the way from Race Point to Wellfleet, over ten miles, and that's a right smart passel of fish. In 1830 the U.S. mackerel catch was 99 million pounds, but that was chicken feed compared to what was to come later. Eighteen eighty-five was one of the greatest years in mackerel history; the catch in Massachusetts alone was over a hundred million pounds, most of it from the Cape Cod area.

Provincetown had a mackerel fleet of over one hundred schooners, and hundreds of other boats from all over New England made Provincetown Harbor their headquarters during the mackerel season, which lasted from June through October. Thoreau described the unsurpassed beauty of the mackerel fleet as it rounded Long Point with hundreds of sails billowing in the wind.

Whiting, flounders, herring and pollock are among the fresh fish mainstays of today's commercial fishing fleet in Provincetown, and to a limited extent, striped bass, bluefish and giant bluefin tuna. They are all excellent eating. Yellowtail flounder fillets dipped in batter and lightly sauteed in butter are one of Provincetown's gifts to gastronomy. Striped bass steaks broiled in butter are to me the greatest of all fish steaks, and a big old striper stuffed with a dressing loaded with oysters, clams, scallops and shrimp makes for one of the most memorable dinners imaginable.

Yes, yes, yes, no doubt about it, Provincetown is still the fishiest town in the world. It's the gourmet seafood capital of the Atlantic seaboard. The tourists and the overcrowded motels may try to make a summer Coney Island out of it, but they'll never succeed completely. Foremost, first, last and forever it has always been and always will be a fishing village.

PORTUGUESE CREWMEN UNLOADING FISH FROM A GRAND BANKER, 1905

The Coming of the Portuguese

They are *rarae aves,* a strange breed, these Portuguese. Melancholy one moment and singing sad *fados* (fatalistic folk songs), and dancing *camarritas* the next. They can be moribund, taciturn, tight-lipped, pessimistic, fatalistic, or, if something triggers them, they can go into a fiesta mood, singing jolly songs and becoming so talkative you have to hit them with a hammer to shut them up. They have both sensitive taste buds and the iron guts of an ostrich. I used to see the old fishermen around Provincetown drink a fast twelve-ounce glass of muscatel in one swig and chase it with a twelve-ounce stein of beer, one of the weirdest combos that was ever invented. But on a cold winter day, this "highball" had the impact of a sledge hammer, a five minute cure for frostbite, chillblains, arthritis, or any of the other ills which afflict the fisherman.

The Provincetown fisherman knows more profanity in more languages than any other breed in the world, and he can cuss five minutes without saying the same word twice. But he cusses with such a beguiling grace and naivete that he can shout all night on Saturday and go to Mass on Sunday with a conscience as clean as new-washed bedsheets.

God alone knows who the Portuguese are descended from. They are a blend of Phoenicians, Greeks, Romans, Carthaginians, Moors, Vikings, Celts, Iberians, Basques, Gallegos, Spaniards and Jews (most of the Jews of Spain fled to Portugal during the Inquisition). And this potpourri makes for a helluva spice.

No two Portuguese are just alike; each is a character on his own hook, a universe unto himself, which is why they are so damned interesting. The more you study them the less you'll know; a Portygee is a paradox wrapped in an enigma. You could never find two John Gaspies, or two Didda Rodericks, or Frank Cables, or even Colonel Corns.

In the beginning, Provincetown was a campground and summer resort of the Wampanoag Indians. Then the Pilgrims, Puritans and other Yankees came along and killed off the Red Men or absorbed them. Then the Portuguese came along and absorbed the Yankees and everybody else. In Provincetown, Portuguese usually means Azores Islanders. From 1800 to 1850 the whaling captains would sail to the

WHALING VESSEL MOORED AT DYER'S WHARF

The whaling ships brought the first Portuguese to Provincetown.

Azores with skeleton crews, and sign on a bunch of Islands natives to make their full complement. Whaling voyages were so long, the pay so low, and the work so dirty and arduous that the Azoreans were the only ones with guts enough to stand it. When the boats returned to Provincetown, the Portuguese crews would jump ship, put down roots and become fishermen; sometimes they'd have to toil for several years to save passage money to send back for their families.

I don't know why, but many of those Islanders seem to have had no family names before they got here. A man could bear the family name of either his mother or his father, and nomenclature was confused, and many of those who did have names promptly Anglicized them: Cabral became Cable, Pereira was changed to Perry, Gaspar to Gaspie, Rodriguez to Roderick, etc. But names were still a problem; there were so many Joes, Tonys and Manuels among the Santos, Silvas, Souzas, Cabrals and the rest, that the Provincetown Portuguese became, as a matter of necessity, the most prolific and creative inventors of colorful nicknames in the country. Here are samples. Mention any one of these and a native will know immediately the man you're talking about: Louis Ding, Dory Plug and his brother Joe Buckets, Crapoo, Boobah, Canesa, Scarry Jack, Friday Cook, Vardee, Flyer, Boyzine, Sou'wester, Didda, Didit, Squirts, Colonel Corn, Skunk, Bobo, Tarts, High, Blaney, Corky, Hot Dog, Flip, Hamananka, Ducky, Zeke, Pigeon, Hy-Stericks, Barber, Dope, Shag, Peacy, Jazz Garters, Fletas, Flinx, Blue, Iron Man, Casaretta, Burgundy, Parthenon, Manny the Guinea, Rocky, Whitey, Blondie, Below, Slippery, Joe Sax, Meely, Phat, Carp, Pilhasca, Khaki, Tanglefoot, Ty Cobb, Doctor Foo, Popeye, Willy Alley, Hot Times, Goddam, Fall River, Cabbage, Squid, Honka, Squash, Arboo, Shoemaker, Shockers, Beeska, Spinach, Mutt, Pidge, Valero, Cheynee, Four Master, Charlie Mex, Tony Cheroot, Bunny, Sonny, Captain John, Maline, Boozie, Blindie, Jack Ripper, Cull, Doodie, Kaka, Narchie Burr, Jessie Burr and so on till the cows come home.

Transplanting the Azores Islanders to Provincetown was a great step forward because they brought with them their beautifully rambunctious cookery (*cozinha*), and this husky, euphoric cuisine has quietly worked its way into Cape Cod and New England cookery in general. When somebody says, "Saute some onions until they are soft,

UNLOADING THE CATCH

The fish were hauled to the drying yards on wheelbarrows.

add some tomatoes, garlic, a pinch of cominos, etc.," then you can know you're off on a Portuguese kick.

Portuguese cooks are, without a doubt, the most fantastically inarticulate cooks in the world. They don't talk about their food; no Portuguese cook that I know of has ever written down a recipe because they have no measurements of quantities or standards of cooking times. They play by ear and intuition, like Dizzy or Miles blowin' a horn. They're laconic. Ask 'em how long you cook it, and they'll say, "till it's done." I have been observing Portuguese cooks for  twenty-five years and I find that they have the following relative units of measurement: (1) a little, (2) some, (3) a bit more, (4) a lot, (5) plenty, (6) enough. Of course it would have been a little more picturesque if I could have given the original Portuguese words for these measurements. But it's a lot easier to understand the Wampanoag tongue than the Azorean dialect.

Also, the Portuguese are great mumblers; when they don't know an answer or don't want to tell you, they'll give you a mumble and a shrug, which leaves you feeling that you got an answer of sorts, but didn't comprehend it. It's much better to get a friendly mumble than a blank stare and cold silence.

Since the times of Vasco da Gama and Prince Henry the Navigator, the Portuguese have been great voyagers, and though they are generally a rough peasant and fisherman stock, their cooking is as cosmopolitan as any in the world. From the Orient they brought back and used all kinds of exotic herbs and spices: basil, thyme, mint, coriander, cumin *(cominos)*, hot peppers, saffron, allspice, cloves, and garlic.

Grinding poverty has always cursed the Portuguese, especially in the Azores, hundreds of miles from the mainland. They have had  to make shift with whatever materials were at hand. But they always compensated for their adversity with inventiveness. An acute and permanent shortage of fuel led them to become masters of "the simmer"—a long slow cook that never boils or bubbles, and consumes a minimum of fuel and is ideal for thick soups, stews and sauces. Total lack of refrigeration led to perfection of the marinade and heavy use of spices to preserve food. Salt pork and dried codfish are two of the staples of Portuguese cuisine. Their lack of beef, lamb and other

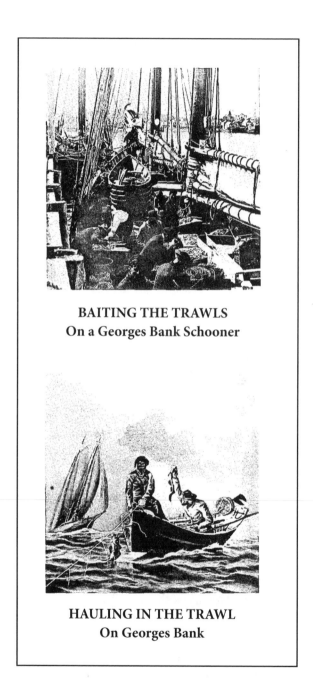

BAITING THE TRAWLS
On a Georges Bank Schooner

HAULING IN THE TRAWL
On Georges Bank

meats forced them to become the world's greatest seafood cooks, and the things they can do with fish and shellfish are almost miraculous. Their two great sausages—linguica and chourico—are among the best sausages of the universe. They are used sparingly to flavor a wide variety of soups, stews and sauces.

When they can afford it, they use olive oil in their cookery, though some prefer lard or vegetable oils. Many Portuguese cooks use garlic and wine very freely and generously; others do not use these elements at all, relying for flavor on herbs and spices. Their favorite vegetables are onions, tomatoes, potatoes, and sometimes garlic. Nine out of ten Portygee dishes start off with onions sauteed in oil, with tomatoes and seasonings added later. This is the famous *molho tomate* (tomato sauce) which could give zest to a pair of old boiled tennis shoes.

Their most famous marinade is the *vinha d'alhos,* pronounced "vinyer thyles"; it literally means "wine of garlic." It's the beautiful spicy garlicky marinade which makes Portuguese food seem like witchcraft or black magic. The stew Macbeth's witches brewed would have been a gourmet's *pot au feu* if the ingredients had been subjected to this Portuguese marination process. One could almost concede that an old dish rag could be made palatable by "galvanizing," which is what the Yankees call the spicy soak, and it's as good a name as any.

In the days before refrigeration *vinha d'alhos* was used to keep fish and meats from spoiling; you could keep a fish fresh in it for several days, likewise pork chops or beefsteaks. And the spices and garlic made the foods taste so good that the system has persisted in spite of the refrigerator. What a beautiful term is "wine of garlic"! To me garlic is the happiest member of the whole vegetable family. I love its flavor and its fragrance. It has many ancient mythical and mystical significances; it's a cure-all for illness and disease, a preserver of good health, a tonic and thickener of the blood, and the ancient Egyptians four thousand years ago knew of its aphrodisiacal qualities.

The simplest vinha d'alhos is two cups of water to one cup of vinegar (pure vinegar would be too sharp) plus salt, crushed black peppercorns, a few crumbled bay leaves, a good many crushed cloves of garlic, a chopped onion and a wide variety of spices and herbs of your own choice, but especially a half teaspoonful of crushed cumin seeds.

HIGH LINE SCHOONER MOORED TO A WHARF IN THE EAST END

Many cooks would use a ten-cent package of mixed pickling spices, plus the cominos. I have found that the small packages of commercial crab and shrimp boil spices, plus the cominos, make a beautiful *vinha d'alhos*.

A more elegant marinade would use a good bottle of white wine instead of water, one cup of vinegar, a package of mixed spices, cominos, a dozen cloves of garlic crushed, a chopped onion, thyme, basil or any other herbs except oregano, which is too strong for this business. Soak your fish fillets or steaks in this mixture for thirty minutes, which is long enough to make them zoom. Too long a soak will soften the flesh of the fish. You can't marinate a fresh mackerel or it will become soft and mushy, but you can marinate cooked mackerel (see the *molho cru* recipe on page **225**).

To cook the fish remove the fillets from the marinade and brush off all the seeds and herbs, dry them with paper towels and broil them, or dip them in batter and saute them gently. Use bacon grease for cooking them because the soaked-up vinegar would cause butter or oleomargarine to curdle. (Marinate pork chops in vinha d'alhos for two or three days and when you cook and serve them you can call it "transcendental pork chops" because they'll be on a higher plane than ordinary pork chops.)

The Portuguese love hot peppers better than anybody under the sun except the Cajuns of Louisiana, or perhaps the Mexicans, Malaysians and Indonesians. I pride myself on being something of a hot pepper aficionado and I really dig the Portuguese *piri piri* hot sauces. There are many *piri piri* sauces but the standard is usually olive oil and hot peppers; to go with our Provincetown seafoods I have developed a *piri piri* of my own which goes thus:

Take two small bottles of pickled "pepper sauce" peppers; red is preferred but the green ones are just as hot or hotter. Pour off the vinegar, take out the peppers and mince them finely, put in a sauce pan. Dice a small can of pimientos and add them to the pan, pour in a bottle of chili sauce, add a half cup of olive oil. Heat slowly and stir gently to emulsify the mixture. If it's not hot enough to suit you add another bottle of pickled peppers chopped, or crushed red pepper seeds. When you spread a blanket of this sauce over a broiled mack-

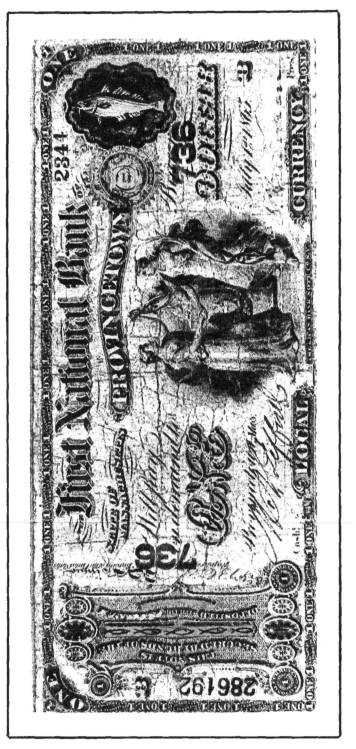

"THE FISH DOLLAR"

It has always packed a wallop in Provincetown's economy

erel, or haddock fillet, or striped bass steak, it's hotter than hellfire, but delicious and you'll never forget it.

It's in the making of those slowly simmered soups and stews that the Portuguese outdo themselves. *Sopa verde* (cabbage soup) and *sopa de couvres* (kale soup) cooked with chourico or linguica sausage are national institutions of the Portuguese. They should be allowed to simmer for at least four hours. Six hours is better, and eight or ten is best of all. It's also a good trick to put a little cabbage in your kale soup and vice versa. These famous soups are first cousin to turnip greens pot likker in which Southerners love to dip their cornpone, but as an old pot likker fancier myself, I am forced to admit that the Portuguese versions are vastly superior.

Portuguese squid stew is so different from anything else that it's not a dish for John Q. Public. Your first dish shocks you; your second numbs you, but around the fifth or sixth dish you begin to realize its distinctiveness. Then you'll thaw out, and from then on, brother, you are hooked. Squids are also good when stuffed with linguica or shrimp or smoked country ham.

The good old musty flavor of smoked pork or country ham is one of the trademarks of Portuguese (or Spanish) cookery and gives it an unmistakable savour. It's like the difference between a Smithfield and an ordinary ham. Something in the slow curing process breaks down the enzymes or introduces bacteria that give the well-cured pork its aroma and flavor, totally different from the uncured salt pork and hams that are forced on us by the supermarkets. This is one of the reasons that it is so difficult to recapture true Portuguese and Spanish flavor in the United States. A little bit goes a long way. Portuguese cooks put a little salt pork in everything but ice cream and malted milks.

Just as the national dish of Spain is *paella* called after the utensil that it is cooked in, so Portugal has its *cataplana*, one of the most formidable weapons in the arsenal of gourmandize. It's basically two skillets hinged, and when folded shut they fit tightly together. After cooking on one side for awhile you can flip it over and cook on the other and all the juices and sauces that were on the bottom will now be on top and will seep downward to saturate the basic ingredients.

Ameijoas na cataplana à la Provincetown (littleneck quahaugs in the shell, cooked in a cataplana with tomatoes, onions, finely chopped

LOW TIDE, 1895

The steeple on the Center Methodist Church was damaged by the Portland Gale in 1898 and had to be removed.

linguica, garlic and a medley of herbs and spices) is one of the most delicious dishes I've ever eaten, and I will be forever grateful to the Portuguese Provincetown lady who introduced me to it. If you can't find a cataplana, you can make do with a skillet with a tight lid, or a Dutch oven pot.

And so-o-o-o, when you give it a long hard look lasting for several years, you can see that the mystique of Portuguese *cozinha* is not mysterious at all. These people simply put their soul into their cooking, and they enjoy the eating of it. What could be ordinary food takes on a magic aura, it's hokus pokus with vittles at its very best. And it helps make old Provincetown one of the best little towns in the western hemisphere.

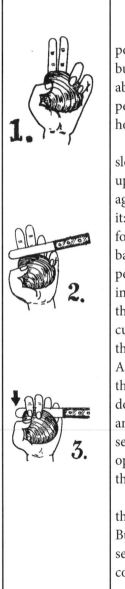

HOW TO OPEN QUAHAUGS

Do not try to open quahaugs with a kitchen knife or a pocket knife; you can end up with a badly gashed hand. You can buy a good clam knife at any hardware store on Cape Cod for about a dollar; these knives have a thin strong edge which readily penetrates the slot between the shells of the quahaug. So here's how to do it:

Lay the quahaug on the palm of one hand with the shell slot facing upward; keep the index finger and the middle finger upright. Take the knife in the other hand and lay the blade against the slot between the shells. Now here is the whole trick of it: you do not exert any pressure with the blade of the knife, you fold the two upright fingers over and press with them against the back of the knife blade; this will cause the front of the blade to penetrate between the shells. Once you have the knife blade well in between the shells, move it backward slightly until the point of the knife is under the top shell; then slant the point upward and cut the two adductor muscles inside the shell. If you do not keep the knife pointing upward, you will split the clam's body in half. After cutting both muscles lift the clam's top shell up, and using the point of the knife, rake the clam's mantle inside the top shell down to the bottom shell. Run the knife under the clam's body and sever the bottom of the adductor muscles. It's now ready for serving on the halfshell or for use in cooking. It is important to open clams over a flat pan which will catch the escaping liquor; this stuff is the best part of the clam.

Of course the simplest way to open quahaugs is to steam them, which is fine if they do not have to be cooked anymore. But for chowders, stuffed clams and other dishes that require a second cooking it is better to use fresh clam meats; too much cooking will destroy the clam's flavor.

CHAPTER I
The Shellfish

THE FIRST PAGES of any Provincetown or Cape Cod cookbook would have to be about quahaugs, *Venus mercenaria*: he's our typical sea creature, and our tastiest gourmet morsel. And be careful of what you call him. South of Massachusetts and Rhode Island, from New York and New Jersey on down to Maryland, they call him a "clam," but in New England clam usually means the softshell steamer clam, *Mya arenaria*, and no real Cape Codder would ever call a quahaug a clam—although he might use the term loosely when speaking of all the burrowing shellfish as a group.

If you scratch a quahaug out of the sand on Provincetown's clam flats you can probably rest assured that the ghost of John J. Gaspie will be watching you from the great beyond. If a still small voice says to you, "That quahaug's too little, put him back!," you'd better do so pronto. As longtime shellfish warden and clam authority extraordinary, he was Mr. Quahaug in Provincetown.

Quahaug is derived from "poquahock," a Wampanoag Indian word. The Indians were fanatical in their admiration of the quahaug;

in the summertime thousands of mainland Indians would migrate to Cape Cod to bask in the sunshine and feed on the shellfish. They used the purple part of the linings of quahaug shells to make "suckanhock" beads, the black money which had twice the value of white money, or "wampum." 'Way out on the western plains early explorers found this bead money in circulation among the Sioux, Chippewas and the like, and much of it was probably minted right here on Cape Cod.

In the early days Provincetown, Truro and Wellfleet had many enormous shell mounds, kitchen middens where the Indians had piled up shells for centuries; one of these near Pilgrim Spring (shouldn't it be called Indian Spring?) covered several acres of ground. The early settlers burned shells to make lime and plaster. This limemaking used enormous quantities of wood and much of the virgin forests that originally covered the lower Cape were consumed in this manner. Even before the Revolutionary War, Truro had passed laws forbidding lime burning, not to save the quahaug shells but the valuable wood lots. These were probably the first forestry conservation laws ever passed in the New World.

If the Indians hadn't taught the Pilgrims how to dig quahaugs they would all probably have starved to death that first hard winter in Plymouth. Ever since that time, especially during depressions, a lot of other folks would have gone hungry except for a bucket of steamed "'hogs." Like the shmoos, they were a self-perpetuating bounty. But only up to a certain point. During the depression of the early '30's, when money was so very very scarce, a barrel (three bushels) of quahaugs would fetch two dollars, so the desperate com-

CHEAP LUCRE   COHOGS

mercial clam muckers raked Provincetown mudflats as clean as a hound's tooth. And to cap it off some sort of epidemic killed off most of the eelgrass which produces the microscopic diatoms on which quahaugs feed. This double disaster made quahaugs so scarce that many people thought they were extinct. But around 1940 the eelgrass began to make a comeback, and so did the quahaugs and so did the dollars. The current wholesale price for a bushel of littlenecks is $34 ($102 per barrel), and they must be purchased from commercial clam farmers or fishmarkets. This is one of the sharpest comebacks of almost any commodity on the market except call girls. From stepchild of the mudflats the lowly quahaug has become the glamour item of the seafood world. Provincetown learned its lesson in ecology the hard way, and there will never again be commercial digging here. In the wintertime each resident family that has the two dollar permit is allowed one ten-quart bucket of quahaugs a week, and they know they're lucky to get that, and they treasure them.

If the quahaug doesn't survive it's not because he ain't tryin'. A mature quahaug two and a half inches long will produce two million eggs per year; an acre of shoreline with an average of twenty two-and-one-half-inch quahaugs per square foot will throw out 800 billion eggs a year. If only a small percentage of these reached maturity there would be enough quahaugs for everybody, but they don't

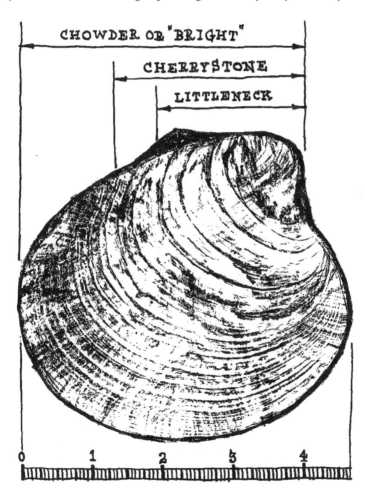

and there just aren't enough quahaugs to go around. Several quahaug farms have opened on the Cape during the past few years but clam farming is a big gamble due to so many complex biological factors. The quahaug will not cooperate unless he has plenty of current bringing him diatoms and plankton for food, and he needs a suitable balance of sand and mud in his bed for comfort. His growing areas must be protected from rough tides and too strong currents which would tend to wash him out of his burrow. And there's the problem of seed. A quahaug farmer has to plant good seed to stock his farm and it is very difficult to obtain. Natural seeding, cashing in on the tremendous number of eggs, has not been perfected yet.

Quahaugs are divided into three classifications according to size, as shown in the illustration on page 41. The small tender littlenecks are the best for general purposes and the cherrystones are close behind. The large "chowders," as the name denotes, are excellent for making chowder; cut them up with scissors or put them through the coarse blade of a grinder.

QUAHAUGS ON THE HALFSHELL

The best of all ways to eat a littleneck or cherrystone quahaug is right off the halfshell. Chill it in the shell, in ice, then insert a clam knife between the shells and sever the adductor muscles, remove the top shell and sever the muscles again under the quahaug's body to make it loose. Apply a little lemon juice and a few drops of Tabasco sauce and wolf it down right off the shell and drink the liquor. This is said to be one of the world's greatest aphrodisiacs. (See page 38 — How to open Quahaugs.)

STEAMED QUAHAUGS

The next best way to eat littlenecks and cherrystones is to steam them. Take a good-sized pot and put a cup of white wine in it, slice a good-sized onion therein and add a three-inch piece of linguica sliced, a teaspoon of fresh ground black pepper and half a teaspoon of crushed red pepper seeds. Put in a ten quart bucket of quahaugs and steam just until the shells are open. Serve in the shells with melted butter on the side, and cups of the broth; this liquor is the most delicious part of the quahaug . . . it is nectar—ambrosia—fit for the Gods on Olympus.

PHIL COOK'S PORTUGUESE QUAHAUG PIE

1 quart quahaug meats, chopped
½ cup quahaug liquor
2 tbsps. linguica, finely chopped

1 lb. linguica (to make liquor)
2 onions, chopped
2 tbsps. flour
crushed red pepper seeds
pie crust

Put the pound of linguica in a pot and cover generously with water. Boil rapidly for thirty minutes. Take out the linguica and store it for future use—it's the pot liquor that you want here.

Saute the onions in a little butter until soft, add the two tablespoons of chopped linguica, add the quahaug meats and the half cup of quahaug juice. Mix it up well, add enough of the linguica pot liquor to just cover the mixture, stir and adjust salt flavor if necessary, add fresh ground black pepper and a very light sprinkling of crushed red pepper seeds. Line a deep pie pan with pie crust (or a skillet if you don't have a deep pan). Pour the mixture into it. Cover with pie crust, brush with milk or beaten egg to glaze it. Punch a few holes with a fork to allow steam to escape. Bake in a preheated 400 degree oven for half an hour or until the top is browned. This is just about as good as Provincetown Portuguese food can get.

PEPPER PICKLED QUAHAUGS

I've always prided myself on my ability to eat hot peppers. I've visited the Tabasco factory in Louisiana and devoured with gusto those flaming little morsels out of which they make the famous sauce, and I survived, in spite of acute Mexican heartburn. But there is a Portuguese red pepper from the island of St. Michael, Azores, growing in a few gardens in Provincetown, that will put anything from Louisiana or Mexico to shame when it comes to sheer unadulterated hotness. One of my Provincetown friends, Bill Fields, sometimes brings me a share of his pepper crop and I use it to make pepper pickled quahaugs, a very foolish item, since only about one person in ten can stand the heat of them; but if you happen to be that one out of ten, you'll love 'em. Here's how to make a quart.

PEPPERS

Make a mild brine by dissolving ½ cup of salt in 2 cups of water, take quart ¾ of fresh shucked quahaugs and quart of ¼ hot fresh Portuguese peppers (cut the stem end off the peppers so the brine can enter), and cook them in the brine for ten minutes. Cool and store in the refrigerator until ready to use. This is a delicious hors d'oeuvre or snack on a freezing cold winter evening.

STUFFED QUAHAUGS I

4 dozen quahaugs	4 medium onions, chopped
1 loaf Portuguese or Italian bread	1 green pepper, chopped
	1 piece celery, chopped
2 tbsps. linguica, finely minced	4 tbsps. fresh parsley, chopped
1 stick butter	½ cup white wine
4 cloves garlic, finely minced	salt and fresh ground black pepper to taste

STUFFED
QUAHAUG

Open the quahaugs with a clam knife and save all the liquor; keep the matching shell halves together. Put the quahaugs through the coarse blade of a grinder or chop them up by hand with scissors. Melt the stick of butter in a skillet and saute the onions, garlic, pepper and celery until soft. Add the parsley and linguica and stir it in well. Add the wine and the clam meats and stir them in, cooking for five minutes longer.

Break the loaf of bread up into small pieces and wet it down with the quahaug liquor. Let it soak a short while and then knead it into a soft paste, free of all lumps; if more liquid is needed to achieve paste consistency, add some white wine. Add this paste to the ingredients in the skillet and mix thoroughly; season with salt and pepper. Stuff the mixture into paired quahaug shells. Close the shells and tie together with several loops of cotton string. Store in the refrigerator until ready to use. To serve, remove the string and the top shell from the stuffed quahaug, brush with melted butter and brown under the broiler. At the end, brush with melted butter again and sprinkle with a few drops of sherry just before serving.

Solemn warning: Don't go getting fancy and adding sage or poultry seasoning or other strong herbs to quahaug stuffing. Give the beautiful creatures a chance to assert their own good flavor.

STUFFED QUAHAUGS II

1 qt. quahaug meats, ground, and their liquor

1/3 bottle dry sherry

2 cups bread crumbs

½ of a small box of saltines, crumbled

½ cup lemon juice

½ lb. butter, melted

½ cup chopped parsley

6 cloves garlic, minced

paprika

Place the ground clams and their liquor in a large bowl, add the bread crumbs, crumbled saltines, lemon juice and sherry. Melt the butter, add garlic to it, add parsley. Mix this up and add it to the clam mixture; stir all the ingredients well. Fill the clam shells with the mixture and sprinkle with paprika. Bake in a preheated 350 degree oven for thirty-five minutes or until they are browned on the tops and crisped on the sides.

QUAHAUGS WITH SAFFRON RICE

2 dozen cherrystone quahaugs and their liquor

½ cup chopped onion

½ cup chopped celery

1 tbsp. chopped parsley

1 clove garlic, minced

½ stick butter

¼ tsp. imported saffron or 1 tbsp. American saffron flowers

salt and fresh ground black pepper

½ lb. rice

Shuck the quahaugs and save their liquor. Cut the meats up coarsely with scissors and set aside. Melt the butter and saute the chopped onion and celery until soft, add the parsley and stir it in, then the clams and their liquor; cook for ten minutes.

Serve very hot on a mound of saffron rice which has been cooked as follows: Fry the raw rice in a little oil until it has become golden, add to the skillet a quantity of hot water equal in volume to the rice; add the saffron and bring it to a rolling boil, stirring it around. Then cover the skillet and lower the heat and cook for about twenty minutes until the rice has absorbed the water and saffron. You can add a Portuguese touch to this by adding slices of linguica or chourico to the clams in the sauce.

SOUL MATES

MUSHROOM STUFFED LITTLENECK
(OR CHERRYSTONE) QUAHAUGS

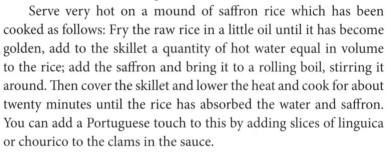

2 dozen littlenecks (or cherrystones) in the shell	*½ cup heavy cream*
1 cup of their liquor	*2 egg yolks*
½ stick butter	*1 clove garlic, finely minced*
1 medium onion, finely chopped	*1 tbsp. chopped parsley*
6 large fresh mushrooms, chopped	*dash of Tabasco*
	pinch of nutmeg
3 tbsps. cornstarch	*salt and fresh ground black pepper*
	sherry

Open the littlenecks and save one cup of their liquor. Cut the clam meats with scissors. Melt the butter and saute the onions, garlic and mushrooms until they are soft, add the cornstarch and stir it in well; then add the clam liquor and the cream, stirring constantly.

Add the clam meats, parsley, Tabasco, nutmeg and salt and pepper to taste. Cook for five minutes and add the egg yolks and cook five minutes longer at very low heat.

Place clamshells on the bottom of broiling pans and fill each shell with the mixture; sprinkle lightly with bread crumbs and place under the broiler flame until lightly browned. Using an eye dropper, drop 4 drops of sherry on each clam just before serving. Serve with a good white wine well chilled.

A SKILLET CALLED A CATAPLANA

Ameijoas na Cataplana using the littleneck quahaugs of Cape Cod is to me one of the world's greatest seafood dishes. The Portuguese words mean "clams in a cataplana," and the cataplana, which I described in the Introduction, is a type of double skillet designed especially for steaming clams. I've been cooking cataplana clams for about ten years using an ordinary twelve-inch skillet. And for years and years I swore that if I ever got to Portugal the first thing I was going to buy myself was a cataplana. So when I finally made it over there last year, the first thing I did was to find a good metal worker's shop and purchase a beautiful handmade cataplana.

While in Portugal I ate at some of the best restaurants on the Algarve Coast and I sampled the *ameijoas na cataplana* in the region of its birth. Frankly, I was a bit disappointed. Those clams they have in Portugal and Spain are only about the size of your thumbnail, and the meats inside the shells are about the size of a matchhead. Eating them is a very slow and tedious process. A man would have to eat a gallon or two to assuage his appetite.

So it gave me quite a shock to find that the Cape Cod cataplana using our native littleneck quahaugs is a much better dish than the ones in Portugal. I am a chauvinist on the subject. Our littleneck quahaugs are without a doubt one of the world's greatest shellfish—salty, gamey, full of flavor, chewy but not tough. When I got that cataplana pan back to Cape Cod, I found it was a little too light and flimsy for our quahaugs, so I went back to using a heavy twelve-inch skillet with a lid on it, and hung the cataplana on the wall where it makes a nice decoration and conversation piece. The only thing it contributes to the following recipe is its name.

One thing to understand in advance is that this dish has to be cooked one serving at a time. You can't speed it up or mass produce it. And to serve it you need large deep soup bowls of one quart capacity that will hold both the clams and the sauce-broth.

AMEIJOAS NA CATAPLANA
[Portuguese Clams]
1 serving

24 littlenecks in the shell
½ stick butter
¼ cup linguica sausage, diced
¼ cup chourico sausage, diced
2 strips bacon, fried brown and crumbled
¼ cup white onions, chopped
¼ cup scallions' green leaves, chopped
1 clove garlic, minced
¼ cup green pepper, finely chopped

2 tbsps. fresh parsley, chopped
¼ cup fresh sliced mushrooms
¼ cup fresh tomato, diced
½ cup molho tomate (see below)
¼ cup white wine
2 cups fish broth or bouillon
¼ tsp. black pepper
dash of Tabasco
no salt required—the clam liquor furnishes that

Melt the butter in a 12 inch skillet and saute the linguica and chourico cubes until lightly browned, add the crumbled bacon, onions, scallion leaves, garlic, green pepper, parsley, mushrooms, fresh tomato and black pepper; saute, stirring frequently, until the vegetables are limp and transparent. Add the white wine and stir it in. Scrape the bottom and sides of the skillet to dissolve any brown particles clinging thereto. This stuff imparts a wallop to the sauce.

Add the *molho tomate* and Tabasco and stir them in. The Portuguese and Spanish call this delicious mishmash a *sofrito*, and it forms the background for many of their best dishes. Smooth the sauce out in the bottom of the skillet and lay the littlenecks on top of it. Pour two cups of fish broth over the clams. Cover the skillet and cook until the clam shells open. Discard as suspicious any clams that do not open. They may have gone to their reward, or it may be just a mudfilled shell that could play hell with your dish if it came open and spilled its contents into the pan.

Take a slotted spoon and transfer the clams to a large deep soup bowl. The clam liquor that has mixed with the sauce really gives it zing. Lift the skillet and pour this sauce over the clams in the bowl, but stop when there is about a half cup residue left in the skillet. This last part will contain whatever sand the clams had in them, hence it should be discarded. Serve it piping hot to guest number 1. Then repeat the process for guests number 2, 3, 4, 5, 6 . . . , and by the time you're finished you'll be pooped out.

This is a festive dish. I suggest you serve a Lancer's Portuguese Champagne along with it.

Note: The above cataplana sauce also goes beautifully with softshell steamer clams or mussels. Add a few anise seeds when you're using mussels. All these shellfish release a liquor into the sauce which makes it approach the sublime (well, almost!).

MOLHO TOMATE
[Tomato Sauce]

1 large can of pomodori	*1 cup water*
pelati tomatoes	*2 tbsps. vinegar*
3 medium onions, slivered	*1 tbsp. sugar*
1 green pepper, chopped	*¼ tsp. crushed cumin seeds*
2 cloves garlic, finely	*1 pinch each of basil, thyme,*
minced	*and crushed red pepper*
½ cup chopped parsley	*seeds*
½ cup olive oil	*salt and fresh ground black*
1 cup red wine	*pepper to taste*

Saute the onion, green pepper and garlic in the olive oil until they are soft but not brown; add the parsley and stir it in. Add the tomatoes (squeeze them up to pulverize them) and all the rest of the ingredients; turn the heat up high to bring it to a boil, stirring briskly to mix everything well.

Now lower the heat to as low as possible and simmer for one or two hours, stirring now and then to prevent sticking or scorching. "Simmer" as defined by the Portuguese is a low slow thing; it doesn't even bubble.

QUAHAUGS CASINO (THE CLASSIC METHOD)

2 dozen fresh shucked
  quahaugs on the half shell
½ cup grated onion
½ cup diced green pepper
1 clove garlic, finely
  minced

1 tbsp. anchovy paste (or
  chopped fillets)
1 stick butter
salt and fresh ground black
  pepper to taste
bacon

CASINOS

Melt the butter and saute the green pepper until soft, add the garlic, onion, and parsley and saute a little longer; add the rest of the ingredients except bacon and mix thoroughly. Spoon the sauce over the quahaugs, lay a one-inch square of bacon on top of each, preheat the oven to 400 degrees and bake until the bacon becomes crisp.

QUAHAUGS CASINO a la MITCH

4 dozen fresh shucked
  quahaugs on the half shell
1 package chopped frozen
  spinach
1 package chopped frozen
  kale
4 tbsps. fresh parsley,
  chopped
1½ sticks butter
½ lb. bacon

1 cup bread crumbs
½ cup Parmesan cheese
1 tbsp. anchovy paste (or
  chopped fillets)
2 tbsps. Worcestershire sauce
½ tsp. Tabasco sauce
½ cup fine old Madeira or
  Marsala wine
salt and fresh ground black
  pepper to taste

SPINACH

Steam the spinach and kale with a cup of water until it is soft. Pour off the excess water. Add the butter to the pot and melt it. Add all the other ingredients except the bacon. Cream the mixture with an eggbeater or a blender. Fry ¼ lb. of bacon until good and brown, crumble it up and stir it into the mixture.

If the quahaugs are small littlenecks or cherrystones, use them whole; if they are large cut them into quarters. Place the quahaugs on the half shell under the broiler flame for a minute or two until they are about half cooked. Remove from the broiler and cover each quahaug with a good layer of the blended sauce. Cut the remaining ¼ pound of bacon up into small pieces. Lay a piece on top of the sauce of each quahaug. Return to the broiler and cook until the bacon is browned.

QUAHAUG FRITTERS

1 lb. quahaug meats, put
through the grinder
1 small onion, minced
1 tsp. parsley, minced
1 tbsp. minced celery
2 eggs, well beaten milk

1 cup flour
1 tsp. baking powder
¼ or ½ tsp. Tabasco sauce
½ tsp. salt
a little fresh ground black
pepper

Sift the dry ingredients together. Add the eggs and enough milk to make a thick batter. Add all the other ingredients and mix well. Drop by teaspoons into deep hot oil, brown until golden. Serve hot on toothpicks. This will make 16 to 18 little clam fritters that will melt in your mouth.

SPAGHETTI WITH QUAHAUG SAUCE

2 dozen fresh shucked
cherrystone quahaugs
and their liquor
4 tbsps. olive oil
2 cloves finely chopped
garlic

1 tsp. oregano
2 tbsps. butter
pinch crushed red pepper
seeds
1 lb. spaghettini (or linguine)

In all of Italian cucina, my favorite dish is one of the simplest: spaghetti with Provincetown quahaug sauce! Heat the olive oil in a large wide skillet, add the garlic and saute it until it begins to brown (be careful not to burn it). Add the clam liquor, crushed pepper and oregano. Cover and simmer slowly for five minutes. Chop the clams and add them to the skillet. Cook for several minutes over high heat.

While all this is going on, cook the spaghettini in boiling salted water in another pot. Cook it from 8 to 12 minutes or until it becomes "*al dente,*" firm and not overcooked and soggy. Drain it quickly when it's done and put it in the skillet with the clams and sauce. The butter is optional; add it if you think it's needed for moisture. Toss the spaghettini and clam sauce carefully for 30 seconds. This mixing well is one of the most important parts of the preparation. Serve on hot plates. This batch should feed four people or two gluttons.

BROILED QUAHAUGS
(Serves 2)

2 doz. littleneck or	*6 slices bacon*
cherrystone quahaugs	*Tabasco*

Many people prefer this simple broiled quahaug dish to the more elaborate clams casino.

Open the quahaugs, over a pan to catch the juices. Cook the bacon in a skillet until it is ¾ done; cut the strips in 1-inch pieces. Place rock salt on 2 sizzle platters or pie pans and place the clams on the halfshell on top of the rock salt. Spoon the juice which you caught in the pan over the clams. Add 1 drop of Tabasco to each clam. Lay a piece of the bacon on top of each clam. Place them under the broiler flame until the bacon is browned. Serve at once.

QUAHAUG BISQUE
(Serves 6)

3 doz. littlenecks or 1½ doz.	*1 pint milk*
cherrystone quahaugs and	*1 pint cream*
their liquor	*1 stick butter*
1 large onion, chopped	*3 tbsps. flour*
2 scallions and 2 inches of	*salt and fresh ground black*
their green leaves, chopped	*pepper*

Open the quahaugs and save their liquor. Now it's almost sacrilegious to ask you to do this, but this soup has to be clear and light colored, so-o-o split the bellies of the clams and rinse out the contents. (I'll never ask you to insult a clam like that again.) Place the clams, onions and scallions in a blender and cream them. Melt the butter in a skillet and add the clam-onion mix. Cook for about 5 minutes, stirring constantly. Add the flour and stir it in, browning it a little. Add a cup of the clam liquor. Stir well. Add the milk and cream and heat to just this side of the boiling point, stirring until it thickens. Serve in preheated soup bowls, sprinkling on top a few chopped chives or chopped parsley a little dash of paprika and a small piece of butter.

Life is a Clambake

JOHN J. GASPIE
Lord Protector of the Quahaugs

Every man at one time or another in his life runs into a friend who is more than a friend, a teacher who helps to mold and shape his whole way of life and thought, for better or worse. Socrates taught Plato and Aristotle shaped Alexander the Great. Me, I had John J. Gaspie, and what a tutor! Father Gaspie taught me a few things about the sea and its creatures that I will never forget.

I met him on my very first afternoon in Provincetown twenty-seven years ago: he was plodding gingerly down the wrong side of Commercial Street, swinging his heavy walking stick to swoosh the tour-  ists, children and dogs out of his path. Close at his heel came his "Genuine Kentucky Redbone" dog, Koochicki (which means "nice dog" in Hungarian). I learned later that his daily promenade to the store for a can of soup or loaf of bread was as important in his own life as Frederick the Great's daily inspection of the Palace Guard, and in a relative way, just as momentous. Although the stick was swinging I knew at a glance that it was just a bluff—that he loved those tourists, kids and dogs, every one of them. So I went up to him and said, "I bet you won't hit me with that damn stick," and he said "Oh yes I will!" And he gave me a sharp rap across the buttocks and we both busted out laughing, and he said, "Mate, you look hungry, come on home and eat some tinker mackerel." And so we were off. From ships and shoes and sealing wax to cabbages and kings, and from Buddhism to pragmatic relativism, we talked and talked for the next fifteen years, about practically every subject under the sun.

But most of it was about fish and shellfish, and how to catch and cook them.

That first summer we set up a nefarious enterprise: we became nocturnal clam bootleggers. At night we'd sail out to Long Point in his dory, and we'd snatch out the clams, and peddle them next day to the restaurants. Then we'd head straight for the bars and get loaded (remember how beer used to cost ten cents a bottle?). We made a remarkable discovery on these trips: we always took Koochicki the redbone hound with us, and it turned out that he was probably the only coon and possum hound in the country who could tree a clam. (Remember, Cape Cod boys have no sleds, and the hounds have no coons.) Chicki would gallop up and down the beach in the moonlight following the spoor of the quahaug, and then he'd sit down, and we'd go dig under him and the sand would be crawling with clams. Some scoffer always screams "Liar! Liar!" when I tell about this, but it's the gospel truth. The sensitivity of the schnozzle of a redbone is almost transcendental, and Chicki knew which side his bread was buttered on; he always got a pound of raw hamburger out of our daily wages of sin. He could do something else I never saw another dog do. He could eat a big mackerel, raw or fried, bones and all, and why they never perforated his gizzard was more than I could figure out.

Chicki was as big a lecher as Gaspie was a staid and prudish gentleman, and you can still see his great-great-grandchildren loping down Commercial Street with the proud and arrogant bearing of a true redbone. . . .

Never throw a lighted cigarette butt on the sidewalk in Provincetown on a windy day. It's a wooden town and you could burn it to the ground. The following anecdote illustrates what can happen when you obey that rule assiduously. (My good friend, the late Charlie Murnane, who was fire chief in Andover, was very fire-conscious and he used to make Gaspie tell this tale over and over.) The bars had closed late one night and Gaspie and I were staggering down Commercial Street. We stopped on the corner in front of Lewis's New York Store to catch a breath and get our bearings. Gaspie and I had been having an argument about clams and were sort of on the outs. As we stood there I remembered the stern warning about fires, so I took my cigarette and ground it out on a fire plug. Only it wasn't a fire plug, it was a big ole black dog who was sitting there quiet as a statue; he gave a god awful yell and "Cockaloo." Pierce, the gendarme, was standing right behind us. He snapped the bracelets on me and said "I've got you at last!" Gaspie hollered, "Keep him in the cooler for a week—cruelty to animals and tryin' to burn the town down!"

I was an artist and writer in my youth and this somehow led to my membership in Provincetown's Beachcomber's Club, although they were a pretty snooty bunch. They hold a meeting every Saturday night and one of the members cooks a gourmet dinner. About twenty years ago they asked me to cook supper for them, so Gaspie and I dug clams for two whole days and we shucked them and made forty gallons of the finest chowder you ever tasted in your life. We made it a day in advance so it could age and "ripen." (Mind you, we had culled out all the dead clams before making the chowder. In such a big batch of clams there are always a few who are dead from natural causes.) On that gray Friday just as we had turned off the gas, Sal Del Deo, who was the cabin boy in those days, came running in and said that some of the high-minded members of the Crimp Gang had ruled that Gaspie couldn't come to the dinner next day. Manny Zora was going to tell Portuguese stories and he just couldn't do it with John J. Gaspie in the audience prompting him and heckling him. (There was a long-standing feud between these two because everybody thought that Gaspie was the rumrunner and ship's captain while Manny Zora was just a clam mucker. This griped Manny no end.) Gaspie couldn't have cared less; he had been black-balled from bigger and better clubs than the Beachcombers. But as we started to leave, he said, "The chowder needs a little yeast," and picked up a handful of dead clams and threw them in it. When I came back next day to serve it, the chowder was at a rolling boil—in its own ferment, like Jack Daniel's Tennessee sour mash—and it stank so badly you couldn't get close to it. We threw it over the bulk-head into the briny, and the Beachcombers had to eat sardines out of cans that night. Of course Manny Zora told his stories, very long and windy ones, and although everybody had heard 'em ten times, they laughed and laughed and clapped and clapped. And Gaspie was sitting in a bar somewhere and the other patrons were wondering why that grizzly old man kept laughing to himself; was he looney?

Father Gaspie was, without a doubt, the greatest Clambake Master that Cape Cod ever produced. Every September for many years he and I would give a clambake called "Salute to Indian Summer." Gaspie had a motto: "Never invite over five people to a clambake. If you do, one of them is bound to be a stinker who will spoil the party. Or he might be too hungry and clams do hate a greedy man." But he was seldom able to hold to his ideals; he had so many friends that they all swooped in when they heard he was fixing a bake.

He always told me, "Mitch, when I croak I want you to cremate me and throw my ashes off Pilgrim Monument during a nor'east gale." Since I was out of town when he made his exit I couldn't carry

out his wish. They gave his weather-beaten old carcass a decent burial in consecrated ground and now the grass grows green above him. And green is the memory of him in the minds of the thousands of friends he made as he promenaded through life.

THE JOHN J. GASPIE CLAMBAKE
(Clambake for 150 People)

5 bushels of littleneck clams	*20 cans small Irish potatoes*
40 lbs. haddock fillets	*300 small onions (or 150*
3 cases sweet corn (150 ears)	*medium, halved)*
25 lbs. linguica sausage	*3 gallons dry white wine*
13 pkgs. pork sausage links	*300 bottles of beer*
(150 pcs.)	

So you'd like to give a John Gaspie–type clambake for a hundred and fifty people? The recipe is very simple. Besides the ingredients listed above, you'll need 10 rolls of heavy duty wide aluminum foil, 6 new large-size galvanized garbage cans to cook in, and 6 packages of bicarbonate of soda to scrub the cans.

General rules: About the clams: Always use littleneck clams; they are tender and tasty, and there are about 500 of them in a bushel. As a contrast, the larger cherrystones are tougher, and there are only 200–300 in a bushel, so they don't stretch as far.

About the utensils: A large new galvanized Steel garbage can becomes a good cooking utensil if you'll dump a box of bicarbonate of soda and a half gallon of warm water in it and give it a thoroughgoing scrubdown. The soda neutralizes any residues of the acids which were used in the galvanizing process; without these six 30-gallon cans it would take you several days to cook this clambake in small utensils.

About the "bundles": The John Gaspie clambake uses the "bundle" or packet technique, one good bundle for each guest containing portions of the goodies. Any other system can only lead to chaos and a horrible mess, impossible to serve to a hundred and fifty people. The drawing herewith shows the way to prepare a bundle; it should be compact, neatly arranged and flat so that twenty-five bundles can be packed into the bottom of each cooking can.

So here are the technical details. Wash the clams, discarding any whose shells are cracked or open. Although they look strong, littlenecks' shells are very brittle and crack easily, so handle them with loving care. Cut the haddock up into 150 slices of about 4 ounces each. Cut the linguica up into 3-inch pieces. Peel the onions, and if they are medium size, halve them. Open the containers of potatoes and sausage links. Shuck the ears of corn. Tear the foil in 2-foot pieces.

CONTENTS
of the
"BUNDLE"

To assemble the bundles, use an assembly line technique by placing the goodies in a row on a long table. One cook slaps down a piece of foil, another lays on it an ear of corn, another places linguica and a pork link, another two onions and two potatoes, another lays on a slice of haddock, the last person wraps the bundles neatly and presses them flat, then takes a sharply pointed knife and punches eight holes in each side of the bundle so the cooking juices will cir-culate through it. The bundles are then stacked neatly in the bottom of the can, 25 to each can. Add ½ gallon of wine and ½ gallon of water to each can. Place on the stove, cover tightly and steam for two hours (this long cook is necessary because the bundles are packed compactly). At the end of two hours divide the 5 bushels of clams into 6 parts and place the clams in the top of each of the 6 cans. Steam for one-half to one hour more or until all the clam shells are open. As the clams open up their liquor will seep down into the packets, giving them an exquisite flavor, and the broth that accumu-lates at the bottom of the can will be absolutely ambrosial.

"BUNDLE"

To serve, pour off the clams and the broth into some kind of large container like a wash tub, then dig out for each guest one of the bundles, and give him a helping of the clams and a large cup of the broth. Of course, to give a smaller clambake you merely divide the above list of ingredients into fractions, but make sure that each individual gets a bundle of the type illustrated.

Then pass out the beers and dance the boogie.

And give a few speeches in honor of the late great John J. Gaspie who invented this system of joy.

ZEUS

BROTH

AMBROSIAL!

DIGGING CLAMS ON THE TIDAL FLATS, 1905
On the site of the present West End breakwater

I have read the clambake recipes in all the great Standard cookbooks, but they are weak and full of holes, ambiguities, and downright ignorance. Only the John J. Gaspie system is airtight and foolproof.

A NICE GENTEEL LITTLE CLAMBAKE

Steamer Clams

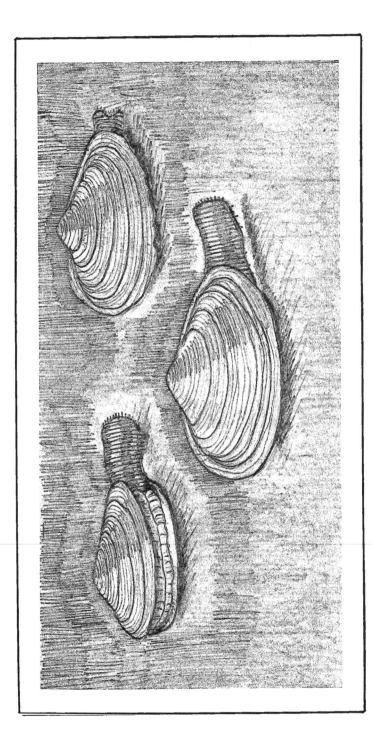

STEAMER CLAMS
(*Mya arenaria*)

It's unfair to all of them to say that one species of clam is better than another, that softshell steamer clams are better than quahaugs, or that they're both better than sea clams, etc. To me they are the best part of Cape Tip Gourmetry, and there's an ideal spot for each of them in our bright lexicon of cooking and eating for the sheer joy of it. Clams are for happy people. They all make excellent chowder, and so does the humble razor clam, if you can find enough of them.

As the name denotes, steamers are best when steamed and served with melted butter for dipping and broth for drinking. Steamer clams often have a good bit of sand in them, and you should always wash them thoroughly in the surf after digging them. After getting them home sample a few and if they are sandy take the rest of them and put them in a wire basket (or even a wooden vegetable hamper will do), cover it and tie a rope to it, and take them out on a wharf and suspend them in the water; leave them there for a day or two and they will blow out their sand. A simpler but less effective way to do it is to soak them in a tub of fresh water and sprinkle salt in the water. And some say sprinkle in a handful of corn meal too. But I don't go for this. The broth will not be as good, and corn meal in a clam's belly does not have time to cook in the short time that it takes to steam them. If you're not afraid of a little sand, go ahead and steam them and eat them right after digging.

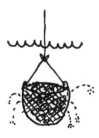

STEAMING STEAMERS

The method is the same as that given for quahaugs. But remember that the shells of steamers are very thin and brittle; handle them carefully. Serve each order of clams with drawn butter and a cup of broth.

TO FRY CLAMS

Dip them in milk, drain off the excess milk. Dip them in the dry clam batter flour and roll them around to coat them thoroughly; place them in a wire mesh basket and shake off the excess flour.

Place the breaded clams in the bottom of a frying basket (they must not touch each other). Fry in deep hot fat until a rich golden brown (never, never a dark brown or they will be hard and tasteless). Drain and serve with tartar sauce.

STEAMER CLAM APPETIZER

DEEP FRYING

36 steamer clams
¼ cup olive oil
1 medium onion, chopped
2 tsps. chopped parsley
juice of ½ lemon

¼ cup bitter black olives,
  chopped finely
2 tbsps. vinegar
black olives, mild

Steam the clams open but leave them on the halfshell. Cut off the siphons with scissors. Mix the olive oil, onion, parsley, olives, lemon juice and vinegar and mix well. Spoon this sauce over the clams on the half shell. Chill and serve as an hors d'oeuvre, with the clams attractively arranged on a tray. Decorate the tray with pitted mild black olives.

STEAMER CLAM COCKTAIL PARTY DIP

FRIED CLAMS

2 doz. steamer clams, and
  liquor
1 small pkg. Philadelphia
  cream cheese
1 pint sour cream
2 cloves minced garlic

½ cup grated onion
1 tbsp. lemon juice
Tabasco
salt and fresh ground black
  pepper

If you're giving a cocktail party and want to serve a dip that is miles ahead of ordinary commercial dips, try making this one with fresh Provincetown steamer clams.

Steam the clams and save ½ cup of the broth. Shuck the clams and snip off their siphons with scissors. Rinse thoroughly under a faucet to remove any traces of sand. Drain well. Place the clams and ½ cup of liquor in a blender, add the onion, garlic, lemon juice,

Tabasco and salt and fresh ground black pepper. (Go easy on the salt, the clam broth is salty.) Cream this mixture in the blender, then add the sour cream and cream cheese. Blend them in. Place the dip in a serving bowl and chill it. Serve with potato chips, Fritos, or small crackers for dipping.

POACHED STEAMER CLAMS (Serves 2)

DIP

36 softshell steamer clams
½ cup clam liquor
1 stick butter
4 tbsps. minced onion
1 jigger sherry

dash of Tabasco
salt (if needed) and fresh
   ground black pepper
toast or Holland Rusk

Shuck the raw clams with a clam knife, holding them over a pan to catch the juice. Cut the siphons off the clams with scissors. Wash the clams well to remove any sand. Set them aside. Strain ½ cup of the clam juice and set it aside.

Melt the stick of butter in a skillet and add the minced onion, clam liquor, sherry, Tabasco, and fresh ground black pepper. Mix well and add the clams. Lower the heat and poach the clams slowly for 15-20 minutes, or until they are well done. Place slices of toast or Holland Rusk on heated serving plates and ladle the clams and sauce over the slices. Sprinkle with parsley and serve at once.

CLAMS
ON RUSK

STEAMER CLAMS ITALIAN STYLE
(Serves 4)

4 doz. steamer clams	*2 tbsps. chopped parsley*
3 sticks butter	*2 tsps. oregano*
4 tbsps. grated onion	*Tabasco*
4 cloves garlic, minced	*fresh ground black pepper*
1 tbsp. wine vinegar	*sherry*
¼ loaf Italian bread	*Parmesan cheese*
clam liquor	

Place the clams in a pot with ½ cup water and steam them until their shells are open. Save the broth. Open the clams and leave the clam lying on the bottom halfshell. Take scissors and snip off the siphons. Hold the clam and shell under a faucet to rinse off any remaining sand; shake off the excess water. Set the clams on the shells aside.

Break the Italian bread into small pieces and wet it down with part of the clam broth. Knead it into a paste free of lumps. Set aside. Melt the butter in a skillet and add the grated onion, parsley, oregano, bread paste, black pepper, sherry and a dash of Tabasco. Add a cup of clam broth and mix well. Place rock salt on 4 metal pie pans. Cover each clam on the halfshell with a layer of the sauce. Cover the sauce with a layer of Parmesan. Place 1 dozen clams on each pan. If you have any clam liquor left, spoon it over the clams. Place the pans in a preheated 350 degree oven until the cheese is light brown. Serve at once, right in the cooking pans.

STEAMER CLAMS FRENCH STYLE

4 doz. steamer clams and their	*2 cloves garlic, finely minced*
liquor	*4 tbsps. grated onion,*
3 sticks butter	*Tabasco*
4 tbsps. lemon juice	*paprika*
1 cup white wine	

The procedure is almost exactly the same as that given in the preceding recipe; it's the sauce that is different. Melt the butter and add the lemon juice, white wine, garlic, onion and Tabasco; do not cook, just mix well. When the clams on their shells are in place on the rock salt, spoon a little of the clam liquor on each clam. Then cover each clam with the sauce. Place under the broiler flame until just heated through. Sprinkle each clam with a little paprika and serve on the hot pans.

The Versatile Sea Clam

The Cape Tip is very fortunate in having a good supply of sea clams, or as they're called in some localities, surf clams, or sea hens. These babies grow up to seven inches long, and they're loaded with rich, sweet meat.

You haven't really begun to be a Cape Tip gourmet until you've learned how to make stuffed sea clams and that delicious classic, sea clam pie. All of the chowders and minced clams that you buy in stores are sea clam products; there aren't enough quahaugs and steamers available any more to keep a clam factory running. But the delicious clam loses so much of its sparkle in the canning process that they really ought to label the cans something else. You won't find a recipe in this book beginning, "Take a can of minced clams . . . ."

The most difficult thing about catching sea clams is to know where, when, and how to find them. John Alexander, who is a walking encyclopedia of Cape Tip flora and fauna, has passed on some facts that may be of interest to my readers.

Unlike the more peaceful quahaugs and steamer clams, the sea clams love the wild pounding surf and the "live" sand that moves and shifts around. They live on exposed outer beaches just below mean low water line, and love the little channels that form between the small bars below low water mark. You spot them by their good-sized siphon holes and their dung deposits. For equipment—if you want to do it right—you need rubber hip boots, a long handled clam rake, and an elongated carrying net bag of the type with a strap for slinging it from the shoulder; any Cape hardware store can sell you these. However, if you're hardy enough, you can go out there and dig them out with your bare hands.

SEA CLAM
BAG

The best time for sea clamming comes twice a month during the high spring tides, when the ebb tides reach the lowest. Obtain the local tide table and look for the minus signs: for instance, -1.8 means that the ebb tide on that day will reach one and eight-tenths feet below the mean water mark, which is zero. That's the time the clams are easiest to get at. The lowest tides around Provincetown are -2.0.

Truro has a good sea clam bed east of Beach Point. Provincetown has some good beds but they are harder to get at. There's a bed off Long Point, but you need a boat to get there. There's a tremendous bed that stretches all the way from Wood End, past Herring Cove Beach to Race Point Light, but it is in pretty deep water and hard to get to. After a big storm Herring Cove Beach will sometimes be covered with sea clams, and people go out there and gather them by the washtub full. During the summer the snorkelers and skindivers harvest a good many; the snorkeler swims along the surface, spotting the beds, and the skin-diver goes down to gather them. If you don't feel up to harvesting your own sea clams you can buy fresh minced sea clam meats in any of the seafood markets; it's the best bargain of all the clams.

SEA CLAM PIE

1 dozen large sea clams	*2 tbsps. flour*
¼ lb. bacon, chopped	*milk*
¼ lb. linguica	*salt and Tabasco*
2 onions, chopped	*pie crust*

To clean the sea clams, insert a kitchen knife between the shells and sever the adductor muscles. Open the shells, being careful to save the juice, and remove the meats. Split the stomach part of the clam and rinse it out; split the siphons and rinse them. Wash the meats very carefully and thoroughly in the clam juice to remove all traces of sand. Grind finely in a food chopper.

SEA CLAM IN A PIE (JUS' KIDDIN')

Put the bacon and the onions in a skillet and saute together until the bacon is brown and the onions soft. Grind the linguica and add it to the mixture. Add the flour and cook slowly, stirring. Add the clam meats. Mix milk and clam liquor half and half and pour enough over the mixture to just cover it, stir and adjust salt flavor; add a few dashes of Tabasco sauce. Line a deep pie pan (or a skillet if you don't have a deep pan) with pie crust and pour the mixture into it. Cover the pie with crust and punch a few fork holes to allow steam to escape. Glaze the top with milk or beaten egg. Bake it in a 400 degree oven for one-half to three-quarters of an hour or until the top is well browned.

Sea clam pie is even better on the second day than on the first: a little ageing gives the flavors a chance to amalgamate.

STUFFED SEA CLAMS

2 dozen large sea clams	*pinch of thyme*
2 loaves hard bread	*1 tsp. Tabasco sauce (it's gotta*
1 cup butter	*be hot!)*
8 cloves garlic, chopped	*1 tbsp. Worcestershire sauce*
fine	*½ cup white wine*
4 onions, chopped	*½ cup sherry*
3 green peppers, chopped	*pimiento*
3 pieces celery or 1 celery	*grated Parmesan cheese*
heart, chopped	*salt and pepper to taste (very*
2 tbsps. chopped parsley	*little needed as the clam*
½ tsp. saffron	*broth is salty)*

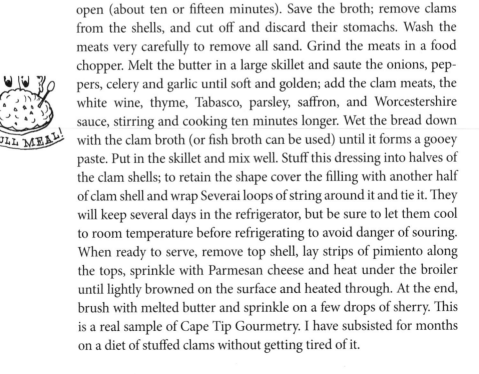

Put a cup of water in a large pot, and steam the clams until they open (about ten or fifteen minutes). Save the broth; remove clams from the shells, and cut off and discard their stomachs. Wash the meats very carefully to remove all sand. Grind the meats in a food chopper. Melt the butter in a large skillet and saute the onions, peppers, celery and garlic until soft and golden; add the clam meats, the white wine, thyme, Tabasco, parsley, saffron, and Worcestershire sauce, stirring and cooking ten minutes longer. Wet the bread down with the clam broth (or fish broth can be used) until it forms a gooey paste. Put in the skillet and mix well. Stuff this dressing into halves of the clam shells; to retain the shape cover the filling with another half of clam shell and wrap Severai loops of string around it and tie it. They will keep several days in the refrigerator, but be sure to let them cool to room temperature before refrigerating to avoid danger of souring. When ready to serve, remove top shell, lay strips of pimiento along the tops, sprinkle with Parmesan cheese and heat under the broiler until lightly browned on the surface and heated through. At the end, brush with melted butter and sprinkle on a few drops of sherry. This is a real sample of Cape Tip Gourmetry. I have subsisted for months on a diet of stuffed clams without getting tired of it.

PORTUGUESE CLAM FRITTERS

*2 cups sea clam meats,
   ground up
2 eggs, beaten
1 clove garlic, finely
   minced
2 tbsps. grated onion
3 tbsps. milk*

*1 tbsp. linguica, chopped very
   fine
¼ tsp. cominos (ground
   cumin seed)
2 tbsps. flour
½ tsp. salt
fresh crushed black pepper*

Drain the chopped clam meats and place in a mixing bowl. Add the beaten eggs and stir well. Add the rest of the ingredients and stir some more. Heat fat in a skillet and drop tablespoons full of the mixture into the hot fat, brown on both sides. This packs a good bit more wallop than ordinary clam cakes.

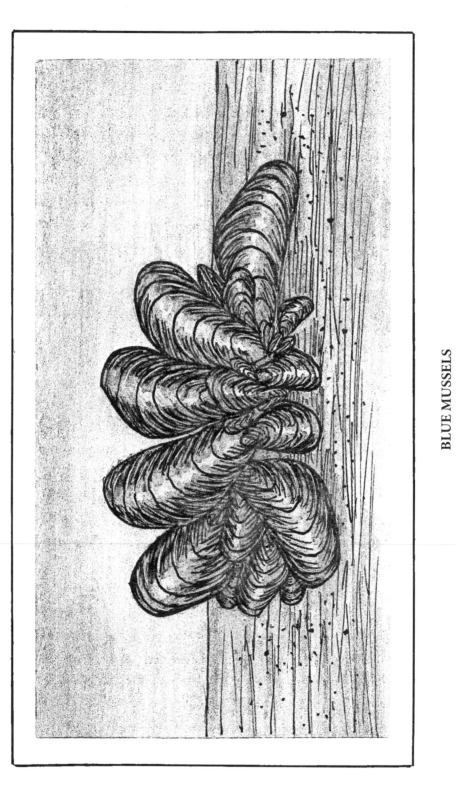

BLUE MUSSELS
(*Mytilus edulis*)

Muscling in on the Mussels

One of the tastiest morsels with which the sea has blessed the Cape Tip is the mussel. A ten-quart bucketful of mussels is loaded with all sorts of gourmet potentialities. Yet it's a safe bet that nine out of ten people on the Cape have never eaten a mussel. This is strictly clam country, and the mussels lie around neglected as orphans. In Europe the shoe is on the other foot: Frenchmen consider it the greatest of all shellfish delicacies. Mussels are also relished by Spaniards, Italians, Greeks, Armenians, Lebanese, and Syrians. One of the greatest of all gastronomic *coups de joie is midia dolma*, the classic Armenian mussel dish.

Mussels are delicious when steamed and served with a variety of sauces, especially remoulade sauce, or when served Italian marinara style, or even when dipped in batter and fried. They have a mild flavor which calls for sharp and snappy sauces bolstered by wine, vinegar, lemons, mustard, garlic, onions, herbs, or what have you.

Provincetown, Truro, and Wellfleet have beds of two types of mussels, the blue mussel and the ribbed, or mud bank mussel. In addition, the scallop boats and draggers sometimes bring in the large deep sea horse mussel, which is excellent fare when properly prepared. Blue mussels are the best of all; they grow in abundance out at the far end of the Provincetown breakwater. There used to be a terrific bed of them out at Race Run, near the lighthouse, but storms and high tides and shifting sands have destroyed most of them, alas.

Through ignorance mussels have been given a black eye and called a health menace, which is probably why the natives are leery about them. The Pacific Coast mussel is dangerous in the summertime because it inhales a small dinoflagellate which upsets its metabolism, but the Atlantic Coast mussel is usually innocent and safe. Unless, of course, it comes from a polluted area, and no shellfish is safe when it's polluted. Just to be on the safe side when steaming mussels in the summer, put enough bicarbonate of soda to cover a Roosevelt dime in the steaming water, and steam them 25 minutes to a half hour. This should be sufficient to kill any bacteria that may

be present. Never gather the small insignificant mussels that grow near the high tide mark and are covered with water only a short time each day. Their meats are skimpy, and they are the most likely to harbor bacteria. The farther out you go, the bigger and better the mussels become. The best ones of all are those that grow in tidal channels and are covered by water twenty-four hours a day. They are big, fat, sassy and full of flavor.

SQUEEZE THE MUSSEL TO TEST IT

Carefully cleaning mussels is a tedious but absolutely necessary chore; you can goof badly with them. Scrub each mussel briskly with a stiff, coarse brush and rinse well under running water. And here, my friends, is a very important point that I learned the hard way: Squeeze each mussel between thumb and forefinger and make sure the shell valves are locked and that the mussel is alive. Sometimes a pair of empty shells will become filled with foul black mud, and the darn thing will look just like a live mussel, until you squeeze the shell and get a handful of mud. If you're careless and one of these stinkers gets into your cooking pot it will be hell to pay. All that scrubbing and rinsing will also assure that your mussel liquor will be clear and drinkable; it's a real nectar to the initiated, and said to be an excellent aphrodisiac.

STEAMED MUSSELS

Take a ten-quart bucket of mussels and scrub and clean as directed above. Take a good-sized pot and put a pint of fine dry white wine in the bottom of it. Slice a big onion in the wine, add 4 cloves of garlic, smashed, 8 or 10 fresh pepper corns, crushed or ground, and a bay leaf. (Now these two items are optional and you can take 'em sometimes as an experiment, or leave 'em, but I have found that they produce a kick: a half teaspoonful of caraway seeds and a 3-inch piece of linguica, sliced.) Put the mussels in the pot, cover and bring to a boil and steam 15-20 minutes in winter, or 25-30 minutes in the summer. Serve the mussels in their shells, piping hot, with lemon butter sauce to which a few drops of Tabasco have been added, and a glass of the broth on the side.

Fifteen years ago Jake Spencer and I threw a steamed mussel dinner for about twenty gastronomes out at the hospitable estate of Colonel Manuel Silva, who has done more in his time for poor artists than any man in Provincetown. We cooked ten buckets of mussels in the above manner in a washtub, and not a single one of our guests complained of their goodness.

Note: Mussels have a tough little mossy umbilical cord with which they anchor themselves to the bottom, or one another. When steamed this "beard" recedes inside the body. It should always be plucked out; the process is called "bearding."

MARINATION

MARINATED MUSSELS

1 10 qt. bucket of mussels	*4 cloves garlic, minced*
1 cup vinegar	*dash of Tabasco*
1 cup olive oil	*2 tbsps. powdered mustard*
1 medium onion, chopped	*salt and fresh ground black*
½ cup fresh parsley, chopped	* pepper to taste*

Steam the mussels and shuck them. Beard them. Soak them in a marinade made from the rest of the ingredients, combined. Since the mussels themselves are so mild, this marinade should have the bong of a kettle drum. Chill before serving as an hors d'oeuvre.

SICILIAN MUSSELS
(1 or 2 Servings)

¾ cup Parmesan cheese	*melted butter*
¼ cup powdered garlic	*molho tomate (see page 49)*

SICILIAN
MUSSELS

Steam 18 mussels until the shells open; remove the top shell, beard them. Arrange the mussels on the half shell on a metal broiling pan, spoon a half teaspoonful of the following sauce over each mussel: Mix the Parmesan cheese with the powdered garlic; mix with enough melted butter and molho tomate to make a thin paste. Place under the broiler until lightly browned. This sauce is as strong as a machine gun but it surely does go good with mussels.

MUSSELS A LA PARMIGIANA

PARMIGIANI

½ bucket of mussels
½ stick butter
2 tbsps. flour
1 pint cream
¾ cup Parmesan cheese

2 tbsps. pimientos, chopped
½ cup fresh mushrooms,
    chopped
2 tbsps. sherry wine

Steam the mussels. Remove the top shells; beard them. Keep them warm and moist. Melt the butter in a skillet, remove from the fire and add the flour, mixing thoroughly. Then add the cream little by little, stirring constantly. Return to the fire and add the grated Parmesan cheese. Add chopped pimientos, chopped fresh mushrooms and sherry wine. Cook very slowly until it thickens, put half shell mussels in soup bowls and pour this sauce over them.

CURRIED MUSSELS

Add one tablespoon of good high quality curry powder to the above sauce and you will give it an East Indian flavor.

MIDIA DOLMA

MIDIA DOLMA

1 10 qt. bucket of mussels
1 cup olive oil
4 medium onions, chopped
2 cups uncooked rice
4 tbsps. pine nuts (pinedos,
    pignoli), chopped
4 tbsps. dried currants

salt and fresh ground black
    pepper
3 cloves garlic, finely minced
2 cups clear consomme
2 cups mussel liquor
1 pint dry white wine

This is one of my favorite dishes in the whole wide world, and it reaches its peak with our fat West End breakwater mussels. There used to be a clutch of small native restaurants in the Armenian neighborhood around Lexington Avenue and 29th Street in New York, and I would go in these places, when I could afford it, and gorge myself on midia dolma. Here's how to fix it:

Heat the olive oil and saute the onions until soft. Add the 2 cups of uncooked rice and cook over low heat for 10 minutes, stirring well. Add the chopped pine nuts, the currants, salt and fresh ground black pepper, and the garlic. Add the consomme and mussel liquor. Cover and cook slowly until the rice is done and the juices absorbed, about 15 minutes. Now stuff this rice mixture into the mussel shells on each side of the mussel meats. Close each shell and tie it with a piece of string. Put the white wine in the bottom of a pot or Dutch oven and steam the bound-up mussels very slowly for 30 to 40 minutes, adding more liquid if necessary. Remove the mussels from the pot, allow to cool to room temperature, then put them in the refrigerator. The next day serve them cold. You'd never hear of starving Armenians if there were enough midia dolma around.

PINE NUTS
(PIGNOLI)
(PINEDAS)

MUSSELS MARINIÈRE (Individual Serving)

CURRANTS

30 mussels	*1 small tomato, diced*
¼ cup olive oil	*2 tbsps. parsley*
2 scallions and their green leaves, chopped	*2 cloves garlic, minced*
¼ cup chopped onion	*½ cup molho tomate (see page 49)*
¼ cup chopped green pepper	*¼ cup dry white wine*
	½ cup fish stock

MARINIERE

Heat the olive oil in a skillet and add the scallions, onions, green pepper, tomato, parsley and garlic. Saute and stir for 3 minutes and add the molho tomate, wine and fish stock. Clean, scrub and test the mussels as previously instructed. Place them in the sauce in the skillet and stir them around well. Cover the skillet tightly and cook until all the mussel shells are open. Discard as suspicious any whose shells do not open. The mussel liquor will add sparkle to the sauce.

Preheat a large 1 quart soup bowl and place the opened mussels in it, ladle the sauce over them. Sprinkle with chopped parsley and serve at once with garlic bread. While eating these the diner should always pluck out the little byssus, or "beard," inside the folds of the mussel's mantle. A good Graves wine, lightly chilled, goes beautifully with *moules mariniere*.

THE "MUSSEL BAKE"

Wash and scrub a bucket of mussels, shuck a dozen ears of corn on the cob. Put a 1-inch layer of corn shucks on the bottom of a large sauce pan or Dutch oven. Now layer by layer place mussels, corn, mussels, corn, until the pan is filled. Put two sticks of butter on top of the last layer. Cover and steam for 20 minutes or until all the mussel shells are open. Serve the mussel bake right out of the pan. No seasoning is needed; the mussels, corn and butter provide their own symphony of blended flavors. Pour off the broth from the pan and dip the mussels in it as you eat them.

STEAMED MUSSELS WITH MAYONNAISE

This is a terrific snack-appetizer. I wandered into La Perla Restaurant on Avenida Cristobal Colon in Granada, Spain, and they served me this as a *"tapa,"* a free snack on the house, with my drinks. It was so good that I kicked myself in the pants for not having thought of it in Provincetown where we have so many good mussels. The secret, of course, is the fresh homemade mayonnaise; if you use a lousy commercial mayonnaise it's an insult to the mussel.

Steam mussels, remove the top shells and leave them lying on the bottom shells. Beard them. Place a little dab (¼ teaspoonful) of fresh homemade mayonnaise on top of each mussel. Serve them on an hors d'oeuvre tray at a party and watch them disappear fast. This is so simple that it's hard to believe it could taste so good.

PORTUGUESE MUSSEL STEW

4 dozen mussels, steamed, shucked, bearded	*4 cups molho tomate (see page 49)*
steamed rice	

Put the mussels into the sauce and serve over steamed rice.

SPAGHETTINI WITH MUSSEL SAUCE

4 dozen freshly steamed and bearded mussels and their liquor
4 tbsps. olive oil
2 cloves garlic, finely minced

2 tbsps. butter
1 tsp. oregano
pinch of crushed red pepper seeds
1 lb. spaghettini

Put olive oil in a skillet, add the garlic and saute it until it begins to turn golden. Add the mussel liquor and oregano, cover and simmer for a short while until the flavors are blended. Add the mussels, cook a little longer. While you are doing this, cook the spaghettini until it becomes "*al dente.*" Drain it when it is done, put it in the skillet with the mussels and the sauce. Toss the spaghettini and the mussels carefully for 30 seconds, add some melted butter if it seems to need moisture; serve immediately on hot plates. La dolce vita?

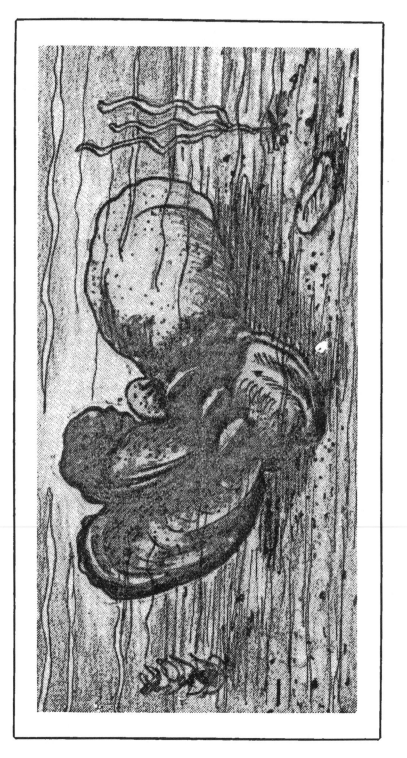

WELLFLEET OYSTERS
(*Cassostrea virginica*)

Hymn of Praise
for Wellfleet Oysters

I've eaten oysters all up and down our coastline from Nova Scotia to Brownsville, Texas. The Antigonish oysters of Nova Scotia are wild, barbarian and gamey flavored; the Long Island Sound and New Jersey oysters are plump and salty; the blue points and Chincoteagues from Chesapeake Bay are very very tasty; and the Gulf Coast oysters from Pass Christian and the bayous of Louisiana are as pampered and fat as their Yugoslavian growers can make them. But to me, the best oyster in the world is the Wellfleet oyster. It is very salty, yet its meat is sweet and gamey; it is not at all flabby and squishy like estuarine oysters which gorge themselves on too much fresh water. The trickle of water from Duck Creek is the only fresh water that touches the Wellfleet oysters, and I believe that this high salinity contributes something to their remarkable flavor.

The history of the Wellfleets goes a long way back. The mainland Indian tribes used to come to Wellfleet in the summertime and, setting up their teepees on the harbor, they'd stuff themselves on oysters all through the season, well past Labor Day and into Indian summer.

Wellfleet was once the oyster and quahaug Capital of the universe. With an enormous harbor that stretched all the way from Duck Creek to Billingsgate Island, it not surprisingly produced more shellfish than any town in New England. The French explorer Champlain and his men gorged themselves on Wellfleet oysters when they landed on Billingsgate Island in 1606; they charted and mapped the place and called it Oyster Harbor. Oysters have always been a notable feature of Wellfleet's landscape, or should I say seascape; the town was even named for the famous Wallfleet oysters of Cornwall. I'll bet the Wellfleet bivalves are tastier than their British counterpart.

The old time statistics on the Wellfleet oyster business are really staggering. From 1830 to 1870, the town had a virtual monopoly on the New England market. In 1870, there were forty schooners busy hauling seed oysters from Chesapeake Bay and mature oysters to Boston and New York. These schooners could carry 2,000 bushels a trip. Most of them were owned and outfitted by dealers who were well known up and down the Atlantic Coast—J. A. Stubbs, H. and R. Atwood, D. Atwood and R. R. Higgins Company, to name a few.

OYSTER LUGGER

In New York in the old days of gourmet-gluttony, such epicures as Diamond Jim Brady, Stanford White, and the other members of their set who dined at Delmonico's, would not touch an oyster unless it came from Wellfleet. In the 1850's Henry David Thoreau came tramping down the Cape and stopped overnight at the house of the Wellfleet Oysterman, and made him a fixture in American literature. But what bugged me was that Thoreau said not a word about the oysters themselves.

One of our typical Wellfleet oystermen today is our longtime friend, Howard Snow. He's a redfaced, smiling Cape Cod Yankee (when he has a hangover his watery blue eyes, oddly enough, resemble oysters on the shell). He lives in the house that his great-grandfather built over a hundred and fifty years ago. Howard is one of the kingpins of the oyster growing business and he'll gladly sell you a bushel if you'll fork over the $25, which is the price they are bringing these days. Compare that with the $10 or $15 which Chesapeake and Louisiana oysters fetch and you'll realize what a luxury those Wellfleets are. There's only a limited quantity of them available and if the price were too low the beds would be fished out in no time at all.

HOWARD SNOW & FRIEND

It has been a well known fact since Greek and Roman times that oysters are one of the most powerful natural aphrodisiacs. Nobody seems to know just why, but it's true. It's dangerous to eat oysters unless your love life is running smoothly and your libido is in perfect balance.

The true epicure believes that the only decent way to do honor to an oyster is to eat him raw and nekkid on the half shell with a squeeze of lemon and perhaps a drop of Tabasco. I solemnly agree, but in addition I think that the oyster is one of the most highly adaptable creatures to artful cookery. But before we go too far let's discuss the problem of opening oysters.

How an Amateur Can Open Oysters Safely

Many people have injured themselves severely by trying to open oysters the wrong way. Professional oyster openers have a heavy lead "s" shaped anvil to hold the oyster steady while they penetrate the side of the shell with a special oyster knife. An amateur has to attack an oyster through its hinge, and the two best tools that he can use are: (1) a small metal beer can opener of the type that punches triangular holes in the tops of beer cans—the curve of its point is perfect for fitting under the hinge of the oyster and providing strong leverage when pressed downward; and (2) a screwdriver which has the strength to pry the oyster open at the hinge without breaking. If you try to do this with a knife the point can easily break and you can stab yourself in the hand, or the knife may slip and cut you. If you don't have an oyster knife or clam knife a small fruit paring knife will suffice for cutting the adductor muscles of the oyster. Here is the sequence of steps:

Lay the oyster on a flat surface and steady it with one hand and take the beer can opener or the screwdriver in the other hand and pry the oyster open at the hinge. You don't have to open it all the way, just make a small slot. Take the small knife and slip it through this slot and sever the oyster's adductor muscle where it joins the top shell; the shell will then lift right off. Next slide the knife under the oyster's body and sever the muscle where it joins the bottom shell. Try not to waste any of the oyster's juice this is the best part; hold it over a small pan when cutting the muscle to catch any juice that sloshes out. And here's a point to remember: At the point where the two hinges join there often accumulates a little crumb of black mud. Wipe it off the shell with the point of the knife. If it falls into the oyster or into the juice rinse it away under a faucet; this stuff is very foul and bitter and can make an oyster taste spoiled if it gets mixed up with it. If an oyster has only a little juice and its gills are stuck to the inside of the shell, discard it as a doubtful specimen. Always serve oysters on the deep side of the shell: it cannot slide off, and the shell holds the juice. Now that I have explained the ground rules of the game you can really enjoy your Wellfleet oysters.

OYSTERS ON THE HALF SHELL

Chill the oysters in the refrigerator overnight. When ready to serve, open them carefully, saving as much of the juice as possible. Cover a serving platter with finely chipped ice, lay the opened oysters on top. Serve with lemon wedges and Tabasco sauce on the side.

WELLFLEET OYSTERS ROCKEFELLER

2 dozen Wellfleet oysters on the half shell
1 bunch chopped spinach, cooked
2 tbsps. chopped parsley
1 stick butter
½ cup bread crumbs

2 tbsps. Worcestershire sauce
dash of Tabasco
1 tsp. anchovy paste (or 2 fillets, chopped fine)
1 jigger Absinthe (or Pernod)
Parmesan cheese

Oysters Rockefeller is one of the world's classic gourmet dishes, and it deserves every bit of its fame. Once you've had it you'll always remember it and your taste buds will do handsprings every time you think back on it. They are usually available only in high-priced luxury restaurants, prepared by snooty chefs in *gros bonnets*, but their formula is so simple you can knock them off in your own kitchen, clad in your underwear, if you choose; when they are ready to serve, put a soothing symphony on the hi-fi, open an old bottle of Clos Vouget and sit down to sheer rapture.

Mix all the above ingredients (except the oysters) and put them in a blender to cream them, or use an egg beater and lots of elbow grease. Open the oysters and place them on their shells on a bed of rock salt in flat baking pans. The rock salt steadies them and keeps the juices from spilling; it also holds the heat longer. Cover each oyster on the shell with a generous blanket of the sauce mixture. Bake for a short while until the sauce becomes slightly brown, then place under the broiler a minute until the spinach has dark dappled spots.

Do not bake oysters too long or their natural juices will evaporate. Serve piping hot in the pans with the rock salt on which they are baked.

WELLFLEET OYSTERS BIENVILLE (Serves 4)

*2 dozen Wellfleet oysters on
   the half shell*
*4 scallions and 2 inches of
   their leaves, chopped (or 1
   chopped onion*
3 tbsps. flour
2 tbsps.butter
½ cup chicken or fish broth

1½ lbs. shrimp, chopped
*1 cup chopped fresh
   mushrooms*
3 egg yolks
¼ cup white wine
½ cup cream
dash of Tabasco
salt and pepper

Oysters Bienville are almost as good as Rockefellers—in fact some gourmets prefer them. Many diners order "6 x 6" (as six of each type at one serving are called).

Place the rock salt on the pans and place 2 dozen oysters on top of the salt, bake until about half done (7 minutes).

Prepare Bienville White Wine Sauce in advance as follows: Saute the scallions in butter until golden, add the flour, browning it; add the broth. Add the mushrooms and the chopped shrimp. Beat the egg yolks, the wine, and the cream together well; put them in the sauce, stirring rapidly to prevent curdling. Add the Tabasco and salt and pepper to taste. Allow to cook for 10-15 minutes. Spoon the sauce over the oysters, covering each oyster well with a whole pile of it. Sprinkle with mixed bread crumbs, paprika and cheese. Bake in the oven until light brown. Eat it in ecstasy!

WELLFLEET OYSTERS FLORENTINE
(Serves 4)

2 dozen oysters	*½ cup cream*
1 stick butter	*1 bunch spinach*
¼ cup flour	*Parmesan cheese*
½ cup fish or chicken broth	*salt and fresh ground black*
3 egg yolks	*pepper*

FLORENTINE

This is one of the favorite dishes of the epicures of Paris; duels have been fought in defense of its virtues. It combines qualities of Rockefellers and Bienvilles in a double layer sauce.

Melt the stick of butter in a skillet and add the flour; cook it slowly, stirring constantly to make a golden brown roux. Now add the fish or chicken broth, beat the cream and egg yolks together and add them; cook over very low heat for about 10 minutes longer, stirring constantly. This is a version of Mornay sauce, the classic French sauce for fish or shellfish.

Cook a bunch of spinach in butter, add salt and pepper to taste. Cream it in the blender or with an egg beater. Lay the deep halves of oyster shells on rock salt in pans. Cover the shells with spinach, lay an oyster on top of each, cook under the broiler flame for about 5 minutes or until the edges of the oysters curl. Next cover the oysters with Mornay sauce, sprinkle generously with Parmesan cheese and place under the broiler flame until the cheese is lightly browned. Serve in the hot baking pans.

EN CASSEROLE

WELLFLEET OYSTERS EN CASSEROLE
(Serves 2 to 4)

2 dozen small Wellfleet	*2 hard-boiled eggs, sliced*
* oysters*	*1½ cups heavy white sauce*
12 saltines	*¾ cup fresh mushrooms,*
½ stick butter	* chopped*
3 tbsps. olive oil	*¼ tsp. Tabasco sauce*
½ cup onion, chopped	*New York or Vermont or*
2 cloves garlic, minced	* Wisconsin sharp cheese,*
	* grated*

Some wizard named Marshall invented this beautiful dish (he must have been in his cups and made a mistake, which is how most great dishes are discovered). Here the common saltine cracker reaches a pinnacle of fame which it will probably never know again.

Put saltines, butter, olive oil, onion and garlic in casserole in preheated 300 degree oven. Bake and stir until the crackers are golden brown. While the saltines are toasting cook the eggs hard and make the white sauce. Drain the oysters and put their liquid in the white sauce for added zip. When the saltines have reached a rich golden brown, fold all of the other ingredients including the oysters into the white sauce and add it to the things already in the casserole, mixing gently. Sprinkle a thin layer of sharp cheese over the top, raise the oven to 350 degrees and bake until the cheese melts or the edges of the oysters curl.

SALTINE

To pull those saltines off their pedestal you can substitute good old New England common crackers, or pilot crackers or split beaten bisquits, and this recipe will still be yum, yum, yum.

FRIED WELLFLEET OYSTERS

Frying oysters sounds like a very simple culinary trick, but far from it. Very few cooks can do it exactly as it should be done. The secret is not to overcook them; a dark brown hard fried oyster is not fit to eat.

The batter is important. If you can get it, the commercial dry batter used by restaurants for frying clams is also excellent for frying oysters. Next best is the yellow corn flour of the type one buys in Italian, Spanish, or Latin American groceries (the Mexicans call it *masa harina*). The clam batter has built-in seasonings; the corn flour should be seasoned with salt and pepper.

ROCKS   OYSTERS
DO NOT OVERCOOK!

Allow twelve oysters for each serving. Drain the oysters. Roll them lightly in the flour. Fry them in deep fat that has been preheated to 260 degrees for 2½ to 3 minutes, depending on the size of the oysters. When done, the oyster will be a light golden brown on the outside, but most important, just heated through and still juicy on the inside. If cooked too long these natural juices will be evaporated and the oyster will be robbed of its distinctive flavor. Serve piping hot with lemon wedges and perhaps chili sauce, but never ketchup. It's sacrilegious to put ketchup on an innocent helpless oyster, no matter how it is cooked or served.

THE "PORE BOY" OYSTER LOAF
(Serves 2)

TONGING FOR OYSTERS

*1 loaf French or Portuguese
  bread, 18" long*
2 dozen oysters

lettuce, shredded
mayonnaise or chili sauce

Long before the invention of submarine and hero sandwiches, the Creoles down in New Orleans had invented an eighteen-inch-long sandwich called a "pore boy," because it was both economical and generous enough to make a full meal. In bygone days, when oysters were both plentiful and cheap, they were the principal ingredient of the "pore boy" sandwich. Nowadays, with oysters so expensive, they call it the "rich boy," or simply oyster loaf.

Split the loaf of bread into halves and clean the "pulp" out of each half, down to within a half-inch of the crust. Toast these halves, then brush generously with butter. Fry the two dozen oysters and pile them up on the bottom half of the bread. Cover them with a layer of shredded lettuce. Swab the inside of the top half of the loaf with homemade mayonnaise or chili sauce (no damn ketchup, didn't we tell you?), and place it in position on the filled bottom half. Cut it in half, now it's ready to go. It serves two people.

For some mysterious reason these taste best at 2 A.M. after a night on the town, served with a big mug of hot chicory *café au lait.*

THE PO' BOY

WELLFLEET OYSTER PAN ROAST
(1 Serving)

1 dozen oysters and their
  liquor
¼ stick of butter
1 tsp. chili sauce

dash of Worcestershire sauce
dash of Tabasco
salt and fresh ground black
  pepper

Melt the butter in a skillet, add the flavoring elements and stir them in. Add the oysters and cook them just until they are plump and their edges are curled. Place slices of toast on a serving plate, place the oysters on the toast and pour the pan juices over them. For those who do not care for fried oysters the pan roast oysters are ideal for filling the "pore boy" oyster loaf.

PIGS IN BLANKETS
(Appetizer for 2)

1 dozen oysters

6 slices bacon

Cut the bacon slices into halves crosswise, fry the bacon in a skillet until three-quarters done but still limp. Wrap each bacon piece around an oyster and skewer with a sharp toothpick. Place the wrapped oysters in a broiler pan and broil them on each side until the bacon is browned and the edges of the oyster inside are curled. Bacon and oysters have a great affinity and this dish makes an excellent appetizer or party hors d'oeuvre.

WELLFLEET OYSTER OMELET
(1 Serving)

4 oysters
1 slice bacon
2 eggs

1 tsp. cream
salt and fresh ground black
  pepper

Fry the slice of bacon brown, drain and crumble it. Pour off most of the bacon fat in the skillet, add the oysters, chopped in quarters.

Cook for only 1 minute, add the crumbled bacon. Set aside. Beat the eggs with the cream, pour into buttered skillet or omelet pan. Make the omelet in the usual manner using the oyster-bacon mix for filling.

WELLFLEET OYSTER STEW
(Serves 2)

6 scallions and 2 inches of their
    green leaves
¼ stick butter

1 qt. milk
1 pint (or 2 dozen) oysters
dash of paprika

This is one of the world's best cures for a hangover. Chop the scallions and their leaves thinly. Melt the butter in a saucepan and saute the scallions until they are soft and golden; add the oysters and their liquor and cook until their edges curl. Add the milk and heat to just this side of the boiling point (never let it boil or it will curdle). Add salt and pepper to taste and a dash of paprika.

WELLFLEET OYSTER BISQUE
(Serves 4)

1 qt. oysters and their
    juices
1½ pints light cream
3 tbsps. flour
½ stick butter

Tabasco sauce
sherry wine
salt and fresh ground black
    pepper

Melt the butter, add the flour and stir, making a roux. Add the cream slowly, bit by bit at first, and stir until very smooth. As it thickens add a little of the oyster broth; keep adding until it's medium thick. Add the salt and pepper and a dash of Tabasco. At the last add the oysters, which have been put through the medium blade of the grinder. (Or you can chop them up by hand if you can get a grip on them.) As a final touch add 2 tablespoons of sherry. Serve in preheated bowls with oyster crackers. This is a moment of glory for the Wellfleet oyster.

WELLFLEET OYSTER GUMBO
(Serves 6)

5 dozen raw Wellfleet oysters	*1 lb. sliced raw okra (or frozen okra)*
6 raw hardshell crabs, cut in pieces	*1 qt. oyster juice (or stock or bouillon)*
1 lb. peeled raw shrimp	*3 tbsps. flour*
6 raw tomatoes, skinned and chopped finely	*5 tbsps. butter*
	2 bay leaves
1 qt. plain water	*1 tsp. thyme*

About fifteen years ago the late great Mr. Roy Alciatore, the owner of Antoine's in New Orleans, gave me his recipe for Oyster Gumbo *a la* Antoine. When made with salty Wellfleet oysters this dish becomes transcendental. We do not have the blue hardshell crab called for in the recipe but you can substitute the local red crabs, or use a half pound of fresh or frozen crabmeat. I wouldn't usually recommend this, but since the Wellfleet oysters are the predominant item in this formula it's better to fudge a little than to go completely without our gumbo.

Use a good-sized pot or Dutch oven and in the bottom of it melt the butter and add the flour, to make a roux. Stir it constantly until the flour is lightly browned, but not scorched or burned. Add the pieces of chopped crab, stir and cook a little. Add bay leaves and thyme. Add the okra and allow it to cook some more until the okra takes on a gummy consistency. Next add the oyster juice and the plain water. (The oyster juice is very important but in case you do not have it, substitute stock, broth or bouillon.) Season with salt and pepper to taste. Allow the gumbo to simmer very slowly for an hour and a half. Ten minutes before serving, add the shrimp and the oysters. Serve in preheated soup bowls with boiled rice (place half a cup of rice in each bowl and ladle the gumbo over it).

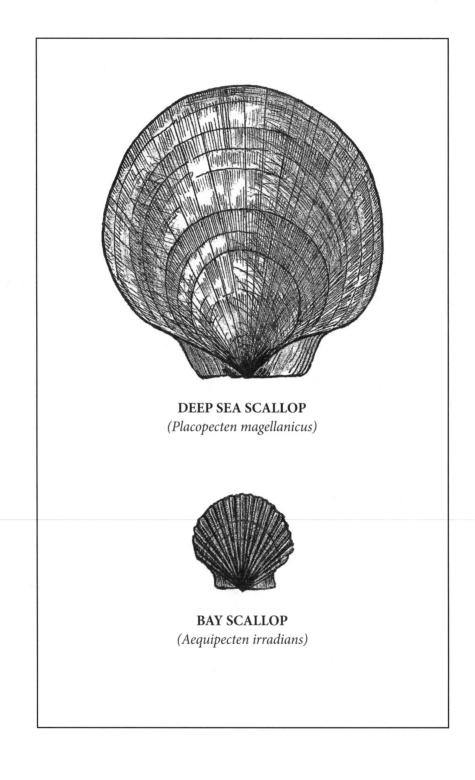

DEEP SEA SCALLOP
(Placopecten magellanicus)

BAY SCALLOP
(Aequipecten irradians)

The Beautiful Scallops

We are very lucky to have an abundance of scallops on Cape Cod. Our harbors and inlets are loaded with bay scallops and several of the draggers in the Provincetown fleet are sea scallop dredgers. You can find both kinds in the fish markets and they're usually fresh out of the sea, which makes a big difference. A scallop that has been frozen and thawed loses much of its flavor and texture, but don't get me wrong: when you're scallop hungry even a frozen scallop is better than none at all.

HE CAN SEE YOU!

Our little bay scallop is one of the tastiest morsels to come from the sea, and the larger deep sea scallop is almost as good. At extreme low tides you can find bay scallops tangled in the eelgrass or jumping around in the tidal pools. The scallop is the only bivalve mollusk who can actually jump and swim; it does so by clapping its shells together rapidly. And it's the only bivalve mollusk with eyes. It has primitive sight organs located at the tips of its gill rakers, and it can see you coming and jump to escape you. It's truly an amazing sight to see these shellfish jumping about in the water; it gives you a shock of bewilderment. These capacities put the scallop higher on the evolutionary ladder than the quahaug, oyster and other bivalves. (Of course the quahaug does have a "foot" and can "walk" considerable distances, but it certainly can't see where it's going. It walks only during extreme emergencies or when it's searching for a more comfortable bed to lie in.) A scallop can migrate for several miles from the place where it was born.

The little bay scallops have a very short life span, only twelve to eighteen months, and this autumn's adults will surely perish during the coming winter. So you should harvest as many of them as the law allows.

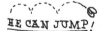
HE CAN JUMP!

Bay scallops hardly ever grow over two inches wide, while the sea scallop can live for a good many years and grow as large as a dinner plate. These beautiful large sea scallop shells are very common in Provincetown and all good scallop cooks will build a collection of them. You can buy them from kids who peddle them on the Street, or from gift shops or, if you're lucky enough to know a scallop fisherman, he will give you hundreds of them free. The ones you get from the scallop fishermen are often covered with sponges, barnacles and other sea growths. They should be scraped clean and boiled in a strong solution of water and bicarbonate of soda for an hour or more so you can get them completely clean and sterile. Never use soap or detergents to clean your scallop shells; they are porous and will absorb chemicals and odors from the soaps, making them useless for cooking. These shells make a perfect baking or serving dish, and are almost indispensible for the classic Coquilles St. Jacques recipes.

What we call "scallop" is really only the adductor muscle of the shellfish; the rest of the body is thrown away. This is a tragic waste. In Europe the whole thing is cooked and eaten. Suppose we ate only the muscles of the quahaug and threw the rest away! We'd be missing something.

Like oysters and quahaugs, scallops are delicious when eaten raw with a little lemon juice, salt, and just one drop of Tabasco. When gathering bay scallops it's hard not to eat them all up as fast as you catch them; they are fresh and salty and have an indescribable tang of the sea in them. When you eat them fresh on the beach they need no sauce at all.

A ten-quart bucket of bay scallops in the shell will contain fifty to sixty of the shellfish, and when shucked will produce approximately two cups of meats. When you go through the labor of gathering them and shucking them you will appreciate what a treasure they are. If sea scallops are large they should be cut up into eighths and each of these pieces will be approximately the size of a bay scallop.

Salute to St. Jacques

In Europe scallops are called Coquilles St. Jacques, "seashells of St. James." The apostle James is said to have wandered from the Holy Land to the northern part of Spain where he preached for seven years. Then he made a bad mistake; he went back to Jerusalem where old King Herod arrested him and beheaded him. His followers recovered his body, returned it to Spain and buried it at the village of

Compostela. He was the patron saint of shellfish and shellfishermen, and the scallop shell became his Symbol (except for some quirk of fate, it could just as well have been the oyster or the clam).

The shrine of Santiago (James again) de Compostela, because it produced many miracles, was the most popular pilgrimage spot in Europe in the eighth, ninth and tenth centuries. Pilgrims on the way to the shrine wore scallop shells on their hats, or tied to a string around their necks. After the Crusades had opened up the Holy Land as a goal for pilgrims, they continued to wear the scallop shell as a badge. It was high crime to rob or molest a pilgrim who wore the scallop shell, and it was considered unlucky not to give him alms to help him on his journey. Maybe if those later pilgrims to Plymouth had worn scallop shells around their necks they would have had more luck, but those roundheads put little stock in abstract symbolism.

·COMPOSTELA·

But to get back to cookery, any dish with scallops as a base can be called Coquilles St. Jacques. They are traditionally served right on the scallop shell. If you don't have a collection of large sea scallop shells you can use small individual casseroles, or ramekins, or pastry shells, or you can just plop the goodies on pieces of toast. If your scallop shells are too shallow to hold a full helping, you can put mashed potatoes in a pastry tube and squeeze a circle of potatoes around the edge of the shell to keep the sauce from slopping over. This is called a tinker's dam, an allusion to the old saying, "I don't give a tinker's dam."

COQUILLE ST. JACQUES, I
(Serves 2 to 4)

TINKER'S DAM

2 cups bay scallops or sea scallops, quartered (1½ lbs.)	¾ cup cream
	¾ cup grated Swiss cheese
	2 tbsps. flour
2 cups dry white wine	1/3 stick butter
¼ lemon	Parmesan cheese, grated
1 bay leaf	salt and fresh ground black
¾ cup milk	pepper

Heat the wine with the lemon quarter, squeezed, and the bay leaf; add the scallops and poach them gently until they are firm and opaque white clear through. Remove the scallops and set aside and keep warm.

Melt the butter in a saucepan, remove from the heat and add the flour and mix well; then add the milk and cream a little at a time, stirring constantly. Add ¼ cup of the poaching wine and stir it in. Return to the fire and add the grated Swiss cheese, stirring until it melts and makes a smooth mixture. Add the scallops and season with salt and fresh ground black pepper to taste. Place the scallops and sauce on four large sea scallop shells. Sprinkle with Parmesan cheese and brown lightly under the broiler flame.

COQUILLES ST. JACQUES, II
(Serves 2 to 4)

¼ stick butter
3 scallions and 2 inches of
   their leaves, chopped
½ cup chopped celery
1 tbsp. chopped parsley
½ tsp. powdered mustard

¾ cup chopped fresh
   mushrooms
pinch of dill weed
salt and fresh ground black
   pepper

Prepare the scallops and the sauce as instructed in the above recipe but omit the cheese from the sauce. Now prepare a vegetable mix as follows:

Melt the butter in a skillet and saute the vegetables until they are soft and transparent. Add the mushrooms, dill, and mustard. Mix well and season with salt and fresh ground black pepper. Add this mixture to the white sauce, and add the scallops. Stir and heat well, but be careful not to boil. Place the mixture on scallop shells that have been preheated. Sprinkle with chopped parsley and serve piping hot. These regal scallop dishes call for a good white or rosé wine, moderately chilled.

COQUILLES ST. JACQUES, III
(Serves 6)

½ lb. lobster meats, diced (from steamed lobster; save 1 cup of the broth)

½ lb. sea scallops, diced and gently poached 5 minutes

½ cup celery, finely chopped

½ cup onion, chopped

½ stick butter

1 clove garlic, finely minced

2 tbsps. flour

1 cup lobster broth

¼ cup sherry

1 tsp. salt

¼ tsp. fresh ground black pepper

1 pinch nutmeg

Melt the butter in a large skillet and saute the onions, garlic and celery until soft and golden. Add the flour and stir until well mixed and browning. Add the lobster broth and stir it in. Add salt, pepper, nutmeg and sherry and cook until blended and thickened. Add the lobster and scallop meats and cook a little longer. Fill the shells (6) with this mixture. Place under the broiler until lightly browned; brush with melted butter and sprinkle with just a few drops of sherry for pungency.

COQUILLES ST. JACQUES
(ON THE HALF SHELL)

SCALLOPS SHISH KEBAB
(Serves 2 to 4)

2 dozen sea scallops
2 dozen mushroom caps
thick slices of Canadian bacon
   or country ham
1 stick butter, melted

juice of 2 lemons
¼ cup dry white wine
salt and fresh ground black
   pepper

Because of their shape, size and flavor, sea scallops are ideal for making shish kebab, that skewered delicacy beloved by Armenians and Greeks. Here's one way to do it:

Place the scallops and mushroom caps in a glass bowl and pour the lemon juice over them. Sprinkle with salt and fresh ground black pepper. Let them "set" in the marinade for an hour, stirring them now and then. Meanwhile fry the Canadian bacon until it is three-quarters done but still limp. Cut the bacon into circles the size of the sea scallops (make 2 dozen circles). Now skewer the scallops, bacon and mushroom caps in an artistic, symmetrical manner. Grill on a barbecue grill, or hibachi, or under the broiler flame, turning now and then to cook all sides uniformly. Delicious, and lots of fun!

KEBAB!

BROILED SCALLOPS

Thousands will disagree with me but I state here and now, flatly, that it's a damned shame to fry a scallop; his flavor is so light and delicate that frying in hot fat destroys over 50 percent of the taste, and the batter or bread crumbs in which they are dipped before frying are nothing but surplus baggage. Next time you cook scallops try broiling them in butter, lightly, gently, quickly; this process seals in their flavor instead of burning it out.

SCALLOPS AU GRATIN

1 lb. scallop meats
2 scallions and 2 inches of
   their green leaves
½ cup sauterne
¼ cup sherry

1 cup cheese sauce (see
   below)
toasted bread
2 tbsps. Parmesan cheese
butter as needed

Combine the first five ingredients, put on slices of toast in a casserole. Sprinkle with Parmesan cheese, dot with butter, bake in a moderate 350 degree oven for 10 or 15 minutes or until brown. (To make the heavy cheese sauce, melt a little butter in a skillet, remove from the heat and add a little flour, then some milk little by little, stirring constantly. Return to fire and add some American cheese cubes, cook it and stir it until the mixture is thick.)

Home-grown Escargots

Provincetown has two delicious members of the sea snail family which can give the famed escargots of France a good run for their money: the moon snail, *Lunatius heros*, and the common periwinkle, *Littorina littorea*. The blue moon snail can be found burrowing along like a mole on any of our beaches at low tide. Most of them are small, but they sometimes grow up to two inches in diameter. Those of about one inch diameter make the best escargot bourguignonne. The largest ones are pretty tough and require tenderizing and should then be chopped and served as an appetizer in vinaigrette sauce. This snail is a voracious predator on quahaugs, mussels, oysters and other shellfish. It has a rasplike tongue and bores a neat round hole in its victim's shell, then sticks its tongue through and sucks out the body of the hapless shellfish; whenever you see a clam shell on the beach with a round hole in it, it means the moon snail got him. You save the lives of many other shellfish whenever you catch a moon snail and eat him.

The little common periwinkle is the best flavored of all snails. It's the tiny little fellow found crawling all over the rocks at low tide.

The breakwater in Provincetown's West End is crowded with them. It is extremely popular all over Europe; in Sicily they are called "*lumache*," in Brittany they are known as "*bigournoux.* " Some homesick Europeans first brought this snail here in 1840 and it has now spread all over the New England coast, much to the delight of gourmets. But the public in general takes very little notice of it, and the average person doesn't even realize it is edible.

ESCARGOTS BOURGUIGNONNE
(With Moon Snails)

Capture as many moon snails as you can of ¾ to 1-inch diameter. Put them in a pot and cover with salted water. After the water has come to a boil cook for 30 minutes. Douse them in cold water to cool them, then pick them out of their shells, discarding the "operculum," the horny brown door of the shells. Pinch off the stomach at the back end of each snail and discard. Split the snail down the belly to clean out the intestinal tract; rinse it out thoroughly because there is always some sand in there. Take a wooden mallet or paddle and pound each snail carefully a few times to tenderize it (don't pulverize it, please). While you are cleaning the snails boil the empty shells in a strong solution of bicarbonate of soda and water to purify them, then rinse them well.

The Sauce

½ lb. butter	3 tbsps. finely chopped
1 medium onion, grated	parsley
6 cloves garlic (pressed through	¼ cup dry white wine
a garlic press)	salt and fresh ground black
	pepper

Melt the butter in a skillet and add the garlic and onions. Cook for 2 to 3 minutes and add the parsley, wine and salt and pepper. Cover the bottom of baking pans with rock salt (or you can use regular snail baking trays if you have them). Take each snail shell and spoon some of the butter sauce into it, then shove a snail into the shell and cover it with some more of the sauce; sprinkle with a little granulated garlic and then with a layer of Parmesan cheese. Place the snail in its shell on the rock salt in the baking pan. When the pan is fully loaded, place it in a preheated 350 degree oven and bake until the layer of cheese is melted and lightly browned. Serve them piping hot right in the baking pan. Provide guests with nut picks or toothpicks to dig the snails out of the shells. They are usually served as a hot appetizer, but they are so rich and delicious you can make a full meal of them.

MOON SNAILS VINAIGRETTE

½ cup vinegar
1½ cups olive oil
1 small onion, minced

1 tbsp. fresh parsley, chopped
salt and fresh ground black
   pepper

This is a good way to utilize the larger, tougher moon snails. Boil, clean and tenderize the meats as instructed above. Make a vinaigrette sauce by combining the listed ingredients. Dice the moon snail meats and marinate them in the sauce for 2 or 3 hours. Serve cold as an appetizer. Spear the chunks of meat out of the sauce with toothpicks.

PERIWINKLES ITALIENNE

1 gallon periwinkles in the
   shell
½ cup olive oil
2 medium onions, chopped
6 cloves garlic, minced
1 8 oz. can tomato sauce
   (puree)
½ cup red wine

1 No. 2 can tomatoes,
   squeezed up
2 tbsps. fresh parsley,
   chopped
½ tsp. each of oregano, basil,
   thyme and cominos
salt and fresh ground black
   pepper

Saute the onions and garlic in olive oil until soft, add the tomato sauce (puree) and tomatoes, chopped parsley, oregano, basil, thyme and cominos (ground cumin), red wine, salt and pepper. Simmer for an hour until the acidity of the tomatoes is reduced; add some water if necessary. Add the periwinkles to the sauce and cook for 30 minutes more. One guest can eat fifty or more periwinkles easily. Dig them out of the shells with a toothpick, dip them in the sauce and eat them, feathers and all.

EPICURE
WITH PERIWINKLES

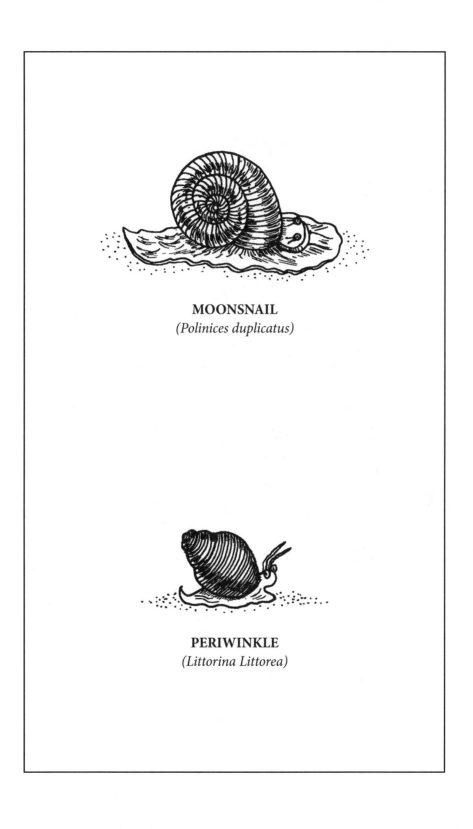

MOONSNAIL
(Polinices duplicatus)

PERIWINKLE
(Littorina Littorea)

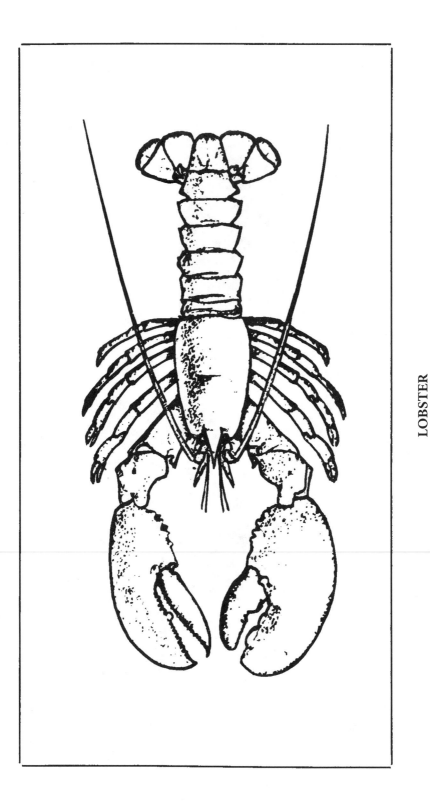

LOBSTER
(Homarus americanus)

CHAPTER II
The Crustaceans

I N MY OLD AGE when I'm retired, I'd like to run the world's most exclusive lobster house. It would be a little old one-room shack on stilts above the water, 12 foot by 12 foot, with just enough space for a stove and a rough table that would seat six people. There would be a trap door in the floor and a ladder leading down to my lobster storage box in the water. My menu would consist only of the five classic lobster dishes, with now and then a little madhouse experimentation. Admission would be by invitation or reservations made two weeks in advance (this should weed out the screwballs, rubber-neckers, etc., who are always "just looking around, thanks"). The joint would probably lose money hand-over-fist but I'll bet it would make gastronomic history, and at least it would be plenty of fun.

To my way of thinking, the five classic methods of cooking lobster are: (a) broiled, (b) steamed, (c) Newburg, (d) Thermidor, (e) lobster salad (remoulade).

Provincetown Started It!

EARLY
GOURMAND

The lobster industry in America had its beginnings right here on the tip of Cape Cod, and Provincetown was the first lobster center of New England. The earliest market records available show that large-size Provincetown lobsters were selling in Boston in 1740 for three half-pence each. The industry didn't really get started until around 1800 when the fishermen had perfected their techniques and the general public was affluent enough to develop a lobster taste.

For the next fifty years, Provincetown had a virtual monopoly of the Boston and New York markets, and they were just as jealous of their resources as they are today. In 1812, the people of Provincetown had a law pushed through the state legislature barring out-of-state fishermen from coming in and exploiting their bonanza. In those days, the lobsters were so thick on the beach at low tide that the citizens would go out on the beach and fill baskets and wheelbarrows with them. They sold them for a cent apiece, and what they couldn't sell they'd feed to the pigs. (Provincetown smoked hams in those days must have had a delightful lobster tang.)

Maine did not have a lobster fishery until around 1840, when the Provincetown men went up there and showed them how to catch 'em, much the same way that Provincetown and Truro men had gone down to Nantucket and New Bedford to teach those folks how to catch whales. In those days, Provincetown was the richest town per capita in New England because of its bountiful fisheries. Unwilling to share their resources, its people were generous enough in spreading their know-how (probably a subtle Yankee strategy to make their neighbors stay in their own back yards).

Biggest lobster news of recent years has been the revelation by scientists that no matter how many lobsters are caught locally they can't be overfished and depleted. Our Cape Tip lobsters are migratory, and they are only the fringe of a much larger migratory group. If we caught every lobster in our local waters it wouldn't damage the mainstream source of supply. In an interview, Tom Morrissey, a biologist for the Massachusetts Division of Marine Fisheries, stated: "This is a relatively unexploited population, and it seems that increased fishing will not diminish the catches in future years. In Maine and Canada where approximately 90 percent of the available crop is caught each year there has been no decrease in the quality or quantity of the lobster population." This came as a real shocker to most of us home grown conservationists who thought that skin-divers and other predators were dooming the famous Provincetown lobster to extinction.

BROILED LOBSTER

I don't need to tell you that the most important thing in preparing to cook a lobster is that it must be alive and kicking. If it's sleepy, it means that its flavor has already begun to deteriorate; if it's dead, it can give you food poisoning.

Split the live lobster down the back. Don't be chicken—it doesn't hurt it. Fold it open and remove the "lady" (the gravel-filled stomach bag) at the head, and the intestinal tract down the back. Lay it on a broiling pan and brush lightly with butter; place in the broiler about 4 inches below the flame. For a 1½ pound lobster, approximately 15 minutes is sufficient; larger lobsters require more time. A broiled lobster is done when the flesh has begun to turn golden and lost its transparent quality, and is firm to the pressure of the index finger. (A good chef walks around the kitchen pressing everything with his index finger; in time, the digit becomes as sensitive as a mine detector.) Serve with drawn butter and lemon wedges.

To make drawn (clarified) butter, heat a pound of butter in a small pan. Skim off the foam carefully and let it sit still until all the water, salt and other adulterants sink to the bottom of the pan. Pour off the clear butter, leaving the white residue in the bottom of the pan.

STEAMED LOBSTER

You often hear people (and cookbooks) telling of "boiled lobster." Actually, to boil a lobster is a sacrilege. It makes his tomalley a mushy mess. The word is STEAM. Put ½ inch of water, a table-

spoon of salt and a tablespoon of vinegar in a pot and bring it to a boil, put the live lobsters in, cover and steam for 15 minutes for one-pound lobsters, add 5 minutes for each pound with larger lobsters. If you have any doubt whether the lobsters are done, take one of them out and break the tail halfway off. If the tail meat is transparent and soft, it needs more steaming. If the meat is opaque marble-white and firm, then it is done. Be careful not to overcook lobsters, as it destroys their delicate flavor. Another way to tell if a lobster is done is to force open its curled up tail and straighten it out; release it quickly and if it snaps back into place with a sharp "clack" then the lobster is done. Split the lobsters, remove the "lady," de-vein, and serve on a platter with clarified butter and lemon wedges. Use a hammer or a nut cracker to crack the claws. Putting the vinegar in the water is an old Cape Cod trick that I learned from Cyril Patrick, Jr. It not only helps the flavor, it makes the shells a beautiful brilliant red.

LOBSTER À LA NEWBURG

I've wrestled for years with various classic Newburg recipes, twisting them around to find one that I really felt proud of. I eliminated eggs from the formula; with good butter, cream, brandy and sherry, the sauce is rich enough. Omitting the eggs simplifies the cooking process also. And there's the evaporated milk that I've added; everybody who ever ate a chowder knows that one-half milk plus one-half evaporated milk gives a much better chowder than plain milk does, and it does something for Newburg sauce, too. And I've thrown in a few chopped fresh mushrooms just for the hell of it. The purists will howl but here's my formula which has pleased many gourmets:

NEWBURG

Newburg Sauce
(Serves 8)

½ stick butter
6 tbsps. flour
1 pint cream
1 pint milk
1 pint evaporated milk
1½ tsps. salt

½ tsp. fresh ground black
  pepper
¼ tsp. nutmeg
½ cup sherry
½ cup fresh mushrooms,
  chopped

Melt the butter in a saucepan, remove from the fire and stir in the flour; mix it well with the butter, now add the cream a little at a time at first, stirring constantly. Then add the milk and evaporated milk. Return to the fire and cook slowly, stirring all the time. Add salt and pepper, nutmeg, sherry and mushrooms (the mushrooms are strictly optional and it's better to go without than to use canned mushrooms). Keep cooking and stirring and scraping the bottom (to prevent scorch) until it thickens, and there's your sauce—8 cups for 8 servings.

The Cooking Process
(2 Helpings)

¼ stick butter
2 cups lobster meat chunks
2 tbsps. brandy

2 cups Newburg sauce
toast triangles
rice

Don't try to cook over two helpings of lobster Newburg at a time; it fouls things up.

Melt the butter in a skillet and add the lobster meat chunks and brandy. Flame the brandy. Saute gently until the meats are lightly cooked. Add 2 cups of the Newburg sauce and cook for 3 or 4 minutes longer, stirring carefully so as not to break up the lobster chunks. Makes two generous helpings. Serve it in individual casserole dishes with toast triangles and rice on the side; serve a good light wine to counteract the richness of this dish.

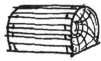

The Mysteries of Thermidor

More baloney has been written about lobster Thermidor than almost any lobster formula. The authoritative gourmet writers can't even agree on which Paris restaurant invented it, and the methods they give for cooking it are much too involved and impractical. As Thoreau said (and so did Escoffier), "Simplify, simplify!" Except for the cheese, onion, and mustard flavors, the Thermidor sauce is close cousin to the Newburg. Serving it in the lobster shells is a frill, of course; it's just as good in individual casseroles, or on toast, or in pastry shells. And most important—where I disagree with the authorities: broiling the lobster is better than baking it because it enhances the flavor without drying out the meat. Another folly is that many restaurants try to make a lobster Thermidor look like a Baked Alaska by covering it with a thick layer of Mornay sauce (white sauce and cheese). This is uncalled for; it's better to put cheese in the original sauce in place of the traditional egg yolks. So now that we've dispensed with the authorities, let's get busy.

LOBSTER THERMIDOR
(Serves 4)

2 2 lb. lobsters	¼ tsp. Tabasco
½ cup grated onion	½ pint cream, ½ pt. milk,
½ cup fresh mushrooms,	½ pt. evaporated milk
chopped	½ cup sherry
½ cup minced parsley	1 oz. jigger of good brandy
½ cup grated mild American	¾ tsp. salt
cheese	¼ tsp. fresh ground black
¾ stick butter	pepper
3 tbsps. flour	lobster fat and tomalley
1 tbsp. powdered mustard	Parmesan cheese

Twist the claws off the lobsters, steam the bodies and claws until done—about 15 or 20 minutes. After they have cooled a bit remove the meats; split the bodies and remove the tomalley and fat from the shells to add to the sauce. Keep the shells intact and save them. Dice the meat to bite-size pieces and set aside. In a small skillet melt ¼ stick of butter, add the onion, mushrooms and brandy and saute until the mushrooms are soft; stir in the parsley. Set aside.

In a large skillet or heavy saucepan melt ½ stick of butter, remove from the fire and add the flour and powdered mustard; stir it to a smooth paste. Add the milk just a little bit at a time at first and stir it in thoroughly; add the cream and evaporated milk and stir some more. Return to the fire, add the cheese, Tabasco, sherry, salt, pepper, lobster fat and tomalley, and the sauteed onion mix. Cook  slowly, stirring constantly and scraping the bottom until the cheese is all dissolved and the mixture has thickened. Add the lobster meats and cook and stir for 2 or 3 minutes longer. Fill the shells with this mixture. Sprinkle Parmesan cheese generously on top and place under the broiler until the Parmesan is lightly browned.

Lobster Remoulade

Listen, my children, and I will tell you about one of the greatest of all seafood sauces used for steamed lobster, boiled shrimp and other crustaceans. It's a marinade and dressing all in one. The magic things it does to these creatures is almost unbelievable.

It's called remoulade, pronounced "ruma-lahd." There are all kinds of funky, fake, red, yellow and brown versions of it served in unscrupulous restaurants from Paris to Patagonia. There are lousy overspiced and embalmed versions of it sold in jars in gourmet stores and supermarkets. The real item is like Hollandaise sauce—it has fresh eggs in it and will go bad if you try to keep or preserve it. The secret of this sauce is its homemade mayonnaise: Don't try to cheat and use flabby commercial mayonnaise. It just doesn't work.

REMOULADE SAUCE

1 qt. homemade mayonnaise (see below)	2 tbsps. capers
	3 hard cooked eggs, chopped
2 cloves garlic, finely minced	1 tsp. anchovy paste (or chopped fillets)
2 tbsps. chopped onion	2 tbsps. fresh parsley, chopped
2 tbsps. chopped sour pickle	1 tsp. paprika

Mix it all together well and if it is not zingy enough add more salt and more lemon juice or vinegar to make it sharp as a razor. Cut lobster meats into bite-size chunks (or use whole boiled peeled shrimp, steamed mussels, etc.) and marinate overnight in the remoulade sauce.

Served chilled, either as an appetizer or a full dinner.

Mayonnaise for Remoulade

4 egg yolks	½ cup lemon juice (or vinegar)
1 qt. olive oil (or vegetable oil)	
¼ tsp. Tabasco	1 tsp. salt
1 tbsp. powdered mustard	fresh ground black pepper

Beat the egg yolks and the flavoring elements together, continue beating and add the oil one drop at a time, and then in a very slow steady stream as the beating continues. Do this until all the oil is absorbed. If it curdles or is too thick it means you have added the oil too fast. Start over again using a new egg yolk in the mixing bowl and add the curdled mixture to it slowly. The final mixture should be firmly creamy, smooth and full-bodied.

LAGOSTA A PORTUGUESA
[Portuguese Lobster]
(1 Serving)

1½ cups lobster meat
1 cup molbo tomate
  (see page 49)

2 tbsps. imported brandy
2 tbsps. butter
½ tsp. chopped parsley

Native Cape Cod lobsters have a great affinity for the *molbo tomate* and for flaming brandy which adds to the piquancy of this dish. Steam lobsters until they are about three-fourths done, shell them and pick out the meats, fat and tomalley. Cut the meat up into chunks. This dish should be cooked only in individual or double portions; it just can't be mass produced.

Melt the butter in a skillet, add the lobster chunks and stir them around; add the brandy and flame it. After the flame goes out add the parsley and keep sauteing and stirring for about 2 minutes more. Add the molho tomate, raise the heat a little and cook and stir until all the elements are well blended. Serve in preheated individual casserole dish with slices of toasted Portuguese, French or Italian bread.

LOBSTER FRA DIAVOLO
(Serves 4)

2 1½-2 lb. live lobsters
½ cup good olive oil
½ cup chopped green
  peppers
2 tbsps. chopped parsley
  (flat leaf type)
1 lb. linguini (or spaghettini)
  pasta

2 cloves garlic, chopped
1 tbsp. dried basil (or 2 tbsps.
  fresh basil, chopped)
2 cups pomodori pelati
  tomatoes
2 tbsps. tomato paste
dash of crushed red pepper
  flakes

Lobster Fra Diavolo is one of the bright gems of Italian cookery. Its method differs from region to region and in the United States the techniques have been so "Americanized" that it's hard to find an authentic recipe for the dish. The well known artist

Ed Giobbi has furnished us with an authentic formula which was created by his grandfather in Abruzzi, Italy. *Bellissimo*!

Use a pot large enough to hold everything, including the whole live lobsters. Put all the ingredients except the linguini and lobsters into the pot and bring to a boil. Add the live whole lobsters and cover, turn the heat very low and simmer gently for 1½ hours. Stir it often, scraping the bottom of the pot. Make sure the heat is not too high or it will scorch (better put an asbestos pad under it to play safe). The sauce will be thick but not as thick as meat sauce; it will be light and delicate and enhanced by the flavor of the lobsters.

About 10 minutes before the sauce is done, start cooking the linguini (or spaghettini) in boiling salted water. Cook until it is "*al dente*," then drain it quickly to prevent overcook. Place linguini on hot plates and pour the sauce over it. Split or chop the lobsters, remove their "ladies" and veins, and serve them on the side, spooning part of the sauce over them.

LOBSTER BISQUE À LA MITCH

2 1½ lb. live lobsters	1 cup evaporated milk
2 onions, chopped	1 small can tomato sauce
3 scallions with half their green	(puree)
leaves, chopped	3 qts. fish stock or bouillon
1 celery heart, chopped	¼ tsp. nutmeg
1 stick butter	¼ cup sherry
2 tbsps. flour	salt and fresh ground black
1 cup cream	pepper to taste

The magic in this dish comes from the flavor imparted by the baked lobster shells. Place the fish stock or bouillon in the bottom of a pot and bring it to a boil; plunge the live lobsters in and cover and steam for 20 minutes. Remove the lobsters, pick out all their meats, the fat, the tomalley and coral; dice the meats and set all this aside.

Preheat the oven to 450 degrees and place the lobster shells in a pan and bake them for 20 minutes, or until they are well browned but not burned. Remove the shells and pound into small pieces in a mortar, moistening with a little of the stock from the pot. Place the pounded shells and the juice into the stock in the pot in which the lobsters were cooked; boil it rapidly for about 15 minutes or until approximately 1 quart of the liquid has evaporated. Strain off the liquid through a double cheesecloth and set aside.

Melt the stick of butter in a skillet and saute the onions, scallions and celery until soft and golden; add the flour and stir it in until it browns lightly. Add the tomato sauce and stir it in; add the strained stock and ½ the diced lobster meats, and all of the fat, tomalley and coral. Add the nutmeg and adjust salt and pepper. Cook the mixture slowly, stirring constantly until it thickens a little. Put it in a blender and cream it. Fold into this mixture the ½ pint of cream and the ½  pint of evaporated milk. Add the remaining diced lobster meat and the sherry. Put it all in a saucepan and heat to the boiling point. Serve in preheated bowls with slices of fried Portuguese, French or Italian bread.

Why the evaporated milk? some gourmets will ask. It prevents curdling and allows you to bypass using a double boiler, and furthermore it gives backbone and body to either bisques or chowders. That's why!

Crabs

There is a movement underway in government and fishery marketing circles to find a market for the New England red crab. This should not be hard to do at all because this crab is such good eating the public would buy them up as fast as they hit the sales counters. The problem is not so much a matter of finding a market as establishing a fishery and getting the crabs on sale while they are still alive and kicking.

NEW ENGLAND RED CRAB.

No one goes out deliberately to catch these crabs; they have always been a by-product of the lobster trapping business and a few are brought up in the trawls of the draggers. The lobster men used to regard them as pests; they would crawl into the lobster pots and occupy the space reserved for the lobsters. The lobstermen would dump them out on the floor of the boat, bash them with a club and throw the carcasses overboard. (In my opinion it would have been better to bash the lobsters and keep the crabs, because they are a tastier morsel.) Locally the lobstermen are now selling their crabs to the retail fishmarkets, and these in turn are selling them to the public as fast as they can get them. Compared to the outrageous price of lobsters, the crabs are a real bargain for the consumer, that poor jerk who is being gouged mercilessly these days for his two-bit dollars.

The best way to cook crabs is simply to boil them. It sounds like a contradiction but lobsters are best when steamed and crabs are best when boiled. The crab has a very tight shell and it needs boiling so that the spices and salt of the cooking liquor can penetrate inside to the meat.

Sometimes a lobsterman or fisherman will bring a couple of buckets of crabs into Cookie's Tap, and Joe will boil them and serve them up free. It's a great pastime for a lazy afternoon to sit around eating boiled crabs and washing them down with innumerable cold beers; you need time on your hands and no worries on your mind to really appreciate this.

HOW TO BOIL CRABS

If you have about 36 crabs, heat enough water in a pot to cover them and to this water add 2 packages of commercial crab boil spices (or 2 small packages of mixed pickling spices), 2 or 3 roughly chopped onions, 3 or 4 pieces of celery with the leaves on, a handful of parsley, a cup of salt and a tablespoon of cayenne pepper. Boil this stuff vigorously for ½ hour to make a good rich liquor. Dump the crabs into the pot, making sure they are all alive and kicking. Don't worry, it doesn't hurt them; they have a very rudimentary nervous system and a vocabulary limited to a hiss, which should leave you with a clear conscience.

After the water returns to a boil cook them for 25 or 30 minutes. When they are done the smell issuing from the pot is just like that of corn on the cob. Fish them out and cool them. (If you have more crabs to cook you can use the broth in the pot over and over; the stronger it gets the better the crabs will taste.) You can serve them immediately or refrigerate them and serve them very cold.

How to Eat Boiled Crabs
(A little melodrama in seven acts)

1. ACT I. Lay the boiled crab on the palm of one hand and grasp the legs in a firm grip between the thumb and the side of the hand. Place the other hand over the top of the crab and grasp the shell by the point and pull upward gently at the point area. The shell will lift right off.

2. ACT II. Take a knife (or use your fingers) and scrape off the "dead man's fingers," or gills, and discard. Dispose of the gizzard, the cellophanelike bag in the top of the body cavity, also the intestinal tract, the hard wormlike mass in the body cavity. Next break off the mouth parts at the front and discard, also the "apron" or genitals on the bottom of the shell. Now everything else is edible. The creamy yellow stuff in the body cavity is the crab's liver; like the tomalley of a lobster it is a great delicacy and should be spread like mayonnaise **3.** on lumps of white crab meat to serve as "sauce."

ACT III. Don't just pull off the crab's shell and throw it away; it's often a treasure house of the most delicious part of the crab, the stored away crabfat. Dig into the corners of the shell with your index finger and bring out the lumps of creamy yellow fat; as with the liver **4.** use it as a sauce on the white meat—it has a sharp acid flavor which contrasts beautifully with the meat's blandness. Twist off the claws, crack them with the handle of a table knife, and eat the meats.

ACT IV. When you get the crab's body cleaned off it will be composed of two partitions or sections, one on each side, each section tapering to a sort of crown. Take a sharp knife and cut off the top of each of these crowns.

ACT V. After cutting off the crowns you will have a perfect cross section of the crab's body, showing the meat in all the compartments as clearly as a draftsman's drawing. Break the body into **5.** two halves, and then, using the legs as handles, break each half into segments and bite off the meat. Then crack the legs with your teeth and eat the meats therein. (Your dentist may not approve of this, especially if you have bridgework or wear dentures.) A good crab eater is very conscientious about it; he doesn't waste the slightest bit of the delicious meat.

ACT VI. Boiled crabs should be washed down with voluminous quantities of good cold beer.

ACT VII. PLEASANT DREAMS!

STUFFED CRABS

2 lbs. crabmeat

12 crab shells

½ cup chopped parsley

1 green pepper, finely
   chopped

1 clove garlic, minced

1 large onion, chopped

3 cups bread crumbs

1 stick of butter or more,
   melted

sherry

salt and fresh ground black
   pepper to taste

One of the best ways to cook crabs is to stuff them, cram them, with their own meat. And crabmeat dressing makes an excellent stuffing for flounders, striped bass, blues, and other piscatorial treasures.

Depending on their size and weight it takes about two blue crabs to produce enough meat to stuff one crab shell, and with the Cape Cod red crab it takes three or more. Picking the meats out of boiled crabs is really a tedious chore, but it's a labor of love, and the final results are worth it. Of course you can buy canned or frozen crabmeat but it won't have the crabfat in it, or the fresh flavor, and since you won't have the shells you'll have to cook it in a casserole or pastry shell ramekins.

STUFFED CRAB

Mix the vegetables with the bread crumbs, add melted butter, add crabmeat and salt and pepper to taste. Mix well and divide into 12 parts and fill the crab shells with the mix. Bake in a 350 degree oven until golden brown. Before serving, brush the tops with melted butter and sprinkle with a few drops of sherry.

STUFFED CRABS AU GRATIN
(Serves 6)

2 lbs. meat from boiled crabs	pinch of nutmeg
12 crab shells	1 cup milk
¾ cup grated Swiss or Gruyere cheese	1 cup cream
	2 tbsps. flour
½ cup chopped fresh mushrooms	1/3 stick butter
	salt and fresh ground black pepper
½ tsp. powdered mustard	

Crabmeat has a great affinity for cheese and cheese sauces. Here's a good cheesy stuffed crab formula.

Melt the butter in a skillet, remove from the heat and add the flour. Then add the milk little by little, stirring constantly. Add the cream the same way. Return to the fire and add the grated cheese, stirring to make a smooth mixture. Add the mushrooms, mustard, nutmeg, salt, and fresh ground black pepper. Place a layer of this sauce in the bottom of each crab shell, then fill the shell with crabmeat; then cover the top with another layer of the sauce. Bake in a moderate oven until lightly browned on top. This is ambrosial enough for the Gods on Olympus. Wash it down with a good white Chassagne-Montrachet or some such liquid treasure.

If frozen or canned crabmeat is the only kind you can obtain, then you can fill pastry cups or individual casseroles with this mixture and it will still be delicious.

CRAB CAKES

1 lb. crabmeat	1 clove garlic, minced
¼ stick butter	1 tsp. Worcestershire sauce
1 small onion, finely chopped	½ tsp. powdered mustard
	2 egg yolks
3 tbsps. flour	dash of Tabasco
¾ cup cream	salt and fresh ground black pepper
1 tbsp. chopped parsley	

Melt the butter in a skillet and saute the onion, parsley and garlic until soft and transparent. Add the flour and stir it in well. Mix the cream with the Worcestershire sauce, mustard and two egg yolks; then stir this mixture into the skillet and mix well, cooking and stirring a short while longer. Add the crabmeat and stir it in gently so as not to break it up. Remove from the fire.

After the mixture cools shape it into small cakes. Dip these cakes in beaten eggs, then in bread crumbs, and fry in deep hot fat until lightly browned. Be careful not to fry too long or the flavor will be destroyed. Serve with a good homemade tartar sauce, or home-made mayonnaise, or a mild tomato sauce (no ketchup please!). Wash these cakes down with a good white or rose wine or a "green" Portuguese *vinha*.

CRABMEAT IN PASTRY SHELLS

You can make the above mixture and use it to fill pastry shells or ramekins; sprinkle with Parmesan cheese and bake in a moderate oven until the cheese is browned. If miniature pastry shells are used, it makes a great hot hors d'oeuvre for a cocktail party.

CRABMEAT AU GRATIN EN CASSEROLE

1 lb. crabmeat chunks
2 scallions and 3 inches
  of their green leaves ,
  chopped
¼ cup sauterne
1/8 cup sherry

1 cup au gratin sauce
  (see recipe above)
toasted bread
Parmesan cheese
butter

Combine the first five ingredients. Cover the bottom of a casse-role with toast slices and place the crab mixture on top of the toast. Sprinkle with Parmesan cheese. Bake in a 350 degree oven for 10 or 15 minutes or until the top is brown. This calls for a good white wine as accompaniment.

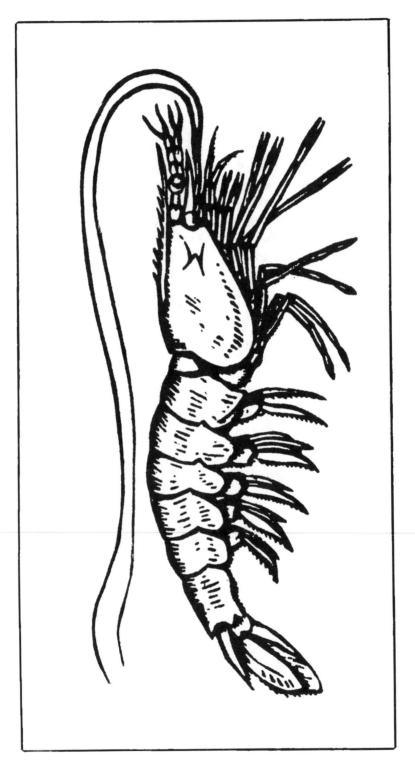

GULF OF MEXICO SHRIMP

The Succulent Shrimp

There's no doubt about it, shrimp have become the most universally popular seafood item in America today. Lobsters have a limited range and their price is usually exorbitant. Fresh saltwater fish are available only on the seaboards, close to where they are caught. Fish do not freeze as beautifully as shrimp. A housewife in Podunk, Iowa, who never heard of haddock or mackerel can get all the good frozen shrimp she needs at her supermarket. And now New England is getting in on the act! People have been hollering lately from Maine to Massachusetts that we have shrimp in our waters, too. And they're catching and marketing millions of pounds of them, and calling them shrimp. But it's a misnomer: these things are really prawns. When cooked the meats are soft, spongy and tasteless in comparison to real Gulf of Mexico shrimp. So read the label carefully when you buy frozen shrimp.

I spend the four coldest months of the year in New Orleans, the shrimp capital of the world, where we eat 'em for breakfast, lunch, dinner and 'tween meal snacks. When you're close to the source of supply and can get 'em fresh with their heads and shells on, the best of all ways to cook shrimp is to boil them, peel them yourself, plop them down your gullet and wash them down with plenty of good cold beer. As a jubilant festive occasion the Shrimp Boil is the southern equivalent of the Cape Cod clambake.

About eighteen years ago I organized a boiled shrimp and beer club called the Guild of Chimney Sweepers (in honor of Charles Lamb's annual dinner which he threw for the young chimneysweeps of London). Each year on the Saturday before Mardi Gras (Fat Tuesday), we throw a big shrimp boil for our friends. At our last big party we boiled 400 pounds of shrimp for 200 guests and gave them, for lubrication, 1,400 cans of beer. For music we had Kid Thomas and his Algiers Stompers, the famous old gut bucket jazz group from Preservation Hall, and the Olympia Funeral Marching Band. We struck a bronze medal as a souvenir of this joyous shindig which is pictured on page 131. It all just goes to show you what a helluva mys-

tique can be built up around the beautiful shrimp. He's as sacred to gourmets and Bacchanalians as the quahaug and the steamer clam.

When boiling shrimp by the hundreds of pounds you should divide them into 25-pound batches and boil one batch at a time. Trying to cook more at one time is foolhardy; the ones in the center of the pile will come out raw. Put a 25-pound batch in a pillow case, and put them in the pot of boiling liquor; make sure that they are loosely packed so that the hot water can circulate around all of them. We found by trial and error that the ideal cooking time is approximately 25 minutes. Of course this will be much less for smaller batches. Use the same cooking liquor over and over for each new batch; it gets richer and richer all the time. Allow 2 pounds or more of shrimp for each guest; a really hungry chimney sweeper can eat at least 6 pounds any old day.

CHIMNEY SWEEPERS BOILED SHRIMP
(Serves 5)

10 lbs. shrimp, whole, with heads on

1 gal. water (or enough to cover)

1 cup salt

1 lemon, sliced

½ bunch celery and leaves, chopped

2 big onions, chopped

½ head of garlic, chopped

4 tbsps. Worcestershire sauce

2 pkgs. commercial shrimp boil spices or 1 pkg. of pickling spices

1 tsp. cayenne pepper (or more if you like it hot)

Let the water with all the vegetables and seasonings boil rapidly for 20 minutes to make a good strong liquor. Put the shrimp in the liquor and when it comes back to a boil cook for 10 or 15 minutes or until the shrimp are hard and firm and peel easily. If undercooked they will taste fishy, if overcooked they will become shriveled and hard to peel; it takes a little practice to tell. When the shrimp are done remove them from the pot to the sink and run cold water over them to stop the cooking process.

Sauce for 10 lbs. Boiled Shrimp

2 bottles chili sauce
(no ketchup, please)
½ bottle horseradish
½ cup fresh parsley,
chopped

½ tsp. celery seeds
½ tsp. toasted poppy seeds
salt and fresh ground black
pepper
Tabasco to taste

Peel the shrimp and dip 'em in this sauce and wolf 'em down. Drink plenty of beer to help the process along.

SHRIMP BOILED IN BEER

If you will substitute beer for water in the boiling process above, the shrimp will taste even better. Costs a little more but the good things in life always come dear.

SHRIMP JAMBALAYA
(Serves 4 to 6)

2 tbsps. shortening

4 scallions and 2 inches of their
  green leaves, chopped

2 tbsps. parsley, chopped

1 green pepper, chopped

2 white onions, chopped

2 cloves garlic, minced

3 oz. can tomato paste

1 can of tomatoes, squeezed up

2 cups boiled rice

2 lbs. raw shrimp, peeled

salt and pepper

enough Tabasco to make it
  sizzle

JAMBALAYA

Saute the chopped vegetables in the shortening for a few minutes, until soft. Add the tomatoes and tomato paste. Simmer for a few minutes more and add the raw shrimp. Cook slowly for 10 minutes, add the boiled rice, the salt and Tabasco. Simmer for 15 minutes more.

SCAMPI CREAMED
(Serves 6)

72 raw shrimp, peeled

½ stick butter

3 tbsps. flour

1 pint cream

2 cloves garlic, minced

½ cup dry white wine

the juice of a lemon

salt and fresh ground black
  pepper

The Italians call shrimp "scampi," and the things they can do with the succulent little scamps is nothing short of miraculous. Here's one of my favorite formulas.

Melt the butter in a skillet, remove from the fire and stir in the flour; mix well. Add the cream a little bit at a time, slowly at first. Return to the fire, cooking slowly and stirring constantly. Add 2 cloves of garlic very finely minced, salt and fresh ground black pepper, the juice of the lemon and ½ cup of fine white wine. Keep cooking and stirring until the mixture thickens. Taste it and adjust seasonings. It should be sharp, salty and garlicky. At the end, dice a tomato into very fine cubes and stir it in; the tomato should just heat through and not cook. This makes enough sauce for six helpings.

Allow 12 medium-size shrimp for each helping. Heat some butter in a skillet and saute the shrimp approximately 1½ minutes on each side. Be careful not to overcook them or they become hard and tasteless. Take 6 individual casserole dishes and place 12 shrimp in each; cover them with sauce and stir well. Sprinkle the top with Parmesan cheese and brown it quickly under the broiler. Serve with toast triangles.

AVOCADO

SHRIMP STUFFED AVOCADOS

4 avocados	*2 cloves garlic, minced*
1 cup shrimp tails, boiled, peeled and diced	*peppers (optional)*
	¼ cup Marsala wine
1 cup crabmeat (or scallops), diced	*Parmesan cheese*
	2 tbsps. olive oil
1 tbsp. chopped parsley	*salt and pepper to taste*
1 medium onion, chopped	

Here's another delicious dish that I came across once in a small Italian restaurant.

Cut the avocados in half and remove the seeds. Heat olive oil in a skillet and saute the onion and garlic until soft. Add the parsley, shrimp, crabmeat, condiments and wine and continue cooking and stirring until they are well mixed and the flavors blended. Fill the avocados with this mixture and pile up a mound of it on top. Sprinkle with Parmesan. Place oiled aluminum foil in the bottom of a baking pan and place the avocados on it. Bake in a medium hot oven until the tops are browned. This is great served either hot or cold.

SESAME

SHRIMP WITH SESAME SEED

The black slaves who were imported against their will into the South brought with them the seeds of two African plants which have worked their way into "soul food" cookery, namely okra and sesame seeds. Among organic gardeners and macrobiotic food buffs sesame seeds have come into a great deal of prominence lately, but they've been here quite a long time. Dip shrimps in egg batter and then dip them in sesame seeds, picking up all the seeds that cling to them. Saute in butter until lightly brown. Don't overcook. The flavor is unique.

SWEET AND SOUR SHRIMP MILBY
(Serves 4)

2 lbs. shrimp, peeled
½ stick butter
1 cup honey

juice of 2 lemons
rice or noodles

Like many other Provincetown artists Frank Milby is a whiz kid in the kitchen; he likes to doodle, to freewheel it and play by ear with his taste buds as a guide. And nine times out of ten his experiments turn out beautifully. Here's one of them.

Melt the butter in a skillet and saute shrimp 1½ minutes on each side; add the lemon juice and honey and simmer for a few minutes more. Serve with rice or noodles.

BARBECUED SHRIMP
(Serves 4)

5 lbs. fresh shrimp with
heads on if possible or
5 lbs. frozen unpeeled
shrimp

6 sticks butter
6 heaping tbsps. black pepper

This dish is so simple that it is hard to believe it is absolutely one of the very best seafood concoctions in the whole world. It's nothing at all except shrimp, butter and black pepper. If you try to add anything else like herbs, spices, Worcestershire or other condiments you'll spoil it for certain. It is important to use fresh shrimp with their heads and shells on if you can find them. The tomalley inside the shrimp's shells is like the tomalley of a lobster and it adds a real punch to the sauce in the pan. However, if you can't find fresh shrimp, frozen unpeeled shrimp will make a dish that is almost as delicious, and better than most any shrimp dish you could find in a restaurant. At first glance it seems as if I'm calling for too much black pepper but as you'll discover later, it's just right; the heat cooks out of it (well, sort of). So try this out:

Wash the shrimp and drain them as completely as possible on paper towels; water would damage the sauce. Spread the shrimp in a big flat baking pan (or even a turkey roasting pan will do). Place the sticks of butter on top of the shrimp, sprinkle on the black pepper (it should be a thick layer, 1/16 to 1/8 inch deep). Place in a preheated 350 degree oven and cook for 45 minutes, stirring gently and turning the shrimp over every 15 minutes to make sure that all of them become saturated with the sauce.

The shrimp are brought to the table in the pan they are cooked in, and the guests gather around the pan and pick out their own shrimp, peel them and dip them in the sauce. Provide plenty of good hot French or Portuguese bread and dip chunks of bread in the sauce. This will feed four people sumptuously, and if you're not allergic to black pepper we think you'll like this dish.

BARBECUED SHRIMP, II
(One Serving)

18 shrimp tails in the shell   *black pepper*
1 stick butter, melted

Use what is called 20 count shrimp (20 to the pound). Arrange the shrimp on a metal sizzle platter. Pour the cup of melted butter over them. Sprinkle with a generous layer of black pepper. Place under the broiler flame for 4 minutes, turn each shrimp over and sprinkle on more pepper. Broil for 3 minutes more, or until well browned. The  guest should peel and eat these shrimp with his bare hands: messy, but delicious, and believe it or not they are not too hot—the black pepper does not penetrate the shells (well, not too much!).

FRIED SHRIMP AND ANCHOVY

1 lb. peeled raw shrimp	*beer batter (see below)*
1 can rolled anchovies	*tartar sauce (see below)*

The Spanish are very fond of shrimp and they're fond of anchovies too, so what could be more natural than that they should combine the two? This is a "tapa" (appetizer) that I was served at La Peria Restaurant in Granada.

Cut the anchovy rolls into halves. Take a shrimp and shape it into a circle. Take ½ an anchovy roll and embed it in the center of the circle; spear all the way through with a toothpick. This holds the anchovy in place and makes the shrimp keep its shape (see the marginal drawing). After all the shrimp have been fixed in this manner, dip them in beer batter and fry in deep hot fat (375 degrees) until light golden brown. Do not overcook or the flavor will be destroyed. Serve with homemade tartar sauce.

Beer Batter

1 cup flour	*1 tsp. salt*
1 cup beer	*1/8 tsp. black pepper*
½ tsp. baking powder	

Place the beer in a mixing bowl and sift the flour, salt, baking powder and black pepper into it. Mix it well, adding a little more beer if necessary. You can use it immediately but it will work better if you let it "set" for a couple of hours. It will keep for several days in the refrigerator and a little fermentation improves its flavor.

Tartar Sauce

1 cup homemade mayonnaise   *2 tbsps. chopped sweet pickle*
   (see page 112)   *1 tbsp. finely chopped parsley*
2 tbsps. finely chopped onion *juice of ½ lemon*

Mix all the ingredients well and chill before using. A home-made tartar sauce tastes so much better than the embalmed commercial varieties that there is no comparison at all.

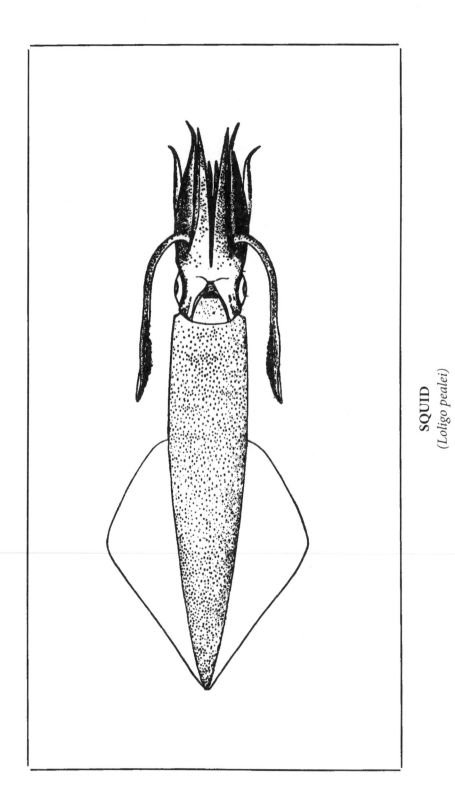

SQUID
(Loligo pealei)

Homage to the Homely Squid

I make no apologies for the homely squid; it doesn't need them. In the hands of a skillful cook this octopusfaced monstrosity is one of the world's greatest seafood delicacies. But poor thing, nobody knows how to cook him, except a few million Chinese, Japanese, Siamese, Vietnamese, Indonese, Micronese, Melanese, Javanese, Balinese, Nepalese, Polynese, Portuguese, Italians, and Spaniards.

We Americans are so vain, cocky, and arrogant that we think many great foods are inedible just because you can't buy them at the drug store lunch counter. We think we know it all, but we miss an awful lot while the rest of the world goes right on enjoying itself. We need to revamp our thinking on a lot of things, including food and cookery. And now that the sermon is finished let us proceed.

The common squid, *Loligo pealei* the scientists call him, abounds in the waters around Cape Cod and our fishermen sometimes catch enormous quantities of them. Many of them are thrown back as "trash," others are sold as bait to the sport fishing boats, the crew members may take them home for their wives to cook, and a few of them end up at Cookie's Tap, which is the only Portuguese restaurant in Provincetown with the time and patience to make squid stew. Squid is the favorite food of the striped bass and sometimes the bass will drive large schools of them into Provincetown Harbor. The poor squid will be so frightened and exhausted they will jump right out of the water onto the beach, and the townspeople will gather them up by the basketful. The town's population of 876,543 seagulls will have a picnic, too. But these bonanzas are infrequent and if you want to get squid you'll just have to ask a fisherman friend to save you some of his catch.

SQUIDS À LA MUFFLER

Provincetown's fishermen are sometimes so busy with the fish that they don't have time to stop to fix lunch, so Captain John Santos and Vic Pacellini tell me they take small tender squids and lay them on the hot exhaust pipe and muffler of the boat's engine. In a few moments they are brown and crisp as a potato chip. They eat them whole, feathers and all, spitting out the "beak," the hard mouth part of the squid. These beaks are what cause ambergris to form in a whale's belly; they scratch his innards and the ambergris forms around them and he vomits it all up. If a man swallowed some of these he might produce some homemade ambergris, an enterprise worth investigating because the stuff—used as a base in expensive perfumes—is worth a hundred dollars an ounce.

SQUID RINGS

FRIED SQUID RINGS

Everybody has eaten French fried onion rings, but few people have had the joy of eating fried squid rings. The squid's body is a cylinder and can be cut up into perfect circles. Pull the tentacles and head off, clean out the inside of the body cavity and remove the cellophane-like backbone called the "pen." Slice the body up into circles ¼ inch wide. Dip these rings in beaten egg, then in flour, and fry in deep hot fat. Keep all the rings separate from one another or they will stick together. Cut off the tentacles just in front of the eyes and dip and fry these, too—to me this is the best part. These fried squid rings and tentacles are good for hors d'oeuvres, or a snack or a full meal; the squid's meat is very rich and nutritious. Serve with a homemade tartar sauce.

WOK

SQUID FRIED RICE

The Japanese and Chinese are past masters at the art of squid cookery. Squid fried rice is as good as ham fried rice any old day.

Clean the squids, chop their bodies and tentacles into small dice, fry and set aside. Cook 1 cup of rice in 2 cups of water, with a teaspoon of salt (see instructions on the package). Spread the rice out on a flat pan and heat it in the oven a moment to get rid of excess moisture. Heat some peanut oil in a wok or heavy iron skillet, add chopped dried mushrooms, chopped green onions and part of their green leaves, chopped parsley, small green peas, the rice, the squid, some soy sauce and a little monosodium glutamate (I never fool with this stuff except in Chinese cookery). Toss it all around constantly until it is heated through and the rice begins to brown. Serve at once with a little hot saki in small cups to wash it down.

SWEDISH SQUID

The Swedes are good at all forms of seafood cookery and they discovered that squid and spinach have a great affinity for each other.

Butter a pyrex dish or casserole and place a thick layer of spinach on the bottom. Clean squids and split them and spread them out flat. Place a layer of squid on top of the spinach, then another layer of spinach on top of that, and so on, until the dish is nearly full. Cover the top with grated Parmesan cheese mixed with bread crumbs. Bake in a hot oven for 30 minutes or until the squid is tender and the top is well browned.

MITCH'S DELUXE STUFFED SQUID
(Serves 6 or More)

2 dozen large squids	*1 piece celery, chopped finely*
1 lb. shrimp tails, chopped	*2 cloves garlic, minced*
6 strips bacon	*3 cups bread crumbs*
2 medium onions, chopped	*salt and fresh ground black*
4 scallions and 2 inches of their	* pepper*
* green leaves, chopped*	*butter*
2 tbsps. chopped parsley	*sherry*

Clean 2 of the squids and dice the meats of the body and tentacles finely. Fry the bacon in a large skillet until crisp and brown, remove and drain it on a paper towel, then crumble it up. Pour off half of the bacon fat in the skillet and in the remainder saute the onions, scallions, celery, garlic, and parsley until the vegetables are soft and transparent. Add the diced squid meats, chopped shrimp, and crumbled bacon and cook for 10 minutes longer, stirring constantly. Season with salt and fresh ground black pepper. Add the bread crumbs, wet the mixture with enough chicken broth or bouillon to make a heavy paste of it. This is your stuffing; set it aside.

The cleaning of the squids is a tricky business because we want to keep the head and tentacles on so the squid will look whole and pristinely alive after it is cooked. So split the body carefully and clean out the innards and cellophane-like backbone. Remove the beak-like mouth part just below the eyes. Rinse thoroughly.

THE SQUID SHOULD LOOK... ...ALIVE!

SEW HIM UP WITH SURGICAL SKILL

Stuff the squids with the dressing, filling them only 2/3 full; the dressing will expand and the squid will shrink, so if you overload them, they will burst during the cooking. Take a needle and strong thread and sew them up in the best surgical manner, working from the tail upward, and when you reach the top put a couple of loops through the head to keep it from falling off. Lay the squid on a square of heavy-duty foil, sprinkle with a tablespoon of melted butter and a teaspoon of sherry, dust with salt and pepper. Lift the edges of the foil, roll them up and crimp them tightly; then roll up and crimp the ends.

When finished you will have a hermetically sealed cylinder. Bake in a 400 degree oven for 30 minutes, or a little longer if the squid are large. Take them to the table in their foil wrapping and serve each guest two or three squids, according to his capacity. Stuffed squid should be washed down with a good full-bodied red wine.

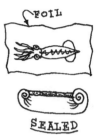

Of course a squid cooked in the above manner is actually steamed, not baked; this method is used to avoid excess shrinkage. But some people prefer them actually baked naked, even though they shrink up to less than half their former size. Fifteen years ago the Portuguese ambassador in Washington sent me the following recipe and I must admit that it is very good, but due to loss from shrinkage it will not serve over four people. Or it can be used as a side dish or hors d'oeuvre for a seafood buffet.

PORTUGUESE STUFFED SQUID

16 squids	*1 cup olive oil*
lean bacon, diced	*1 cup white wine*
1 chopped onion	*3 tbsps. tomato paste*
chopped parsley	*boiled potatoes, sliced*
3 yolks of eggs	

Use small tender young squids. Wash the squids and remove their heads and wing flaps. Remove the backbone and clean out and rinse the inside of the tube bodies. Chop the tentacles and wings finely and weigh. Add half the weight of chopped lean bacon and fry together in hot fat with chopped onion. When cooked, add salt and fresh ground black pepper and the yolks of 3 eggs. Mix well and stuff the squids with this mixture. Hold with a toothpick. In a baking dish make a sauce with the olive oil, white wine, tomato paste, and salt and pepper. Place the squids in the sauce and bake for 30-45 minutes, basting frequently. Place sliced boiled potatoes in the baking dish and serve very hot.

VIC PACELLINI'S STUFFED SQUID

12 squids
12 slices bacon
1 lb. chicken livers
1 8 oz. can tomato puree

1 cup white wine
salt and fresh ground black
*   pepper*

Place the bacon in a skillet and fry it gently until it is three-quarters done but still limp. Remove from the pan and set aside. Saute the chicken livers in the bacon fat in the skillet until they are three-quarters done, season with salt and pepper. Remove the livers, drain on paper towels and chop them up coarsely. Clean the squids as instructed in the first stuffed squid recipe, keeping the heads on.

For each squid take a strip of bacon and line the bottom of the stomach cavity with it, then cover with chopped chicken livers until two-thirds full. Sew them up. Place the squids in a well-greased baking pan; the side with the bacon should be facing upward. Sprinkle with tomato puree and the white wine. Bake in a 350 degree oven for 30 to 45 minutes or until the squids are browned and tender. When you eat this, cut it crosswise in slices so you'll have a little piece of bacon with each bite.

STUFFED SQUID ITALIAN STYLE
(Serves 2 to 4)

4 good-sized squids

The Stuffing:
6 slices bread, moistened and
*   kneaded*
2 cloves garlic, minced
1 tbsp. fresh parsley, chopped
2 tbsps. olive oil
1 tbsp. grated Parmesan cheese
chopped tentacles and wings of
*   the squids*

The Sauce:
½ cup olive oil
1 tbsp. chopped parsley
1 clove garlic, sliced
2 cups tomatoes
½ tsp. oregano
1 cup green peas
steamed rice

This is another of artist Ed Giobbi's Italian masterpieces.

Clean the squids by removing the heads and wings. Carefully turn the tubes inside out, and scrape and wash them. Be sure to remove the backbone. Turn them right side out again. Cut off the eyes and the beak-like mouth part from the tentacles. Chop the wings and tentacles and put them in the stuffing. Mix the bread, garlic, parsley, olive oil, Parmesan cheese, tentacles and wings; stuff the squids with the mixture (sew up the opening to keep it from oozing out). Heat the half cup of olive oil in a skillet and saute the stuffed squids, adding salt, black pepper, crushed red pepper, garlic and parsley. Keep sauteing over moderate heat until the squids begin to brown. Then add the tomatoes and oregano, cover the pan and simmer very slowly for 30 minutes or until the squids are tender. Add the peas and cook another 10 minutes. Serve on hot plates with steamed rice on the side.

PORTUGUESE SQUID STEW

See page 151 in the chapter on soups and stews.

WATERFRONT VIEW FROM THE EAST END, 1895

CHAPTER III
Beautiful Soups
and Stews

Soo—oop of the e—e—evening,
Beautiful, beautiful Soup!

—The Mock Turtle

SHELLFISH, crustaceans, fish—they make the world's greatest soups and stews. Dig back in your memory and try to think of the best soup or stew you ever ate; was it a chowder, a gumbo, a bouillabaisse, *sopa de pesce*, green sea turtle soup with sherry wine? The list is endless. The culinary possibilities of shellfish and fish in soup and stews are infinite; they blend well with one another, they produce their own stocks, sauces and flavoring elements. If the recipes for all the great seafood soups and stews in the world were gathered together in one volume, it would make a hefty tome, very interesting reading, practical to use—good cooking and good eating. Someday, when we finally run out of beef and pork, our cooks will be forced to turn to food from the sea. Then they'll realize what a lot of fun they've been missing all along. Let us start off on the subject of chowder.

A Chowder is a Chowder is a . . .

Everybody on Cape Cod has his own ideas about how to make clam chowder. Chowder is like people: sometimes it's very good, and sometimes it's plain lousy. It's okay to go dashing off on experimental tangents, but sooner or later you'll realize that the hidebound method of the old-time Cape Codders is the best. The Provincetown quahaug chowder recipe given below is over a hundred years old, but it's just as good today as on the day it was written.

Quahaugs make the best of all chowders; their meats are so tasty and chewy they never let you forget they are there, and their liquor adds such a clam-flavored zing to the liquid in the chowder that this dish stands out as the epitome of Provincetown's seafood gourmandise. The important thing to remember is that chowder will sour very easily if you don't handle it properly, especially when made in big batches. Never leave the cover on a pot of chowder while it's cooling; the condensation will spoil it. Never put a chowder in the refrigerator until it has completely cooled to room temperature. If it is cooling on a flat table or shelf, put a spoon or fork under the pot to tilt it slightly and allow air to circulate underneath the pot. If a skin forms on the top of it, skim it off carefully. A chowder always tastes best on the second or third day, but many a chowder becomes a fermented mess before it reaches the second day. I must have ruined dozens of gallons of fine chowder until a wise old chef came along and whispered these secrets into my wooden ear.

TILT THE POT

It is also important to remember that quahaugs must not be overcooked, or they will become tasteless and tough. That's why you'll never get a really good quahaug chowder in a restaurant; it is so light and delicate that it can't stand the prolonged heat of a steam table in a restaurant kitchen. So you shouldn't be lazy and steam your chowder quahaugs open to get at the meats. Open them with a clam knife according to the instructions given on page 38. After you've shucked 1½ quarts of meats, chop them up coarsely with scissors or a sharp knife.

QUAHAUG CHOWDER
(Serves 6)

1½ qts. chopped quahaug meats
1¼ lb. salt pork, cut in small cubes
3 medium onions, chopped
2 large potatoes, diced
2 tbsps. flour

1 qt. milk
1 pint evaporated milk
2 cups quahaug liquor
salt (if necessary) and fresh
   ground pepper
water as instructed

Fry the salt pork in the chowder pot, adding a little water to keep it from getting browned. When the pork is almost done, add the onions and a little more water and cook until they are soft; then add the potatoes and enough water to just cover. Simmer until the potatoes are done. Add the quahaugs and 2 cups of quahaug liquor. Dissolve the flour in a little milk and add it to the pot, stirring it in well. Cook a little longer and there's your basic chowder. When ready to serve add the milk and the evaporated milk and heat it through, but don't boil it. Add salt if necessary (remember, the salt pork and the quahaug liquor furnish much salt) and fresh ground black pepper to taste. Serve in large bowls with pilot or common crackers.

PORTUGUESE CLAM CHOWDER (MILKLESS)
(Serves 6)

1 10-qt. bucket of cherrystone
  or littleneck quahaugs
¼ stick butter
1 medium onion, chopped
2 cloves garlic, minced
2 fresh tomatoes, diced
1 qt. fish stock or bouillon

½ cup chopped fresh parsley
1 1" piece of linguica, sliced
  thinly
¼ tsp. saffron
¼ tsp. ground cominos
1 cup dry white wine
salt and fresh ground black
  pepper to taste

Shuck the quahaugs and save their liquor. Cut the meats up with scissors and set aside. Melt the butter in a saucepan and saute the onion, garlic and linguica together until onion is soft; add the tomatoes and parsley and stir them in. Add the fish stock, the clam liquor, the saffron, cominos and wine. Cook rapidly for 10 minutes to blend all the flavors. Lower the heat a little and add the clam meats and cook 10 minutes longer.

Serve in large preheated soup bowls with Portuguese garlic bread on the side. You can add zest to this soup by adding desalted pieces of dried codfish, or fresh cod, haddock, hake or whiting chunks; then you can call it *calderaida*, Portuguese seafood stew.

PORTUGUESE FISH CHOWDER (MILKLESS)
(Serves 6)

1 6-lb. cod	*¼ tsp. saffron*
1 medium onion, chopped	*½ tsp. cumin*
4 medium potatoes, diced	*2 qts. water or fish stock*
2 tbsps. diced salt pork	*1 tbsp. cider vinegar*
1 garlic clove, minced	*salt and pepper to taste*

In a pot fry the pork, add the garlic and onion, and saute until soft and translucent. Add the water (or stock), the saffron, and cumin. Bone the fish and cut it up in pieces; add it to the pot. You may add the fish's head too and remove it later. Add the potatoes, and salt and pepper; cook for 20 minutes at a slow boil. At the end add the vinegar and stir it in. Serve in large preheated soup bowls with pilot crackers or common crackers.

MANHATTAN CLAM CHOWDER

1 10-qt. bucket of quahaugs (or
   steamers if you can't find the
   quahaugs)
¼ lb. salt pork, diced
2 medium sized onions,
   chopped

1 cup chopped celery
½ cup chopped parsley
1 32 oz. can plum tomatoes
dash of Tabasco
1 bay leaf, pinch of thyme, basil
   and oregano

Shuck the clams and save their liquor. Fry the pork cubes in a skillet, adding a little water to keep the pork from getting too brown; remove the pork and put it in the chowder pot. Put the celery and onions in the pork fat in the skillet and saute them until soft and translucent; add them to the pot. Squeeze up the tomatoes into the pot. Add the clams and the clam liquor. Add the parsley, bay leaf, thyme, basil, oregano, Tabasco and fresh ground black pepper. (Do not add the salt until the end, as the clam liquor is very salty and it intensifies.)

The ingredients in the pot should be just covered by the liquid (½ inch); add water if necessary to achieve this. Simmer on the very lowest fire for 5 hours; this is the very slow classic Italian or Portuguese simmer—it does not boil or even bubble. Stir it now and then and add more liquid if necessary. At the end of 5 hours, remove from the fire, cool it down to room temperature, then place it in the refrigerator to age overnight. This "aging" is very important in bringing out the flavors of a Manhattan chowder. Heat it next day, serve with saltines, or pilot crackers or common crackers. Devour it with glee.

FISH HEAD CHOWDER
(Serves 6)

Milkless chowders, fish and shellfish soups and stews, bouillabaisse, *calderaidas*—these specialties are found in sea-coast fishing villages throughout the world, and they are usually best when made by the fishermen themselves. Since they are so close to the sea, Provincetown's Portuguese fishermen are especially adept at this no-nonsense cookery, and it usually turns out that the simpler the formula the better the savor of the food. Here is Captain Seraphine Codinha's recipe for fish head chowder:

Take 2 big codfish heads and 2 big haddock heads and put 'em in a pot with a gallon of water. Add some fried onions and diced potatoes and boil slowly for 45 minutes to 1 hour. You just couldn't imagine the delicious flavor of this simple stew.

HADDOCK CHOWDER
(Serves 4)

3 lbs. haddock fillets
¼ lb. salt pork
4 potatoes, diced
4 onions, chopped
1 qt. milk or 1 pint cream
   mixed with 1 pint milk

1 qt. fish stock
2 tbsps. butter
2 tbsps. flour
salt and fresh ground black
   pepper
pilot or common crackers

One of the secrets of making a good fish chowder is to use fish stock instead of plain water. To make stock you boil the head, tails, fins and bones, and maybe even a small whole fish, for 30 minutes to extract their essences.

To make haddock chowder: Fry the pork in a skillet with a little water until the pieces are opaque white; remove from the pan. Lower the heat, put the onions in the pan and saute until golden brown; drain off the fat. Put the potatoes, onions and the fish stock in a pot and cook slowly until the potatoes are done; they should be firm, not mushy. While the potatoes are cooking take a skillet and make a roux by cooking the butter and flour together until golden; add this roux to the materials in the pot and stir it in gently. Cut the haddock fillets into 1-inch pieces and add them to the pot. Add the pork, cook slowly for about 10 minutes (haddock must not be overcooked or its flavor is murdered).

Do not add the milk or milk-cream mixture until just before serving. When you do add it, heat through gently, do not boil. Add salt and fresh ground black pepper to taste. Place a pilot cracker in the bottom of each bowl and ladle the chowder on top of it. Float a little dab of butter in each bowl, add a dash of paprika and a pinch of chopped chives.

CODFISH CHEEK AND TONGUE CHOWDER

24 codfish jawbone halves and
tongues (enough to produce
a quart or more of meats)
2 onions, chopped
4 potatoes, diced
1 pint milk

¼ lb. salt pork, cut in small dice
1 pint can of evaporated milk
pilot or common crackers
salt and fresh ground black
pepper

The cheeks and tongues attached to the jawbones of the codfish are some of the best parts of the fish. They are usually regarded as trash and thrown away, but if you can get a fisherman friend to save you a few of them, you are in for a real treat. They not only make a delicious chowder, but they are excellent when fried (see page 193).

Place the jawbones with tongues attached in a pot and add a little over a quart of water. Cover and boil for 10 minutes. Remove the jaws and tongues and cool for a moment, then pick off the meats from the bones and set aside. Discard the bones, strain the stock and set aside 1 quart of it. Place the diced pork in a skillet and add ½ cup of water, cook until the pork cubes are white and opaque clear through. (Contrary to what many people think, the pork in a good chowder should not be cooked brown; this detracts from the delicate flavor of the fish.)

Add the onions to the skillet and saute until they are soft and translucent. Place the quart of fish stock in a soup pot and add onions, pork and potatoes. Simmer until the potatoes are nearly done, then add the fish chunks and cook for 10 minutes more. Add the milk and evaporated milk and bring to just this side of the boiling point. Adjust the salt and add the pepper. Place pilot crackers or common crackers in the bottom of large preheated soup bowls, ladle the chowder over the crackers and serve at once.

Courtbouillon

I used to try to lead the high life in my youth, but now that I have laid away childish things, I like to get stewed and whip up a stew for a pretty girl, and sing in my best Donald Duck voice: "A loaf of bread, a jug of wine, a pot of stew, and you. . . ." The dolls really hate my singing but they usually swear by my stew. Don't forget that from time immemorial seafood has been known as the best of aphrodisiacs, and a brain food to boot. A dozen cherrystone quahaugs or raw oysters on the halfshell will get you further with a nice girl than a quart of booze. I'm not sure what it will do to your IQ.

No list of stews would be complete without a recipe for *court-bouillon* (pronounced "coobyong"). It's one of the glories of Cajun Louisiana; in classic French cookery a *courtbouillon* is just a fish stock, but in Louisiana it's a whole big stew. Cajun folksingers have about a half dozen songs about redfish courtbouillon, most of which are based on the theme "I want some Coobyong, Mama, and your love and affection"—typical Gallic forthrightness and warmth. Here on Cape Cod we don't have the redfish or channel bass (*Sciaenops ocellata*), but we've got something that makes as good, or even better courtbouillon: our old friend the striped bass, ye squid hound, *Roccus saxatilis*.

COURTBOUILLON

10 lbs. striped bass steaks (cut the fish in 1½" cross sections, keeping the bone)
1 No. 2 can tomatoes
1 8 oz. can tomato paste
¾ cup olive oil
½ cup flour
4 large onions, chopped
6 cloves garlic, chopped
1 cup chopped celery
2 lemons, sliced
3 bay leaves
½ tsp. thyme
½ tsp. allspice
1 chopped green pepper
1 cup fresh mushrooms, chopped
1 cup fresh parsley, chopped
½ tsp. fresh ground black pepper
1 tsp. Tabasco sauce
2 cups Burgundy
2½ qts. fish stock or water
1 lb. rice, steamed

Now at a casual reading you'll say that my damned stew recipes all sound just alike. But there's always a certain something that makes them very different from one another. In the case of courtbouillon it's the roux that makes the difference. The roux is the gravy-like overture to much French and Creole cookery. The great Escoffier said that corn starch made a much more easily digested roux than flour, but I never saw a Cajun cook use it, and I've eaten lots of delicious Cajun food. The secret probably lies in slow, slow cooking. A real good cook is never in a hurry even when he's rushed.

DUTCH OVEN

This dish requires a Dutch oven, but if you haven't got one you can pinch hit with a big plain pot and asbestos pad, and a skillet.

Heat the olive oil in the skillet and when it is hot, add the flour; lower the heat and cook it very gently, stirring constantly and scraping the bottom of the skillet until the roux becomes brown (this will really try your patience but the result is worth it). Now add the onions, garlic, green pepper and celery and cook a little longer. Then add the tomatoes and tomato paste and cook some more. It should be sort of smooth and pulpy. Stir in the mushrooms, salt, pepper, Tabasco, and bay leaves. Put the mixture into the big pot, light the fire and put the asbestos pad underneath.

Stir into it the 2½ quarts of fish stock (or water) and the 2 cups of wine. Add the bay leaves, thyme, allspice, lemon slices, Tabasco, etc., and mix it up well. Let it come to a boil for 10 minutes; add the fish, lower the heat and let simmer for 15-20 minutes until the fish is done and the liquid is the consistency of medium gravy. Meanwhile, start steaming your rice in another pot according to the instructions on the package. Serve the courtbouillon and gravy on rice in deep bowls. Sprinkle chopped parsley over it. The one that gets the greasiest chin is the biggest gourmet.

FLOUR RICE

A Small Restaurant and a Big Stew

This is the story of a small restaurant and a big stew. The restaurant is Cookie's Tap in Provincetown, and the stew is squid stew. Cookie's is one of the few restaurants in New England that still makes a good Portuguese squid stew; it's becoming a lost art. The wives of Provincetown fishermen sometimes make it at home, but not very often: they don't like the muss and fuss of cleaning squids. But the Portuguese are so fond of squid stew that they attach an almost mystical significance to it. A good Portygee would walk two miles through a howling nor'east gale just to wrap himself around a hot bowl of squid stew.

Squid stew is definitely not a dish for an impatient landlubber. The first dish shocks you; it tastes like chopped up tennis shoes to many people. The second dish numbs you. Somewhere along about the sixth bowl you begin to realize that the dish *does* have a unique and distinctive flavor and from then on, brother, you are hooked.

The Lord took away a great *bon vivant* and gourmet back in 1946 when he laid a heart attack on Friday Cook in the prime of his life, only forty-eight years old. His grandfather had come here as cabin boy and cook on Captain Kibby Cook's whaling vessel, and the family adopted the name both of the vocation and the

benefactor. Friday ran one of the most amazing bars and restaurants in America. All the fishermen hung out at Cookie's and they would bring in their "trash" for which there was no ready market: crabs, giant lobsters, squids, butterfish, catfish, wolffish, pollocks, blinkers, conches, tinkers, quahaugs and Lord knows what else. Friday and his wife, Clara (and later, sons Wilbur and Joe) would cook this stuff in all sorts of tantalizing ways, and they'd pile it on the counter. Anybody who didn't look TOO greedy and hungry was invited to help himself. I remember that in my first summer here I didn't spend a nickel on food; I spent my dimes on beer at Cookie's, and the food was on the house. The late John Gaspie, the clamdigging *bon vivant*, would sit with me all afternoon, spinning fabulous yarns as we devoured galvanized tinkers and squid stew, and sipped the foamy. Halcyon days they were.

Friday is gone, but Clara and Wilbur and Joe are still carrying on. As is typical in the strongly matriarchal society of the Portuguese, the mother is the backbone of the business; she works discreetly in the background, but does she produce! Clara Cook is a walking encyclopedia of the tricks and twists of Portuguese cookery. 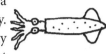 But darn it, not even her own children can get her to write down any of her recipes. In fact she does not have any; she plays by ear, straight from the heart, guided by intuition and her taste buds. *That* is Fine Art. I could never hope to duplicate Clara's squid stew, but here's a formula that will do for a starter.

SQUID STEW

3 doz. squids and their
   tentacles
diced potatoes equal in
   volume to the squids
1 quart red wine
1 quart water or fish stock
(more of these liquids if
   necessary)
1 can tomatoes, squeezed up
1 small can tomato paste

1 onion, chopped
6 cloves garlic, minced
3 tbsps. olive oil
2 tbsps. Worcestershire sauce
pinch of ground allspice
pinch of ground cominos
salt to taste
enough powdered cayenne or
   Tabasco to make it hot as
   hell

Saute the onions and garlic in the olive oil until they are soft and dump them into the stew pot. Put all the vegetables, liquids and condiments into the pot, bring to a boil, then lower the heat and simmer for 1 hour. Then add the squid meats and tentacles; raise the heat to a boil, then lower to the simmer and cook for 1, 2, 3, 4 or 5 hours, according to the amount of time you have on your hands. Stir it now and then, and if necessary add more liquids. Serve in large bowls with hot Portuguese bread.

On a cold winter night a bellyful of squid stew will make you sleep well.

SHELLFISH SOUP
(Serves 6)

1 cup raw shrimp
1 cup shucked mussels
1 cup shucked steamer clams
  (or quahaugs)
1 large onion, chopped
1 large potato, diced
2 cloves garlic, minced

½ cup parsley sprigs, stems
  removed
½ stick butter
1 bay leaf
4 cups fish stock
1 cup cream

Scrub the mussels and clams in their shells. Place the shellfish and the shrimp in a saucepan with ½ cup of fish stock. Steam until the mussels and clam shells are open. Shuck the clams, shuck the mussels and beard them. Set aside. Remove the shrimp from the liquor and set aside. Strain the liquor through double cheesecloth and mix it with the fish stock (for fish stock, see comments on p.158).

Heat the butter in a saucepan. Add the onions and potatoes and cook until tender. Add the fish stock, parsley, saffron, bay leaf and garlic, bring to a boil, then lower to a simmer and add the shellfish. Remove the bay leaf and discard. Simmer for 10 minutes. Ladle into soup bowls. Preheat cream and stir about 2 tablespoons of it into each bowl of soup. Sprinkle a little chopped parsley on top.

TWO FISH SOUP

2 FISH

1 lb. whitefish fillets (haddock, hake, whiting, flounder or cod)
½ lb. mackerel fillets (or blue fish or other fat fish)
6 cups fish stock (made from the heads and bones of your fish)
4 scallions, chopped, with part of their green leaves

2 tsps. fresh parsley, chopped
1 piece celery, chopped
1 small carrot, chopped
1 cup raw rice
2 tbsps. butter
¼ tsp. allspice
paprika
salt and fresh ground black pepper to taste

Victor Pacellini, the Provincetown fisherman-gourmet chef, says that when you make a fish chowder or soup you should always use two different species of fish, one white and lean and the other fatter and richer. This way they'll counterbalance one another and add zip to your "zoop."

Melt the butter in a deep skillet or Dutch oven. Add the scallions, parsley, celery and carrot. Stir and cook until all the vegetables are soft and transparent. Add the fish stock, the rice, the allspice, salt and pepper. Bring to a boil and simmer until the rice is about half done (about 20 minutes for white rice, brown rice takes a little longer). Cut the fish fillets into 2-inch squares and add them to the pot. Cook for 15 minutes longer. Serve in preheated soup bowls with chopped parsley and paprika sprinkled on top.

MUSSEL SOUP
(Serves 4)

1 gal. of mussels in their shells	*1/3 cup dry white wine*
½ carrot, diced	*1 bay leaf*
1 piece of celery, diced	*¼ tsp. thyme*
1 small onion, chopped	*1 clove garlic, minced*
1 tsp. chopped fresh parsley	*4 tbsps. butter*
	1 qt. fish stock or bouillon

Scrub and clean the mussels; put them in a pot with the white wine, ¼ cup water and the bay leaf. Cover and steam them until their shells open. Take the mussels out, shuck the meats and beard them. Set aside; strain the liquor in the pot and set it aside. In the bottom of a saucepan or deep skillet melt the butter and saute the onion, carrot, celery and garlic until soft. Add the parsley and thyme and stir them in and cook a little longer. Add the mussels and their liquor and the fish stock. Heat through and serve in preheated soup bowls with lemon wedges on the side.

A Local Joy

Although this is primarily a seafood cookbook, we must include in this soup section the two soups which are the pride of Provincetown's Portuguese cooks: kale soup and cabbage soup.

SOPA DE COUVRES
[Kale Soup]

2 bunches of fresh kale or 2
  cellophane bags of fresh
  chopped kale or 3 frozen
  pkgs. when fresh kale is out
  of season
½ lb. chourico sausage
1 lb. linguica sausage
a cellophane bag of white pea
  beans

5 medium potatoes, diced
a large soup bone, sawed up so
  the marrow will seep out out
  of it
beef broth or water as needed
dash of red pepper seeds
1 tbsp. vinegar
salt and pepper to taste

Soak the pea beans overnight. Put the beans and the bones in a pot, cover with beef broth or water and boil gently for 1 hour. Add the chourico and linguica sliced in ¼-inch pieces; add kale and cook slowly for an hour more. Add the potatoes and condiments and simmer for as many hours more as you want—the longer it goes the better it tastes . . . 5 or 6 hours is not too much. Always keep the ingredients well covered by adding more hot broth or water if necessary. Remember that a Portuguese simmer does not even boil or bubble; it's probably the world's slowest cook, but it gets spectacular results.

SOPA VERDE
[Cabbage Soup]

2 heads green cabbage
1½ lbs. linguica
1 lb. chourico
1 cellophane bag of white pea
  beans
5 medium potatoes, diced

a large soup bone
beef broth or water as needed
dash of red pepper seeds
1 tbsp. vinegar
salt and pepper to taste

SHRED CABBAGE
THIN AS A HAIR !

Shred the cabbage as thinly as possible (an electric meat slicer set at its lowest focus is ideal for this). Cook as instructed for the kale soup. And here's a tip: Most Portuguese cooks put a little kale in the cabbage soup and cabbage in their kale soup; they mix beautifully. It would require a master taster to tell which of these two soups is the best, but my sympathy leans slightly toward the cabbage.

Variations: No two cooks make these soups just alike. Two typical variations are the use of white butter beans or red kidney beans instead of pea beans.

VIEW OF WHARVES IN THE WEST END, 1908

CHAPTER IV
Some Seafood Symphonies

PAELLA IS, to me, one of the grandest and most delicious of all seafood symphonies. It's the national dish of Spain, the glory of Valencia, Barcelona, and the Mediterranean islands of Majorca, Menorca and Ibiza. After being a paella fancier for twenty-five years and meditating, ruminating and gestating on it, I have come up with the following recipe based on products available in Provincetown. It's definitely a dish for special occasions; it takes a lot of work and it costs plenty of money; if you're either lazy or short of cash, you had better skip this one. Our recipe calls for a large batch of it. You can make a smaller, more economical paella by cutting down on quantities and eliminating any of the items as you see fit. In Spain this dish would be cooked in a large flat pan called a paella, or a large earthenware casserole, but since few home kitchens have this type of equipment you can make do with three utensils: a big skillet, a big stew pot and a turkey roasting pan. After you have assembled all your ingredients, proceed in the orderly stages that we have outlined.

PROVINCETOWN PAELLA
(Serves 10)

A SIMPLE PAELLA

2 doz. littleneck quahaugs in their shells	*1½ cups olive oil*
2 doz. mussels in their shells	*6 cloves garlic, minced*
2 2 lb. live lobsters	*3 onions, chopped*
½ doz. squids	*1 16 oz. can plum tomatoes*
1 lb. haddock fillets	*1 8 oz. can tomato sauce (puree)*
1 lb. fresh or frozen shrimp	*1 green pepper, chopped*
½ lb. smoked country ham	*1 pkg. frozen green peas*
cut in strips (or prosciutto,	*1 small jar pimientos, cut in*
or just plain ham!)	*strips*
1 3 lb. frying chicken, cut up	*½ tsp. Tabasco*
into 10 pieces	*1 cup sliced fresh mushrooms*
½ lb. chorizo sausage	*2 lbs. rice*
(Spanish) or linguica or	*fish stock (see below)*
chourico	*salt and fresh ground black*
	pepper to taste

The Fish Stock Ingredients

4 lbs. fish heads, bones, tails,	*½ tsp. powdered saffron or*
trimmings	*1 tsp. of the stringy type*
4 quarts water	*(if you can't get saffron*
4 cloves garlic, minced	*substitute 1 tbsp. turmeric to*
3 onions, chopped	*achieve yellow color)*
1 cup chopped parsley	*½ tsp. each basil and thyme*
1 lemon, sliced	*4 tsps. salt (or more)*
½ tsp. ground cominos	*½ tsp. fresh ground black*
1 pint dry white wine	*pepper*

Preparation of the Fish Stock

Place all the ingredients for the stock in the stew pot and boil for 30 minutes; while it is cooking you can use it as a medium for cooking the shellfish and crustaceans. Drop the lobsters in and cook them 20 minutes. Scrub very clean the mussels and clams in their shells. Make a "sack" of a double layer of cheesecloth and put the mussels and clams in it; lower it into the pot and cook until the shells are all open, about 10 minutes. Put the shrimp in cheesecloth and lower it into the pot for 5 minutes. All these items will contribute beautiful flavors to the stock. At the end of 30 minutes when all the shellfish have been removed, strain the stock through double cheesecloth into another container and set it aside.

The Seafoods

Take the cooked lobsters and pull off their tails. Take a large sharp knife and cut these tails into slices, shell and all. Set aside. Pull off the claws and separate the end of the claw from the knuckles. Crack all these parts with a hammer, but leave the meats inside them. Set aside. Open the front shells and remove the fat and tomalley. Cream this and mix it with the stock. Discard the rest of the shell.

Keep the opened mussels in their shells but beard them (pull off the little mossy string inside the mantle). Set the mussels and the quahaugs aside in their shells. If necessary peel the shrimp and set them aside. Cut the haddock fillets into 1-inch squares. Clean the squids and dice them, but keep the tentacles whole; cut them off the head just in front of the eyes (these look like baby octopi and they give an authentic "Spanish" look to the paella). Set the squids and tentacles aside.

The Chicken, Ham, Etc.

Cut the chicken up into 10 frying size pieces. Heat ½ cup of olive oil in the skillet and fry the pieces on both sides until about ¾ cooked (15 minutes); set aside. Put the ham, the sausage cut in ¼-inch slices, and the squid meats and tentacles in the skillet and saute until lightly browned. Remove and set aside.

The Sofrito (Vegetables, Etc.)

Heat ½ cup more of olive oil in the skillet and saute the onions, garlic and green pepper until soft and transparent; add the parsley and stir it in. Add the tomatoes, squeezed up, the tomato sauce, mushrooms, pimientos, Tabasco sauce, green peas and lemon slices. Mix well; add a little stock to the pan if it seems dry. Cook slowly for 20 minutes.

The Rice

Heat another ¼ cup of olive oil in the skillet and add the rice. Stir the rice around in the skillet until it becomes golden yellow.

Now here comes the climax. Mix everything together that you have made (except the stock) in the turkey roasting pan; do it gently so as not to tear things up. Add enough of the fish stock to just cover everything. Preheat the oven to 350 degrees. Cover the pan and bake it in the oven for 20 minutes (or until the stock is absorbed). Uncover the pan and bake 10 minutes more. Oh! What a dinner! Serve a good red Spanish or Portuguese wine with it.

Gumbo is a Miracle

Like jazz and the blues, gumbo has an Afro-Caribbean background with a shot of French. The word "gumbo" itself (it was originally spelled with an "o") has in it the overtones of voodoo, mumbo-jumbo and secret ritual; it's a Tshi tribal word from the Gold Coast of Africa, and it stands for okra, the delicious mucilaginous vegetable that serves as the basis of the magical stew. The earliest slaves brought okra seeds over with them to the Caribbean islands, and when it became combined with the seafood of the New World and a few French herbs you've gotcha gumbo. But like jazz and rhythm and blues it's at its best when made by blacks. Some well-springs deep down in them produce the blue notes.

You can leave out several of the elements and still get a delicious mess of goo, but try to get as many of the items as possible. If you're lucky enough to know a fishing boat captain or crewman he may be able to get fresh crabs and shrimp for you; if not, you'll have to fall back on the frozen or canned variety.

Have your butcher saw up the hambone so all the marrow and flavor will seep out.

CAPE COD GUMBO
(Serves 20)

1 2 lb. live native lobster

*1 doz. live crabs (or
1 lb. frozen or canned
crabmeat)*

*2 lbs. fresh or frozen shrimp
in their shells*

*2 doz. fresh shucked
Wellfleet oysters and
their juices*

*2 doz. fresh cherrystone
quahaugs and their juices*

*2 doz. fresh mussels,
scrubbed clean*

1 1½ lb. chicken, chopped up

1½ lbs. stewing beef, diced

*1 hambone with a little
meat on it*

¼ lb. salt pork, diced

3 large onions, chopped

*1 lb. okra (or 2 pkgs. of frozen;
use canned okra only when
you can't find the others)*

6 cloves garlic, minced

2 chopped green peppers

1 cup chopped celery

3 No. 2 cans tomatoes

1 cup fresh sliced mushrooms

1 lemon, sliced

2 bay leaves

½ tsp. thyme

5 tbsps. Worcestershire sauce

*1 tsp. Tabasco sauce (or more
to taste)*

*½ tsp. fresh ground black
pepper*

5 qts. or more of fish stock

2 cups white or red wine

OKRA

The operation calls for three utensils: a big cooking pot, a medium steaming pot and a big skillet.

Fry the salt pork in the skillet until the cubes are brown and their grease is extracted. Remove the cubes and put into the large pot, leaving the fat in the skillet. Put the beef in the skillet and sear quickly to seal in the flavor; remove and put in the pot. Sear the chicken the same way and put in the pot. Remember, this is just a quick process of browning the outside. Now, if necessary, add a little more fat and put the onions, green peppers, garlic and celery in the skillet and saute until golden brown, stirring constantly. Add the okra and continue cooking for a few more minutes, then put it all into the large pot. Start the fire under the large pot and add the tomatoes, 4 quarts of fish stock, parsley, lemon slices, hambone and all the herbs, condiments and flavoring elements except the salt. Cover the pot and simmer slowly for 2½ hours, during which time you will be working with the shellfish and crustaceans as follows:

Put 2 cups of dry white wine into the steaming pot and add the well-scrubbed mussels and cherrystone quahaugs. Steam all the shells open; leave the wine and broth in the pot, remove shellfish and shuck them, beard the mussels and set the meats aside. Put the other quart of fish stock in the pot with the wine broth, bring it to a boil and put in the lobster and crabs and steam them 20 minutes. Add the shrimp in their shells and boil 10 minutes more. Take the crustaceans out and pour the broth into the large pot, except for the last few teaspoons, which will likely contain a little sand from the clams. Shell the lobster meats, saving the fat, coral and green stuff; dice the meats and set aside. Save the shells.

Open the crabs' shells and clean out all the fat in the corners of the shells and save it; save the shells, too. Scrape off the gills of the crabs and discard, clean the entrails out of the body cavity but save any fat or coral. Twist off the legs and flippers and discard. Save the claws; pinch off the mouth parts in front and the genitals behind. The crab's body will now be 2 neatly joined halves, which break into 2 pieces. Set aside; they go into the pot whole. Put the claws of the crabs into the pot now, but save the body halves. Peel the shrimp and save their shells. Bite a chunk off a shrimp and eat it; if it has a strong iodine flavor the shrimp must be deveined. Set the meats aside.

Now here's one of the secrets of a real good gumbo. Put the shells of the lobsters, crabs and shrimps (and shrimp heads if they had any) in a mortar or other heavy container and pound them up with a pestle, or use a heavy champagne bottle or some such instrument. When you get them all cracked up, take out the pieces and tie them up in a double layer of cheesecloth and throw the bundle into the big pot. Strain into the big pot any juices that settled to the bottom of the mortar during the pounding. These shells are a wonderful flavoring element, and along with the crabfat give a real kick to the gumbo.

Shuck the oysters and set aside; put their liquor in the big pot. Now all this stuff in the big pot should simmer gently for about 2½ hours; it should be kept completely covered with fish stock or water—

if it evaporates, add more. Don't try to rush it or it will scorch. If the pot is thin put an asbestos pad under it to prevent scorching. At the end of this time, add all the shellfish and crustacean meats and the half crabs; add the salt. It should still be covered with stock; add more if necessary. Bring back to a boil and simmer very gently and stir lightly now and then for 15 minutes more. Remove the chicken bones, the hambone, and the bag of crushed shells. Taste it and adjust the salt; it should taste good and salty. Serve the gumbo over steamed rice in big deep soup bowls, making sure each bowl gets some of all the elements. Now you oughta accompany this with some fine Champagne and soft music on the hi-fi.

It's a hell of a lot of work, but a labor of love and worth it. Doctor Joe Civetta, the famous surgeon, and I made a potful not long ago at his summer home in Wellfleet, exactly according to the above specifications. The preparations took us all day, but the results justified the effort; his twenty guests were very happy.

Zarzuela, a Shellfish Orgy

Provincetown and the rest of Cape Cod are blessed with such a great number of shellfish and crustaceans that we ought to give thanks each day to Allah, Jehovah, Oceanus, Triton, Neptune or whoever it is that provides us with these bounteous gifts. Because, as everybody knows by now, the quahaugs, steamers, mussels, oysters, shrimp, lobsters and the rest are the most delicious things to come out of the sea. Yes, yes, the fish are delicious too, but when all the chips are down a plain fish just can't stack up against the shellfish and crustaceans. The culinary possibilities of these creatures are unlimited; it boggles the mind. For many years I have been experimenting with hundreds of recipes, trying to find the best ways to cook them—to separate the wheat from the chaff.

Catalonia in Spain is famous for three things: (1) the primitive Romanesque frescoes dating back to the tenth century, (2) Picasso's birthplace, and (3) zarzuela. In the Spanish theatrical world, *"zarzuela"* means variety show, and that is exactly what this dish is. It is a delicious stew of many kinds of shellfish and crustaceans that ranks with France's bouillabaisse and Italy's *zuppa de pesce* as one of the world's great seafood dishes.

And fortunately, we have most of the makings for it right here on Cape Cod. It's one of those improvisational fishermen's dishes, where you make do with whatever you have at hand. But classically, the purist Catalan chefs get into it as many varieties of shellfish as they can lay their hands on. *Nota bene:* Although it is a shellfish dish, if you're too poor to afford lobsters, crabmeat, oysters and shrimp, you can substitute chunks of skate wing, goosefish, haddock, hake, whiting or ling (mud eel) and still get a good stew. So give the dish a trial with Cape Cod products. Frankly, it is as expensive as hell! But as I said, you can do it on a shoestring by making substitutions.

A CAZUELA

Ideally the dish should be cooked in one of those large earthenware casseroles called a *cazuela*, but since these are pretty scarce you can substitute a Dutch oven or a large skillet. Now here we go:

ZARZUELA À LA CAPE COD
(Serves 6)

24 littleneck quahaugs	4 scallions with their green leaves, chopped
24 steamer clams	
24 mussels	3 cloves garlic, minced
48 periwinkles in their shells	½ cup olive oil
	5 tbsps. chopped parsley
3 small squids	¼ cup sliced almonds
24 Wellfleet oysters	1 cup dry white wine
24 peeled shrimp	1 oz. jigger Spanish brandy
8 oz. lobster meat, cut in bite size chunks	4 oz. tomato sauce (puree)
	4 saltine crackers
1 cup crabmeat	½ tsp. saffron (stringy type)
2 medium onions, chopped	fresh ground black pepper
2 tomatoes, diced	fried bread slices

Shuck the quahaugs and oysters and save their liquor. Set the meats aside; strain the juice through triple cheesecloth and set aside. Scrub the mussels and the steamer clams and put them in a pot with

½ cup of water, cover and steam them until their shells are open. Shuck them, remove the beard from the mussels, and take scissors and snip off the "schnozzles" of the steamer clams (they are often filled with sand). Strain the liquor in the pot through triple cheese-cloth and save it.

Boil the periwinkles in salted water for 30 minutes, drain and set aside. Pull off the heads of the squids, pull out the cellophane-like backbone, skin them and remove the flippers; carefully turn the tubes inside out and wash off all the innards. Turn them right side out again and slice the tubes into ¼-inch circles. Cut the wings up into small pieces. Cut the beak and the eyeballs off the tentacles and discard; chop up the tentacles. Set all the squid meats aside. Now you're ready to start cookin'.

Heat the olive oil in a large skillet (or Dutch oven or casserole) until it is smoking, add the onions and 2 cloves of garlic and fry until soft and golden. Add the scallions and their leaves, 2 tbsps. of the chopped parsley, squid meats and chopped tomatoes and stir them in; season with fresh ground black pepper (the shellfish liquors furnish the salt element). Use the stringy type of saffron commonly called among cooks "pussy hair"; pound it to a powder in a mortar and stir into the cooking pan. Add the tomato puree, the dry white wine and the brandy and stir them in; cook a little longer to allow the alcohol to evaporate. Now add the littlenecks, steamer clams, mussels, periwinkles in their shells, peeled shrimp, lobster meats and crabmeat, and stir them in gently. Finally, add the oysters and stir them in very gently.

Now mix the quahaug, clam, mussel and oyster liquors together and pour them into the skillet. There should be enough of it to not quite cover the other things in the pan. Take the remaining 2 table-spoons of parsley, the remaining clove of minced garlic, the sliced almonds and the saltine crackers and put them in a mortar with a little olive oil; pound into a paste and sprinkle this mixture over the top of the things in the skillet.

Now your have your choice of two procedures: you can cover it and simmer it for 15 minutes more on top of the stove, or you can bake it in a preheated 400 degree oven for a few minutes until the top surface is lightly browned; either way it is orgasmic. Take the zarzuela to the table in the container it's cooked in and ladle it out in soup bowls. Serve with bread slices fried in olive oil, and of course a good full-bodied wine, white or red.

WHITE OR RED

Cioppino, an Italian Medley

Much of the very greatest cooking is really very simple, and some of the best seafood dishes in the world are those whipped up by fishermen and natives of coastal regions. These are usually stews, chowders, gumbos or other medleys made up of whatever fish or shellfish happens to be close at hand. Usually the basic ingredients are some sort of "trash" fish, but as the dishes become "classics" they begin to incorporate more expensive ingredients. Today there is no such thing as "trash," and nothin'—but nothin'—is cheap. Oh happy Provincetown! We have nearly all the basic ingredients for the greatest seafood dishes right here amongst us.

Take this joyful Italian dish, *cioppino* (pronounced Joe Peeno): it has kept the fishermen of Italy fat and jolly for many centuries. And when you taste it you will see why it is becoming as popular in American restaurants as bouillabaisse. In the old country they throw everything into the *cioppino* except their rubber boots and dungarees—fish with their heads and tails on, crustaceans and shell-fish in their shells, and so on. The shells add a certain something to the flavor of this dish, and digging out the meats adds to the joys of discovery. I have formulated below a Cape Cod Cioppino that is the typical mixture; you can leave anything out, or add something else that you especially like and it will probably turn out just as good. Make fish stock by boiling heads, tails and even a few small fish for 30 minutes to extract their essences, then strain it.

CIOPPINO
MAKIN'S

CAPE COD CIOPPINO
(Serves 6)

2 live 2 lb. lobsters
5 haddock fillets
5 flounder fillets
6 squids and their tentacles, cleaned and diced
2 doz. mussels

2 doz. softshell steamer clams
2 doz. littleneck quahaugs in their shells
1 lb. fresh or frozen shrimp tails in their shells

The Zuppa

2 qts. fish stock
2 cups dry white wine
1½ cups olive oil
1½ cups funghi seci (dried Italian mushrooms soaked in water for an hour and chopped). If you can't get them use 2 cups sliced fresh mushrooms
2 onions, chopped (if you can find bulb-type shallots, substitute about 8 of them for 1 of the onions)
¾ cup fresh parsley, chopped

6 scallions, chopped, leaves and all (or the white part of a leek, chopped)
6 cloves garlic, chopped fine
2 No. 2 cans tomatoes
1 8 oz. can tomato puree
1 bay leaf
½ tsp. basil
½ tsp. oregano
salt (be careful, the clam and mussel juices are salty)
½ tsp. fresh ground black pepper
sprinkling of hot crushed red pepper seeds

Since we do not have the large earthenware casseroles or iron pots that they use in Italy, this cookery requires three utensils: a large pot, a medium steaming pot, and a large skillet. If the large kettle doesn't have a thick bottom, put an asbestos pad under it to prevent scorching.

Chop the lobsters in their shells into 1-inch chunks, crack the claws but leave the meat in; cut the fish fillets into 3-inch pieces. Heat 1 cup of the olive oil in the skillet and saute the onions, scallions and garlic until soft and golden brown; add the parsley and mushrooms.

·CIOPPINO·

Add the tomatoes, the puree and spices, herbs and condiments. Stir frequently and cook for about 30 minutes or until it loses its acid flavor. Transfer it into the large pot with about 1 quart of the fish stock, and keep it simmering.

While this is going on, wash and scrub the mussels, steamer clams and quahaugs. Put 2 cups of dry white wine in the medium pot and cover and steam for 10 minutes or until all the shells are opened. Remove the shellfish and add the liquor to the big pot (watch out for any small residue of sand that may be in the bottom of the steaming pot). Put the remaining ½ cup of olive oil in the skillet and saute the lobster chunks and claws for 10 minutes to "seal" their flavor. Add to the big pot. Add the chopped squids to the big pot, stir gently and thoroughly; add the fish pieces—no more stirring. Cook 10 minutes, add the shrimp and the remaining fish broth (or enough broth to completely cover everything in the pot) and cook 10 minutes more; add the clams, mussels and quahaugs in their shells at the very last moment—and no more cooking. Don't let this stuff overcook; it must retain the fresh tang of the sea. Have your bowls preheated and ready to receive it, and serve it piping hot; serve with slices of Italian, Portuguese or French bread fried in olive oil.

There are two ways of serving the cioppino: (a) the broth and fish together in large soup bowls, (b) the liquid in one bowl and the assorted fish and shellfish in another. I prefer the former method because it has the peasant gusto. Serve a crisp chicory salad along with it, and a good dry white wine, or even a robust red chianti, claret or valpolicella. For dessert have an assortment of cheese (provolone, bel paese, gorgonzola) and fresh fruit (purple grapes, pears, sour apples, nectarines, peaches) and more good red wine and then some cafe espresso and, and, and. . . .

Beautiful Mess, Bouillabaisse

Since most of my writing and my cooking is concerned with *fresh* seafood, I like to get as close to the source as possible so that my readers can know that I don't copy my recipes off the wrappers of frozen packets or cans from the supermarket. (I always give an UGH! when I read a recipe that begins "take a can of minced clams . . . , or "take a can of tuna . . . ," etc.) So I try at least once a year to make a trip out to the fishing grounds on a Provincetown dragger; that way I can follow my fish from the moment it's caught till it hits my stew pot and is cooked and is eaten by my friends. The flavor of this fresh-caught fish is a revelation—a joy that can only be appreciated by those who have tried it. It also gives me a chance to defend my underdog friends, the "trash" fish. Fully half the fish that are caught by a dragger are shoveled back through the scuppers to be pounced on by the enormous hordes of seagulls that follow the boat.

Not long ago I took one of my annual trips on board the *Peter and Linda* with Captain Seraphine Codinha and crew of Victor Pacellini and Manuel Thomas. We left Town Wharf at 4 A.M. on the dot; it was still dark and we steamed out about ten miles to the west side of Stellwagen Bank, north-northwest of Provincetown. It was whiting we were after and the Captain knew where to find them. After four long drags of over two hours each, the hold of the boat was filled with neatly sorted boxes of whiting, flounder, cod and even a few boxes of goosefish tails and skate wings for export to Europe.

It would be easy to say that when you've seen one drag you've seen them all, but it's not true; every drag is a different adventure—you never know what's coming up next in that net. On our second haul we pulled in a huge tractor tire weighing about 200 pounds; it was probably a bumper off a seagoing tugboat. And in that same haul was a fifty-pound goosefish, the largest I had ever seen. You can bet that old goosefish was using the tire for a nest; they love to hide out in just such curious spots, lying there perfectly camouflaged and wiggling their antennae to attract curious fish within snapping distance of their gigantic maws.

It was a perfect fishing day, the sea was as smooth as glass, and the dogfish weren't overly plentiful as they sometimes are. At 6 P.M. we were back at Town Wharf unloading the catch. And I was able to unload my "haul," about fifty pounds of fish, mostly "trash," that I had grabbed before the seagulls could get it, rich ore from which I intended to refine a bouillabaisse to end all bouillabaisses.

The prime requisite of a good bouillabaisse is plenty of variety, and I really had it: goosefish, dogfish, catfish, monkeyfish (mud eels), skate wings, squids, mackerel, whiting, flounders, gray sole, sculpins, butterfish, schrod, hake, herring and northern red shrimp (prawns)—a total of sixteen kinds. When I got home I dressed the fish and made a batch of fish stock out of the heads and scraps. Then I made a ten-gallon pot of bouillabaisse, and invited about twenty-five friends in to try it. They happily annihilated the whole potful, and no one was squeamish about words like dogfish, catfish, goosefish, and the like. That soup was a symphony.

I can't expect my readers to find such a wide variety of fish, so I will give a recipe with products obtainable at any fish market; whole fish with the bones in, cut into chunks is best, but fillets will do in a pinch.

MONKEY-FISH

BOUILLABAISSE
(Serves 10 or More)

1 lb. haddock	*1 cup olive oil*
1 lb. flounder	*2 onions, chopped*
1 lb. mackerel	*7 cloves garlic, minced*
1 lb. shrimp in their shells	*1 32 oz. can plum tomatoes*
2 doz. shucked oysters	*1 bay leaf*
2 doz. littleneck clams in	*½ cup chopped parsley*
* their shells*	*½ lemon, sliced*
2 doz. mussels in their	*1 cup white wine*
* shells*	*½ tsp. saffron (if not available*
4 scallions and 2 inches	* use turmeric for color)*
* of their green leaves,*	*fish stock as needed*
* chopped*	*salt and pepper*

Saute the onion and garlic in the olive oil until transparent, then put in a large pot or a large earthenware casserole. Add the tomatoes, parsley, bay leaf, lemon slices and saffron. Now add the fish, shrimp and oysters. On top of this lay the mussels and clams. Add the wine and enough fish stock to cover the whole by 2 inches. (You should prepare the stock in advance by boiling the heads, bones and trimmings of the fish along with chopped onions, celery, parsley, thyme, basil, bay leaves, salt and pepper for 30-45 minutes. Strain it.)

Cover the pot, bring to a brisk boil, and cook for 15 minutes; it may take a little longer if you're cooking a really big batch, but don't overcook it. Another tip is to adjust the salt properly, neither too much nor too little; remember, the shellfish juices are salty too. Cover the bottoms of large bowls with thin slices of garlic bread and fill the bowls with the fish, shellfish and soup. Sprinkle parsley on the top.

This is one of the world's greatest stews.

A NOTE ON SUBSTITUTIONS

Most of the recipes in this fish section call for fresh Provincetown fish, but with the perfection of freezing, packaging and fast freight shipping, a supermarket in Podunk, Iowa can sell you fish that is as good as anything found in the coastal regions. The freezing process actually improves the flavor of some fish, such as haddock and cod.

Generally speaking, lean, white, firm-fleshed fish are interchangeable in the recipes we have given, and so are the fat fish. And you can even mix them up. In fact, we actively encourage our readers to experiment, substitute and discover. That's the joy of creative cookery!

Herewith we identify lean and fat fish from oceanfront sections of the country—Atlantic Coast, Gulf Coast, Pacific Coast—and a few freshwater species from inland lakes and streams.

Location	Lean fish	Fat fish
Atlantic Coast	pollack, swordfish, rosefish, whiting, haddock, flounder, fluke, hake, perch, wolffish	striped bass, bluefish, butterfish, mackerel, herring, halibut, tuna
Gulf Coast	red snapper, spot, cobia, croaker, flounder, fluke, channel bass (red fish), sheepshead	mullet, king mackerel, pompano, barracuda, bonito
Pacific Coast		black seabass, lingcod, pilchard, anchovy, salmon, jack mackerel, yellowtail, albacore
Freshwater	carp, trout, black bass, perch, bluegill, catfish, pickerel, pike	buffalo, whitefish, shad

CHAPTER V
The Fishes

EVERY LOCALE HAS its best loved eating fish. Around the Mediterranean it's the red mullet and dried or salt codfish. On our Gulf Coast it's the pompano and striped mullet smoked. Here in old Provincetown the best loved and most delicious fish is the noble haddock. Although it has suffered a terrific decline in the last few years there is still enough of it available to keep seafood connoisseurs happy. In the past, haddock was so plentiful and so low priced that it was considered a poor man's fish, and gourmets took little notice of it. But as its abundance has declined and the price has skyrocketed, it has become a luxury like lobster.

Haddock is one of the finest fish that swims in the seas; its habitat is very restricted and the Cape Tip is very fortunate that it happens to be one of the haddock's favorite summer playgrounds. It brings happiness to the hearts of our fishermen when their trawls come up with haddock in the net; because of its scarcity it commands a good market price. Even the boats themselves can be happy about it. Did you know that each Provincetown fishing boat has a

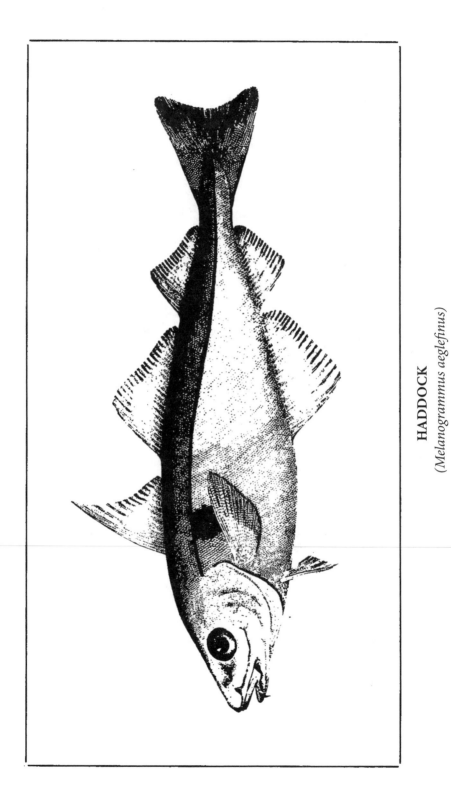

HADDOCK
(*Melanogrammus aeglefinus*)

personality of its own that is almost as close to human as an inanimate object can be? Each boat gets a share of the catch, and it has a bank account in its own name, and it pays for its own outrageous insurance and the never-ending drydocking for diesel engine overhauls, and constant scraping, painting and minor repairs. As it sits on the ways getting the works, like a lady in a beauty parlor, a Provincetown dragger seems to say, "Don't worry, I'm paying for this out of my own pocket; these Portuguese scampering around all over me are my partners."

Haddock is a versatile fish for a cook to handle. It can be boiled, poached, steamed, baked, smoked, broiled and sauteed. The meat is firm and white and flakes beautifully, and its taste is delicious—subtle and delicate and unfishy. But it must not be overcooked or subjected to high heat or its flavor is gone with the wind. A lot of folks won't believe this, but frozen haddock fillets when thawed and cooked right are better than the fresh fillets of many species of fish. Once I cooked thawed-out haddock and served it alongside fresh speckled trout—served it to my friends without telling them what it was—and they unanimously chose the haddock as the tastier fish.

Some of the old-time cooking methods are the best, and here's a real oldie:

PROVINCETOWN BOILED HADDOCK
(Serves 4)

1 6 lb. haddock (leave the head and tail on for good looks)	½ lemon, sliced
	1 tsp. mixed pickling spices
	2 cloves garlic, crushed
1 large onion, sliced	1 cup white wine
2 pieces celery, chopped	salt and fresh ground black
2 bay leaves	pepper

In old Provincetown they used to boil a whole haddock, and to keep it from falling apart they would sew it up tightly in a clean piece of linen with a strap at each end for lifting it. (Rub it first with flour to keep the skin from sticking to the cloth.) The fish was lifted in its shroud into the pan of gently boiling water, which was flavored with the vegetables, spices, and wine. Then when it was done (approximately 30 minutes) it was lifted out and the shroud cut away and the fish would be lying there as pristinely beautiful as the moment it was caught.

The Modern Method

You can do this more simply nowadays by wrapping the floured fish in a double layer of foil and rolling and crimping the edges tightly together. Punch lots of small holes in the foil so the cooking liquid will be in free contact with the fish. Take a turkey roasting pan and place in it enough water to cover the fish; bring to a boil and add the onion slices, celery, bay leaves, lemon slices, pickling spices, garlic, wine, salt and fresh ground black pepper. Boil vigorously for 15 minutes to make a good liquor. Lower the heat to a slow boil, place the shrouded fish in the pan, cover and boil gently for 30 minutes. Remove the fish and deshroud it on a bed of parsley on a platter; make it look alive! And make it look even purtier by decorating with lemon slices, parsley, watercress, radish roses, sliced rings of green pepper, cape jasmine, gardenias, morning glories, etc., etc., etc. Such good Provincetown eatin'!

PORTUGUESE BAKED HADDOCK
(Serves 4 to 6)

1 6-8 lb. haddock, cleaned and beheaded and betailed	½ tsp. saffron
	1 cup white wine
2 onions, chopped	4 tbsps. olive oil
2 small green peppers, diced	chopped parsley
2 cloves garlic, minced	1 onion, sliced
1 cup fresh mushrooms, chopped	1 tomato, sliced
1 can plum type tomatoes	salt and fresh ground black
½ tsp. ground cumin	pepper

The haddock is one of the best baking fish in the world, and Provincetown's Portuguese are just about the best fish bakers there are. The Portuguese don't care too much for aesthetics so they usually cut the head and tail off their fish before baking it.

Heat the olive oil in a skillet and saute the onion, green pepper, garlic and mushrooms just until the vegetables are transparent. Add the cumin and saffron and stir them in; add the tomatoes, squished up, and cook slowly for 20 minutes more. Rub the fish inside and out with salt and pepper and melted butter, and lay it in a greased baking pan. Sprinkle the wine over it, then ladle the tomato sauce over it. Spread slices of fresh tomato and onion over it. Bake for 30-40 minutes in a 350 degree oven, basting now and then with the sauce. Take it to the table right in the baking pan.

MITCH'S BAKED STUFFED HADDOCK
(Serves 6)

1 6 lb. haddock (leave the head and tail on)
1 cup shrimp, sliced
1 cup scallops, diced
2 cups bread crumbs
¼ tsp. thyme
¼ tsp. basil
¼ tsp. cumin
1 tbsp. Worcestershire sauce

3 scallions and 2 inches of their leaves, minced
1 piece celery, finely chopped
1 cup fresh mushrooms, chopped
1 cup white wine
1 stick butter
salt and fresh ground black pepper

Melt the butter in a skillet and saute the scallions, celery and mushrooms until soft, add the thyme, basil, cumin, Worcestershire, wine, and salt and pepper and stir them in well. Add the shrimp and scallops and cook 3 minutes longer. Moisten the bread crumbs with water and knead until they are a paste; stir this vigorously into the mixture in the skillet. This is your stuffing; set it aside.

Rub the fish inside and out with melted butter, salt and fresh ground black pepper. Stuff the fish with the dressing and sew up the slot (or use skewers). Lay it in a wellgreased baking pan and pour a cup of white wine over it. Bake for 30-40 minutes (in a 325 degree oven), or until it begins to brown and the flesh will flake when you stick a fork into it. Place it on a serving platter (a tray covered with bright foil serves well) and decorate it handsomely as described above for the boiled haddock.

A Very Special Haddock Dish

In all my years as a chef in Provincetown restaurants, my most popular dish has always been *haddock amandine*, and I have friends who come all the way from Chatham, Falmouth, and Boston just to beat their gums against it. But most of my haddock-consuming pals are Provincetowners themselves, many of them are fishermen. And brother, when you sell a piece of fish to a Provincetown fisherman you have got it made: when they dine out in restaurants they usually eat T-bone steaks. I modestly advertise it on my menu as "probably the best piece of fish you will ever eat."

"Sauté meunière amandine" is a very old French classic cooking process, and it has been brought to a peak of perfection in this country by Galatoire's Restaurant in New Orleans (probably the best seafood restaurant in the country). But Galatoire's uses fillets of speckled sea trout (southern squeteague, spotted weakfish). I have the personal recipe of seventy-five-year-old Mr. Jules Galatoire, written for me in a beautiful antique script.

When I started cooking we didn't have any speckled trout around Provincetown, so I adapted Mr. Galatoire's recipe to our delicious native haddock and threw in a few sliced fresh mushrooms for lagniappe. And I've really gotten myself into a jam: I, who used to be a lazy Bohemian lying around on the beach all day, am now a chef, and I have to turn out several thousand haddock amandines every summer. By the time Labor Day gets here I'm so tired of looking at them that I wouldn't eat one for a million dollars.

People think I'm sort of coo-coo to publish my trade secrets and recipes, but to me good food is like love, it should be given as wide a distribution as possible. So here we go again.

HADDOCK AMANDINE MEUNIÈRE
(Serves 6)

6 ¾ lb. haddock fillets
milk
flour
½ lb. butter

juice of 2 lemons
¼ lb. sliced natural almonds
4 fresh mushrooms, sliced
   thinly

Take the haddock fillets and dip them in milk, then dredge them in flour (the yellow dry clam batter which is used in restaurants is even better). Shake off the surplus flour. Melt the butter in a large skillet and place the fish in it, skin side up; cook slowly until brown, then flip it over with a spatula and brown the other side. Remember, this is a saute, a slow cook, not a hot fry, which would destroy the delicate flavor of the fish. Remove the fish and place on warm serving plates. Add the lemon juice to the butter in the pan, add the almonds to the pan, add the mushrooms. Raise the heat high and stir and scrape the bottom and sides of the pan to release any browned crumbs; these are delicious. Stir until the almonds turn a light golden brown (don't let them get too brown or they will be bitter); pour this sauce over the fish and serve immediately, piping hot.

FRESH HADDOCK FILLETS VERONIQUE
(Serves 4)

4 fresh haddock fillets,
   about ¾ lb. each
2 sticks butter
12 oz. can white grapes (or
   an equal amount of fresh
   seedless grapes, peeled, a
   tedious little job)

½ cup dry white wine
juice of 1 lemon
1 tbsp. chopped parsley
salt and fresh ground black
   pepper

VERONIQUE

Poach the grapes in the white wine for 5 minutes. Melt the butter in a skillet and saute the fillets for 5 minutes on each side. Place the fillets on hot serving plates. To the pan juices add the lemon juice, chopped parsley, grapes and white wine. Raise the fire and cook 2 minutes more. Ladle the sauce over the fillets and serve at once.

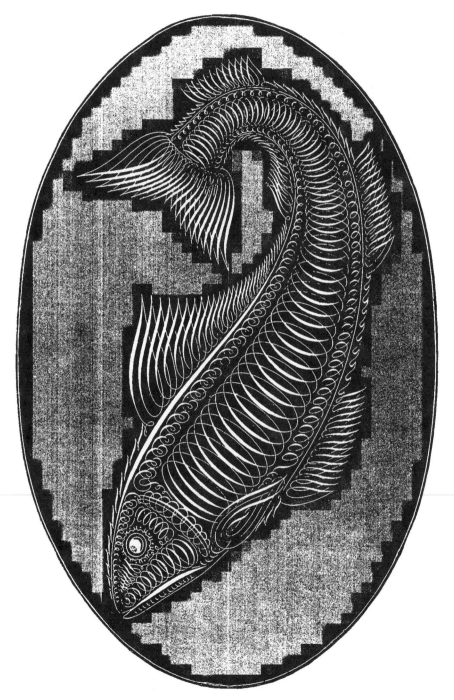

PORTRAIT OF A HADDOCK BY A COLONIAL PENMAN

HADDOCK BAKED IN BUTTERMILK

Lay haddock fillets in a baking pan and cover them with sliced onions. Sprinkle well with salt and black pepper. Cover with buttermilk (the fresh churned kind if you can get it). Bake in a preheated 350 degree oven for 30 minutes or until the fish is firm and flakes easily with a fork. Remove from the pan and place on serving dishes, sprinkle with melted butter and fresh chopped parsley, or fresh dill chopped finely. Serve with small boiled potatoes that have been dipped in melted butter and rolled in fresh chopped parsley or dill.

Let me state right here and now that there is a great affinity between haddock and fresh dill, and you should combine them as often as possible. Affinities are love affairs ordained by heaven. Discovering the affinities of diverse foods is half the fun of fooling around in the kitchen. Such as:

HADDOCK FILLETS WITH
WELLFLEET OYSTER SAUCE
(Serves 4)

4 haddock fillets	*2 doz. Well fleet oysters and*
1 stick butter	*their liquor*
3 scallions, chopped,	*1 tbsp. chopped parsley*
with 2 inches of their green	*½ cup light cream*
leaves	*¼ cup white wine*
1 piece celery, chopped	*dash of cayenne pepper*
finely	*salt and fresh ground black*
1 clove garlic, minced	*pepper*

Melt ½ stick of butter and saute the onions, celery, garlic and parsley until soft. Add the oyster liquor and allow it to evaporate a little. Add the cream and white wine and stir them in, cooking a little longer until the sauce thickens a little. Add the oysters and cook until they are plump and their edges curl. Set the sauce aside and keep it hot. Melt the other ½ stick of butter and place it on sizzle platters or in a broiler pan and broil the haddock fillets for 5 minutes on each side until done. Place on hot serving plates and pour the oyster sauce over the fillets.

The Story of Finnan Haddie

A WEE BIT O' SCOTLAND

Fresh Provincetown haddock has a Scottish brother named Findon Haddock. It is plain haddock, very lightly salted and very lightly smoked. Because of its great flavor and good keeping qualities, it has spread far and wide. There are many landlubbers in the United States who have eaten finnan haddie but who have never tasted a fresh haddock fillet. It is very popular in Canada, especially Nova Scotia, which we sometimes forget means New Scotland. Cape Breton Island is so strongly Scottish that they still wear kilts in some of its isolated mountain valleys, and it is to be assumed that many of them carry finnan haddie sandwiches in their sporrans. A sporran is the funny catfaced satchel that a Scotsman wears in front of his kilts and uses for storage of bottles, guns, dirks, VVO, copies of Bobby Burns's poems and the finnan haddie sandwiches.

EARLY SMOKE-
HOUSE

Findon is a small fishing village on the coast of Scotland, a sort of Provincetown where English tourists, Scots, artists and Bohemians go to cool off in the summer, and some to get up a head of steam and blow their tops. It was here that findon haddock was invented many, many years ago. Its discovery is said to have been by accident, similar to Charles Lamb's essay on the apotheosis of roast pig. A fish shed full of haddock caught fire and burned down. The thrifty Scots who owned the fish house refused to throw away the scorched fish. They ate it themselves, and it turned out to be such a tasty morsel that they wanted to keep it a secret from their neighbors—but you know how fast news travels in a small town. Within no time everybody was burning down his fish house in order to make the new treat. Finally a dumb Irishman who was shipwrecked on their coast taught them to build smokehouses instead of bonfires, and the knowledge came none too soon because half the town was already in ashes. The rest of it is history and the name of Findon is known all over the globe, but they've shortened it to "finnan haddie."

BROILED FINNAN HADDIE

Connoisseurs prefer their finnan haddie simply broiled. Rub the fillets with melted butter, place on a broiling pan or sizzle platter and gently broil on each side for 5 minutes. Brush with lemon-butter sauce and serve piping hot. With hot coffee and crisp toast this is one of the world's best breakfasts.

POACHED FINNAN HADDIE

Take 2 pounds of thick finnan haddie fillets, remove the bones and skin and place the fish in a saucepan; cover it with hot water, and when it returns to a boil lower the heat and poach it gently for 10 or 15 minutes. Drain it and pat dry with paper towels. Place it on a hot serving platter and decorate it with lemon slices and plenty of fresh parsley. Serve a lemon-butter sauce in a dish on the side.

CREAMED FINNAN HADDIE

Take 2 pounds of finnan haddie fillets, remove the bones and skin, flake or dice the meat and place it in boiling water in a saucepan for 5 minutes. Drain it in a collander. Melt ½ stick of butter in a skillet and add 2 tablespoons of flour. Remove from the fire and add 1 cup of milk and 1 cup of light cream, ½ teaspoon of salt, a little fresh ground black pepper, a pinch of nutmeg and a dash of cayenne pepper. Stir the sauce until it thickens, then add the haddock and cook for a few minutes longer. Ladle over toast on hot plates and serve at once. This is great for breakfast, luncheon, 4 o'clock tea, supper, dinner, or a midnight snack, and if you wake up hungry at 2 A.M. it's good even then. You can spark up this cream sauce by adding at various times chopped or sliced onions, celery, chopped hard-boiled eggs, fresh dill or mint leaves, capers, etc.

FINNAN HADDIE IN CHEESE SAUCE

2 lbs. finnan haddie fillets
1½ cups American cheese,
   cubed
thin slices of Swiss cheese
1 tsp. prepared mustard
2 tbsps. flour

1/3 stick of butter
2 cups milk
1 jigger of sherry
salt and fresh ground black
   pepper

Cut the fillets into 1-inch chunks and poach them for 10 minutes; drain and set aside. Melt the butter in a skillet, remove from the heat and add flour, and stir well. Then add the milk a little at a time, stirring constantly. Return to the fire and add the cubed cheese, stirring until it melts and you have a smooth mixture. Add the mustard and stir it in. Add the poached haddock chunks and the sherry. Season to taste with salt and fresh ground black pepper. Place the mixture in an ovenproof baking dish and cover with a layer of slices of Swiss cheese. Bake in a 350 degree oven until the cheese on top is melted and beginning to brown.

Finnan haddie is a great casserole fish. Use your imagination and freewheel it with all sorts of cream sauces and herbs. Like this brainstorm:

FINNAN HADDIE WITH
YOGURT-SOUR CREAM

Cut the haddock into chunks as instructed above and poach it. Mix a cup of sour cream and a cup of fresh plain yogurt. Grate an onion into the mix, add chopped parsley, salt and fresh ground black pepper. Put the haddock in this mixture, pour into a casserole and heat it slowly and gently in the oven. This is very yummy, but you have to be very careful when cooking yogurt or it will fall apart.

The Saga of Skully Joe

Ladies and gentlemen, may I present Skully Joe? Please stand back and give us lots of elbow room; this is a devastating subject. Skully Joe, like atomic fission, is fraught with all sorts of weird dangers. There can be so many heartbreaks between the making of it and the final digestion of it that Skully Joe should not be attempted by the fainthearted. And no matter how much you like it, never try to commercialize it; that would be like an alchemist trying to make brass out of 18 karat gold.

Let me inform any newcomers present that Skully Joe is nothing in the world but hard dried pollock or schrod (baby cod or haddocks). It must have been invented by the Indians; it has the same old chewy quality as pemmican, the pounded and dried buffalo meat which was relished so much by the Plains Indians. It's a safe bet that the Pilgrims thought Squanto was making fun of them when he handed them a Skully Joe and said, "Eat-um." Myles Standish probably raised his arm and said "How?" Answering the salute Squanto raised his arm and said "And how!," and lots of people have been puzzled over the enigma ever since. It's hard to tell just where the fascination of Skully Joe lies, and why the subject won't die and be forgotten once and for all. It's food value is almost nothing, and you have to chew on a hunk of it for about a half hour before it's soft enough to swaller. John J. Gaspie and I always agreed that it had only one reason for existence: IT TASTES SO GOOD WITH BEER. It's ten times better than potato chips, or salted peanuts, or fried pork skins and other thirst-provokers that are foisted off on us beer guzzlers. It has one drawback, though. If you piled two quarts of beer on top of a pound of Skully Joe it would swell up and you'd have the equivalent of a live five-pound fish swimming around inside you. Keep the bicarbonate of soda handy, lots of it!

The day has yet to come when some hostess is daring enough to serve a Skully Joe Dip at a cocktail party. But it could liven things up. Children, too, love Skully Joe; if you leave enough of it lying around the house the kids will get hooked on it and forget about chewing gum and candy bars and the other cavity-producing sweets that keep our dentists so wealthy and happy.

In the old days nearly every family in Provincetown would make Skully Joes, just for the heck of it; it was an unnecessary necessity like rum and hard cider and cherry bounce. Joe Patrick tells me that his great-uncle, Captain Elisha Newcomb, was one of the champion Skully Joe makers in town, and he taught Joe, and now Joe is one of the few experts left. Here's how he does it:

THE MAKING OF SKULLY JOE

You should use cod, haddock, or pollock of 1 or 2 pounds in size. Since it's hard work you should make a batch of a hundred or more. (Don't go mooching them off the poor fishermen; shell out some cash and buy a whole boxful when the price is right.) You don't have to scale them or cut off the fins. Just cut off the head and gut them by splitting down the body to about an inch below the vent hole. After scraping out the innards you hold them under a running faucet, and, using a toothbrush, brush off the stomach lining and blood, and most important of all, the blood clots near the backbone.

Next you make a brine of the quantity needed to cover your fish. The old Cape Cod way of making brine is to lay a medium-sized potato on the bottom of the container, fill it with water and then add salt and stir slowly until the potato rises to the surface and floats. (A quicker way to approximate this is to use 1 quart water to 1 pound of salt.) To make Skully Joes easy to handle you tie them together at the tails by twos with strong cord; they are slick when they come out of the brine, and the cord with a fish on each side also provides a handy way of hanging them up. You soak them in the brine for 12 to 20 hours, then you hang them out in the back yard on the clothesline for 3 days of sunshine. Moisture must be avoided at all costs; take your fish in at sundown to avoid dew and frost, and if it's rainy or foggy do not put them out at all. If there are any bluebottle flies around, they usually won't attack a well-salted fish, but just to be doubly safe you should pack about ¼ teaspoon of salt at the upper end of the split by the tail, which is where any residues of blood or oil are most likely to seep out. At the end of the third day of sunning you can move them to a shed, or an attic or a cellar; drive nails in a rafter or joist, and drape a pair of fish over each nail. (Do not put them in a furnace room or they will dry out too fast.) At the end of 10 days they should be ready to eat.

And there's also the fine old Yankee version of sugar cured Skully Joe. To achieve this effect you add a pint of Porty Reek Long Lick or long tail sugar to each 2½ gallons of brine. Porty Reek Long Lick and long tail sugar, of course, is old Cape Cod lingo for molasses. Or you can just use a pound of sugar. Now this kind of Skully Joe really will draw flies, so you must build a screen box to dry them in. Didn't I warn you this business could become complex?

PORTY REEK

I didn't warn you that Skully Joes throw off a very strong smell. After the cure is finished, they should be stored in air-tight plastic garbage bags and hidden in some far off corner of the house, say the garage, or the tool shed. To eat 'em you take a sharp pocket knife and cut off a chunk and chew on it. Or if you want to be dainty about it and you happen to have an electric table saw, you can saw them up fast into bite-size squares. Dear Emily Post and Amy Vanderbilt, I know your ghosts is shudderin' at this salty old Cape Cod custom of Skully Joe, but that's how it is, take it or leave it.

HIGH!

BACKYARD SKULLY JOE FACTORY

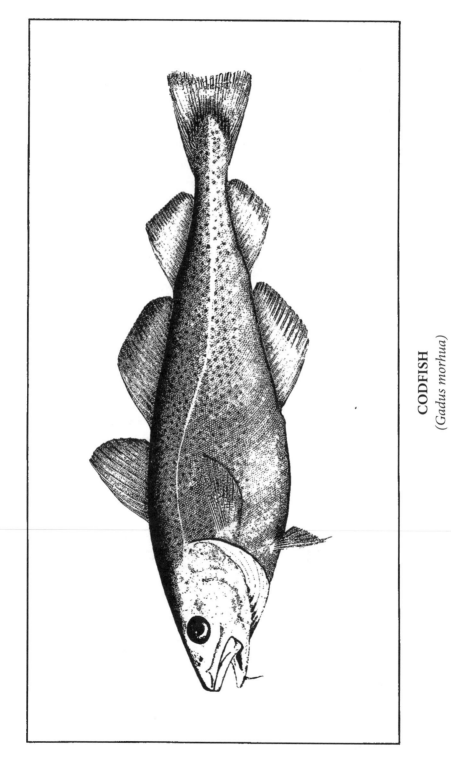

CODFISH
(*Gadus morhua*)

The Sacred Cod

As I stated in the introduction to this volume, the codfish has always been the staff of life for Provincetown. But in the old days, "codfish" nearly always meant salt cod, and the greatest recipes in the world of *haute cuisine* were based on the cured salt fish. (We'll get to these soon.) But the *fresh* codfish is something to be reckoned with, and like its very close relative the haddock, it is delicious; it tastes very much like haddock and it looks like haddock. In fact, the only way an amateur can tell them apart is to remember that the haddock has a black stripe and splotches, while the codfish has a white stripe and freckles. All of the recipes given heretofore for cooking haddock are also applicable to fresh cod. In olden days they were lumped together as a single species; even today the famous "Boston Schrod" can be either a baby haddock or a codfish.

SACRED COD IN BOSTON

Fresh codfish is good year 'round but it's best of all in the winter. Cold weather firms up its flesh and improves its flavor. It is one of the only fish we know of that can be fried in deep hot fat without perceptibly damaging its flavor. Small fish can be filleted. The large fish can be cut crosswise into steaks. Or the fillets from these large fish can be sliced up into cutlets. (See the marginal drawings.)

STEAK

FRIED FRESH CODFISH STEAKS

Dip the steaks in milk, then in flour (or dry clam batter) and fry in deep hot fat. Do not overcook; a rich golden brown is sufficient. Place on a hot serving plate, garnish with fresh parsley and lemon wedges. Serve at once.

STUFFED FRESH CODFISH
(CAPE COD TURKEY)
(Serves 6)

CAPE COD
TURKEY

1 8 lb. codfish
1 cup crabmeat
1 cup chopped shrimp
1 cup chopped scallops
1 diced sweet pepper
4 cloves garlic, minced
1 large onion, chopped, 3
*   medium onions, sliced*
½ cup celery, chopped
1 cup olive oil
4 strips bacon
1 tsp. powdered mustard
1 tsp. Worcestershire sauce
2 dashes Tabasco

pinch of thyme
4 eggs
¾ loaf Portuguese bread (or
*   more if necessary)*
fish or chicken broth
1 stick butter
1 cup white wine
½ cup sherry
3 sliced tomatoes
1 cup chopped fresh
*   mushrooms*
2 tbsps. flour
salt and pepper to taste

Clean and scale the codfish, leaving the head, tail and fins on, just for aesthetics. Remove the backbone in a strip from just behind the head to the front of the tail. This is done by severing each rib carefully where it joins the vertebrae, and then undercutting the spine.

Saute the celery, garlic, and green pepper in butter until soft and golden. Add the crabmeat, shrimp and scallops, Worcestershire sauce, Tabasco, white wine, herbs, and seasonings and saute about 5 minutes more, stirring constantly. Moisten the Portuguese bread until soft and knead with the fingers. Add the beaten eggs to the bread and work them well into it. Fry the bacon strips brown, crumble them and add to the mixture. Put the bread into the sauteed stuff and mix them well. Add fish or chicken broth to make the mixture into a thick paste. Turn off the heat, add ½ cup sherry and 2 finely chopped cloves of garlic, and mix them in well.

Put all this material into the belly cavity of the fish and sew it up. Put the cup of olive oil in the bottom of a turkey roasting pan, with a couple of cups of fish or chicken broth. Lay the codfish in the pan; lay sliced onions and tomatoes on top of it and some more around it in the pan juice. Cover the pan and bake in a 400 degree oven for 45 minutes to 1 hour; baste often to keep it from drying out. About 15 minutes before the fish is done sprinkle the flour and a handful of fresh chopped mushrooms into the juices around the fish. Leave the pan uncovered for the last 15 minutes.

Remove the fish carefully from the baking pan when done and place it on a large serving dish, or a large tray covered with aluminum foil. Stir the pan juices, flour and the rest until they thicken into a sauce (you may have to add more broth at this point). Pour this over the fish, garnish with the cooked tomatoes, onion slices, some sliced truffles, some lemon slices, some parsley, etc. Serve a great wine with it.

CODFISH STEAKS AMANDINE
(Serves 6)

6 codfish steaks, ¾ lb. each	salt and fresh ground black
½ lb. butter	pepper
milk	1 cup fresh mushrooms,
flour	chopped
¼ lb. sliced almonds	juice of 2 lemons

Saute the almonds in butter until light golden, remove them quickly or they get too dark and their flavor is spoiled. Saute the fresh mushrooms lightly and quickly in butter, then mix them with the almonds. Dip the codfish steaks in cold milk, sprinkle with salt and pepper, dip in flour. Melt the butter in a skillet and saute the fish very slowly until brown on both sides. When the fillets are done place them on hot plates. Add the juice of 2 lemons to the butter in the pan, raise the heat a little, add the mushrooms and almonds. Stir constantly until the butter begins to turn golden brown. Spread the sauce over the steaks and serve piping hot.

SAUTE

ALMONDS LOVE FISHES

A Local Joy

Samson slew the Philistines with the jawbone of an ass. Sometimes a Provincetown cook can slay them with the jawbone of a codfish. Codfish jawbones are strictly a colloquial delicacy, something you won't hear about from Craig Claiborne, James Beard, Michael Field or Julia Child. When the fishermen dress a codfish on the boat, they gut him and cut off his head. The body goes to the market but the fisherman gets the head as a bounty, and it's a real treasure. Often he will cut off the lower jawbone, leaving the cheeks and tongue attached, then he will cut the jawbone down the middle and divide it into two parts. When dipped in batter and fried in deep fat, these jawbones look very much like the leg of a chicken or a pork chop, as will be seen in the drawing below.

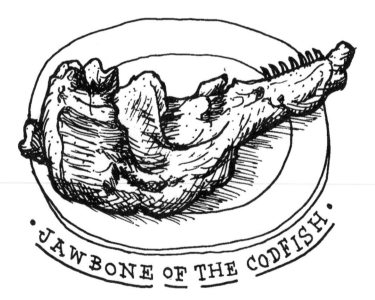

JAWBONE OF THE CODFISH

But they taste better than either chicken or pork chops. Very frequently fishermen will bring a sack full of jawbones into Cookie's Tap. Wilbur and Joe Cook will fry them up and feed them to the steady barflies and to any fortunate visitor who happens to be present at the time. If you have a friend or neighbor who is a fisherman, by all means get him to save you some codfish jawbones and cook them thus:

FRIED CODFISH JAWBONES
(Serves 4)

8 codfish jawbones (halves of   *milk*
    the lower jaw)   *fat*
flour seasoned with salt and   *4 small red pickled pony*
    pepper   *peppers*

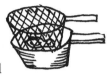

Dip the jawbones in the milk, then dredge them in the flour and shake off the surplus flour. Heat the deep fat and add the pony peppers. Fry the jawbones brown on both sides as you would do fried chicken. Serve immediately and eat with your bare hands: no sauces, bread or other trimmings needed. Wash them down with beer.

The biggest lump of meat in the codfish jawbone is the "cheek," or "sounds" as some people call it. It's about the size of a large scallop, and there is also the tongue clinging to the inside of the jawbone. Cheeks and tongues make one of the best fish chowders in the world (see page 147).

About Schrod

As stated before, schrod (or scrod) are young codfish or haddock of three-fourths to one pound each, and "Boston Schrod" is one of the most popular seafood dishes in restaurants all over New England. It can be fried or broiled. Schrod are also the best fish for making Skully Joes.

BROILED FRESH SCHROD
(1 Helping)

Split and clean a small schrod as instructed for mackerel on page 217. Leave the head and tail on for good looks. Rub the fish with melted butter and salt and pepper. Lay the fish skin side up on a buttered sizzle platter or broiler pan, and place in the broiler 4 inches from the flame. Broil for 4 or 5 minutes until lightly browned, then flip it over and broil the other side until brown. Serve with fresh homemade tartar sauce (see page 131). Garnish with parsley sprigs and lemon wedges.

FRIED SCHROD
(1 Helping)

Split and dress the fish as instructed. Dip in milk, and then in flour (or in dry clam fry batter). Fry on both sides in deep hot fat until lightly browned. Do not overcook; remember that it keeps on cooking after you have removed it from the hot fat. Serve with tartar sauce and lemon wedges; decorate with parsley sprigs.

An Old Provincetown Product

And now we have come to the seafood product that was the economic backbone of Provincetown for over a hundred years, the salt codfish. Although Provincetowners made tons of it for export they ate very little of it themselves, and never developed an extensive salt codfish cuisine; they made an occasional salt codfish hash for breakfast and that was just about it. With all the fresh fish and shellfish around, Provincetowners did not have to lean too heavily on the preserved varieties. As the philosopher Vico says, things go in complete circles; today we have to import both our salt codfish and our recipes for cooking it—primarily from Spain, Portugal, Provence and Italy. These countries have built up an extensive salt codfish cuisine; some of it is truly delicious and it is to these Mediterranean peoples that we must turn for most of our recipes in this section.

SALT CODFISH HASH WITH EGGS
(Serves 4)

1 ½ lbs. salt codfish
¼ lb. salt pork, diced in very
* small cubes*
4 cups mashed potatoes

1 medium onion, grated
fresh ground black pepper
8 slices bacon
8 poached eggs

In the old days, codfish hash was a very popular breakfast dish in Provincetown. It's still good today.

Cut the dried codfish into pieces and soak for 24 hours, changing the water several times. At the end boil the fish for 20 minutes. Drain. Remove the skin and bones and flake the fish. Set it aside. Fry the salt pork until light brown; remove from the pan and set aside. Discard the salty fat in the pan and wipe it out with a paper towel. Fry the bacon in the skillet until crisp; remove and set aside. Pour off half the drippings from the skillet. In a mixing bowl combine the flaked codfish, salt pork, potatoes, onion and black pepper. Press this mixture into a large cake the size of the skillet, fry in the bacon fat in the skillet until it is well browned on the bottom, then carefully, very carefully turn it over and brown it on the other side. Divide it into quarters and serve with poached or fried eggs and bacon.

BRANDADE DE MORUE

1½ lbs. salt codfish (3 cups,
* flaked)*
4 garlic cloves, chopped
1 cup olive oil (or vegetable
* oil)*
1 cup heavy cream

1 cup mashed potatoes
* (or more)*
½ tsp. Tabasco
fresh ground black pepper
toast triangles or Holland
* Rusk*

The people of Provence in the south of France have been eating a codfish hash of sorts for a thousand years. Provencals love garlic and olive oil, and these elements are what gives a punch to their *Brandade de Morue.* Frenchmen believe that salt codfish should be soaked and cooked in fresh rainwater. Just what virginal purity this imparts to the codfish we have never been able to determine. It's getting harder and harder to find clear fresh rainwater in the United States.

Soak the codfish for 24 hours, changing the water several times. Cut the fish up roughly and place it in a saucepan. Cover with cold water, bring to a boil, lower heat and boil gently for 1½ hours. Remove the fish and drain it; remove the skin and bones and flake the fish into small pieces. Set aside.

Place the garlic and olive oil in a blender and mix well. Add the flaked salt codfish and cream it. Add the Tabasco and fresh ground black pepper to taste. Add the cream and blend it in. Pour this mixture into a mixing bowl and mix in by hand enough mashed potatoes to thicken it. The dish can be served hot or cold. Served cold, it makes a good hors d'oeuvre or appetizer at a cocktail party or buffet supper. To serve it hot heat it for 10 minutes in the oven. Serve toast triangles or Holland Rusk along with it. It makes a great breakfast dish when shaped into thick cakes and heated, and served with poached eggs on top and crisp bacon on the side.

BACALHAU ALENTEJO

1½ lbs. salt codfish	¼ cup black bitter olives,
2 medium potatoes, boiled and	chopped
peeled	fresh ground black pepper
2 medium onions, chopped	bacon or country ham
½ cup olive oil	6 eggs

In the Portuguese farmer's version of the codfish hash breakfast, the eggs are mixed right into the hash and bitter olives are added. It's very tasty.

Soak the codfish for 24 hours, changing the water several times. Boil it for 30 minutes, remove the skin and bones, and break it up into bite-size chunks. Dice the boiled potatoes into bite-size chunks also. Heat the olive oil in a skillet until it is smoking, add the onions and cook until soft and transparent. Add the fish, potatoes, olives and black peppers to the skillet, mix them in well and cook for a few minutes to blend the flavors. Add a little milk to the eggs and beat them lightly; add to the mixture in the pan, lower the heat, mix well, and cook just until the eggs are done. Do not overcook. Serve at once with crisp bacon or fried country ham on the side.

CODFISH A LA GOMEZ DE SA
(Serves 4)

1 1½ lb. dried salt codfish
1 cup olive oil
3 medium onions, sliced
1 green pepper, diced
3 medium potatoes, boiled,
*   peeled, sliced*
2 cloves garlic, minced
3 hard-boiled eggs, sliced

¼ cup black bitter olives,
*   chopped*
½ cup chopped fresh parsley
½ cup white wine
fish stock
fresh ground black pepper
Parmesan cheese
pimiento strips

This could almost be called the national dish of Portugal; they serve it everywhere and at all hours, morning, noon and night. I had it once at 2 A.M. and I'll have to admit it exerts a steadying influence after a night on the town, carousing. Gomez de Sa was not a man, it's the name of a cooking utensil, for which we can substitute a Dutch oven or deep skillet.

Soak the codfish for 24 hours, changing the water several times. Cut it up into 2-inch squares. Parboil these squares for 10 minutes. Drain the pieces and remove skin and bone; set aside. In a Dutch oven or deep skillet heat the olive oil until it is lightly smoking. Add the onions, garlic and green pepper, and saute until the vegetables are soft and transparent. Sprinkle in the black olives, the parsley and fresh ground black pepper. This is your *sofrito*. Smooth it out and lay the codfish pieces on top of it; lay the sliced eggs on top of the cod and then lay on the sliced potatoes. Pour in the wine. Pour in enough fish stock to just reach the top but not cover it. Cook at a very, very slow Portuguese simmer for 2-3 hours, adding more stock if necessary. At the end, sprinkle with Parmesan cheese; heat it in the oven a few minutes to brown the cheese. Decorate the top with pimiento strips and parsley sprigs. Serve piping hot right out of the pan it's cooked in.

GOMEZ DE SA

SALT CODFISH DRYING ON A WHARF

Two Georges Banks Schooners moored alongside

SALT CODFISH WITH EGG-CAPER SAUCE
(Serves 4)

1½ lbs. salt codfish
2 strips bacon, fried and
  crumbled
¼ cup American cheese,
  cubed
2 cups milk

2 tbsps. flour
¼ stick butter
4 hard-boiled eggs, chopped
1 tbsp. capers
salt and fresh ground black
  pepper

Soak the codfish 24 hours, changing the water several times. Boil it gently for 20 minutes. Drain, remove the skin and bones and cut the fish into 2-inch squares; keep it hot. Fry the bacon until brown and crisp; drain it and crumble it.

Melt the butter in a skillet, remove from the heat and add the flour; mix well, then add the milk a little at a time, stirring constantly. Return to the fire and add the cubed cheese, stirring to make a smooth mix. Add the chopped eggs, capers and crumbled bacon; mix well. Place codfish pieces on heated serving plates, cover with the egg sauce and serve at once. Serve with assorted boiled vegetables of the type used in a New England boiled dinner.

SALT CODFISH WITH TOMATOES,
ONIONS AND CHICKPEAS
(Serves 4 to 6)

1½ lbs. dried codfish
½ cup olive oil
1 16 oz. can garbanzos
  (chickpeas)
3 medium onions, chopped

1 16 oz. can pomodori pelati
  (plum tomatoes)
3 cloves garlic, minced
salt and fresh ground black
  pepper

Soak the codfish for 24 hours, changing the water several times. Cut the fish into 2-inch squares, removing the bones. Heat the olive oil in a skillet until it is smoking; dip the codfish pieces in flour and fry them brown on both sides; set aside. Saute the onions and the garlic in the remaining oil in the skillet (add a little more oil if necessary) until soft and transparent. Add the tomatoes, squeezed up, and their juice; add the chickpeas. Season with salt and fresh ground black pepper and simmer for 20 minutes. Place the codfish in an earthenware casserole or ovenproof dish, pour the tomatoes, onions and chickpeas on top and bake in a preheated 350 degree oven for 15 minutes. Serve with carafes of vinegar and olive oil on the side for optional use by the guests.

SALT CODFISH WITH GARLIC SAUCE
(Serves 4)

1½ lbs. salt codfish
beer batter (see page 130)
2 cups olive oil
1 doz. cloves garlic, chopped

juice of 1 lemon
2 cups mashed potatoes
salt and fresh ground black
 pepper

Soak the codfish for 24 hours, changing the water several times. Cut it into strips 3 inches long and 2 inches wide. Heat 1 of the cups of olive oil in a skillet. Dip the codfish strips in beer batter and fry them brown on both sides; set aside and keep hot. Place the garlic in a mortar with a little olive oil and pound it to a paste with the pestle. Add the salt and pepper, potatoes and lemon juice and mix well. Add the remaining olive oil a little at a time, mixing constantly. The finished sauce should have the texture of mayonnaise; spread it generously over the fried codfish and serve at once.

BACALHAU WITH MOLHO TOMATE
(Serves 4)

1½ lbs. dry salt codfish
1 cup olive oil
2 cloves garlic, minced
2 cups molho tomate (see
 page 49)
½ cup bread crumbs

1 small jar pimientos, chopped
2 tbsps. sherry
dash of Tabasco
Parmesan cheese
fresh ground black pepper

Soak the codfish 24 hours, changing the water several times. Drain well and cut into 2-inch squares. Parboil these squares for 10 minutes. Remove and drain. Remove the bones. Heat the olive oil in a skillet until it is smoking. Dip the fish pieces in flour and fry until brown on both sides; drain and set aside, keeping them warm. Mix the molho tomate with garlic, pimientos, bread crumbs, sherry, Tabasco and black pepper; stir it well. Place half of the mixture in an earthenware casserole or an ovenproof baking dish. Place the fried codfish squares on top of the sauce and cover the fish with the remainder of the sauce. Sprinkle with mixed bread crumbs and Parmesan cheese and bake in a preheated 350 degree oven for 15 minutes or until the top is browned.

Serve with a good red Portuguese or Spanish wine.

SALT CODFISH WITH EGGPLANT
(Serves 4 to 6)

1½ lbs. dried salt codfish	1 16 oz. can pomodori pelati
1 large eggplant	tomatoes
2 medium onions, chopped	½ cup dry white wine
2 cloves garlic, minced	fresh ground black pepper
½ cup olive oil	bread crumbs and Parmesan
	cheese

Soak the codfish for 24 hours, changing the water several times. Cut the fish up into 2-inch squares. Parboil these pieces for 10 minutes; drain, remove the skin and bones. Set aside. Squeeze up the canned tomatoes in their juice. Peel the eggplant and cut it into ½-inch slices, cut these slices into 2-inch squares.

Heat the olive oil in a skillet or Dutch oven and saute the onions and garlic until soft and transparent. Remove and set aside. Now remove the skillet from the fire and place in it a layer of eggplant (half of it), and on top of the eggplant place half the onions and garlic, then a layer of codfish squares (half of them). Cover with half the tomatoes and sprinkle with fresh ground black pepper. Repeat these layers with the remaining materials. Add the wine. Cover the skillet and simmer very slowly for 1 hour. Place an asbestos pad under the skillet so the lower layer of eggplant will not scorch. At the end, sprinkle the top with bread crumbs and Parmesan cheese and place

EGG-PLANT

it under the broiler flame for a few minutes until lightly browned. Serve in the cooking pan, garnished with butter, black olives, parsley, and onion rings. Serve olive oil and vinegar in carafes on the side so that the guests may sprinkle it on if they wish. Boiled chickpeas or steamed rice make a good side dish for this.

About Moist Salt Codfish

In the supermarkets today you can buy moist salt codfish in one-pound wooden or plastic boxes, or cellophane wrapped packages. This product does not have the exquisite flavor of the bone dry codfish, but it's better than no salt cod at all, and you can use it with any of the recipes for the dry fish. A dried 1 ½ pound fish is equal to 2 pounds or more of the moist fish. This moist codfish combines well with other seafoods such as shrimp in the recipe given below. And, believe it or not, it's delicious when eaten raw as an hors d'oeuvre, thus:

SALT CODFISH APPETIZER

Unpack a 1-pound box of moist salt codfish and hold the pieces under a running faucet to rinse off the excess salt on the outside of the fish. Dry the pieces with paper towels. Take a very sharp knife and slice the pieces crosswise as thin as possible. Arrange these slices attractively on a platter surrounded by lemon and lime wedges. Squeeze a few drops of lemon or lime juice on the slices while eating them. Very good, and thirst-provoking with cocktails, highballs, wine and beer.

SALT CODFISH-SHRIMP STEW
(Serves 4 to 6)

2 lbs. moist salt codfish
1 lb. raw peeled shrimp
½ cup olive oil
2 medium potatoes, boiled,
  peeled and diced
1 cup celery, finely chopped
½ green pepper, diced

1 16 oz. can plum type
  tomatoes
3 cloves garlic, minced
1 cup black whole olives, mild
  type
½ tsp. Tabasco
fresh ground black pepper
fish stock or water

Soak the codfish for 12 hours, changing the water several times. Rinse well. Cut it into bite-size chunks and set aside. Heat the olive oil in a skillet; add the celery and cook until soft. Chop the almonds and add them. Add the garlic, mushrooms, tomatoes, potatoes, black olives, wine and fresh ground black pepper. Simmer for 15 minutes. Place this mixture in a stew pot or Dutch oven. Add the codfish chunks. Cover with fish stock or water to about ½ inch above the top of the stew. Simmer for 1 hour. Add the shrimp and raise the heat and cook 10 minutes longer. Serve in soup bowls with toasted garlic bread. A chilled rose wine is a good accompaniment.

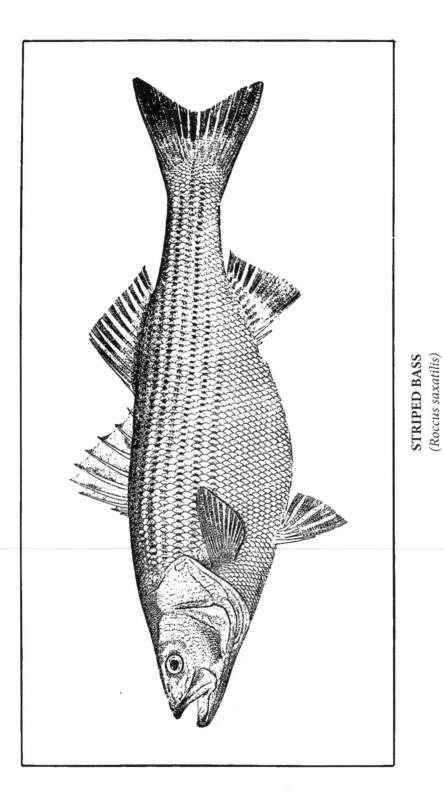

STRIPED BASS
(Roccus saxatilis)

How to Stuff a Squid Hound

This ole Cape Tip is one of the hottest striped bass fishing areas on the Atlantic Coast. Both Champlain and Gosnold during their seventeenth-century visits reported large numbers of stripers here and predicted that this would become a fishermen's paradise. Nowadays when the bass start running, every man in town who is worth his salt drops whatever he is doing and heads for the back shore, and beachbuggies from all over creation start flocking into town. Every night during the incoming tide the fishermen line the shore, patiently waiting for their strikes. It's a sort of fearsome thing to be alone in the dark on the beach and have a big old giant of a squid hound hit your plug; they are so darn strong that it feels as if they might pull you out over the bars and drown you. I'll never forget when I bagged my first one out at Peaked Hill. I was all alone, it was a pitch black night, and when this powerful old lunker struck, I thought I had the Loch Ness monster on the end of my line. I was so excited that I fouled up my reel and had to horse him in by fighting a tug of war, walking backward up the beach, the most unsportsmanlike thing in the world to do to such a noble adversary. But when it's your first bass, and you don't know the ropes, it's about the only thing you can do. When I got him into town and weighed him I couldn't believe the scales, which said he weighed only twenty-five pounds.

CATCHING BASS

Outside of a John Gaspie type clambake there's no Provincetown feast so festive nor jag more joyous than a real stuffed striped bass party.

One of the goals in question is aesthetic. You want to preserve the beauty of the bass so that when he's laid out on the table he looks as fresh and alive as if he'd just jumped out of the water. This is complex and involves a lot of hokus pokus. You don't cut off his head or his tail and you don't scale him; you carve out his beautiful golden eyeball and put it in the refrigerator to keep it fresh and sparkling. Sounds gruesome but it's part of the rigmarole.

Very few ovens or baking pans can accommodate a thirty-five-pound bass, which is from three and a half to four feet long, so you must neatly cut it into halves and stuff and bake each half in separate pans. When it's done, carefully place the two halves back together.

The stuffing is so voluminous that even the largest skillet will not hold it all. It must be cooked in shifts and mixed together just before stuffing into the bass. Some querulous gourmet might ask, "why those browned pork cubes?" It's a trick I learned from the Provincetown Portuguese. Salt pork does miracles in accentuating the flavor of shellfish in a stuffing. So if you have about eight or ten hours of spare time and forty or fifty bucks of spare cash and a thirty-five-pound striped bass, you can have some fun with this recipe. I've kitchen tested it four or five times and it never misfired yet.

STUFFED STRIPED BASS

1 35 lb. bass	1 lb. fresh mushrooms, sliced
4 doz. fresh shucked Wellfleet oysters and their juices	1 celery heart, chopped (about 2 cups)
4 doz. Provincetown littleneck quahaugs and their juices	12 cloves garlic, minced
	4 tbsps. prepared mustard
	4 tbsps. Worcestershire sauce
5 lbs. shrimp, peeled and cut in ½-inch pieces	1 tsp. Tabasco
	1 bottle imported white Burgundy
5 lbs. scallops, quartered	2 loaves Portuguese bread
½ lb. salt pork, finely diced and fried light brown	2 lbs. butter
	2 cups vegetable oil
6 eggs, beaten	4 tsps. salt (or more, to taste)
4 large onions, diced	2 tsps. fresh ground black pepper
2 green peppers, diced	

Since you'll probably have to cook the stuffing in batches, divide all the ingredients into equal parts—as many as you need to fit your skillet—and proceed as follows: Melt butter in the skillet and saute onions, green pepper, celery and garlic until soft and golden, add the oysters, scallops and quahaugs and their juices. Add the chopped parsley and sliced mushrooms, saute for 5 minutes longer, stirring now and then. Add all the other ingredients except the wine and bread and stir them in. Tear up the loaves of Portuguese bread into small pieces, wet them down with the bottle of wine, and make a mush out of them; add this to the other cooked ingredients and mix it all up thoroughly.

Carefully cut the backbone out of the fish and stuff the halves of the bass with this mixture. Punch holes in its weskit with an ice pick and lace it up good with stout cotton cord (careful not to use nylon or plastic; it melts). Cover the bottoms of 2 large baking pans with aluminum foil and wet them down with vegetable oil; lay the stuffed bass halves in the pans and rub them generously with the oil. Preheat the oven to 400 degrees and bake the fish for 45 minutes to 1 hour, brushing it frequently with oil to keep it from drying out.

Cover the top of a table with aluminum foil and make a big bed of fresh green lettuce leaves; lay the halves of the baked bass on this bed, reassembled in a natural posture. Run get the sparkling eye from the refrigerator and replace it in its socket. Call in the photographers and reporters.

After the oohs and ahhs are over with and you are ready to eat, peel the scales and skin off the bass and slice it up into individual portions, and give each guest plenty of stuffing. This is my humble salute to old *Roccus saxatilis*, the squid hound.

TO STUFF A SMALL STRIPED BASS

Now I admit that many of my readers will never see a thirty-five-pound striped bass, but you can often purchase a five- or ten-pound bass in a good fish market. When you find one, divide my stuffing ingredients into appropriate fractions, or use the recipes for stuffing five- and ten-pound haddock and codfish.

BROILED STRIPED BASS STEAKS
(1 Serving)

Many people think bass steak is so good that it needs no adornment other than butter or lemon juice.

Rub the bass steak with melted butter, salt and pepper. Lay it on a buttered sizzle platter or broiling pan, skin side up, and broil until the skin is brown, then flip it over and broil it 5 minutes more; allow a little more time for big thick steaks. To test for doneness, lift the flesh up with a fork and peek inside; if it's opaque white clear through it is done, if the flesh is still transparent it needs more cooking. Brush with melted butter and serve with lemon wedges.

BASS STEAKS WITH SOUR CREAM SAUCE

Broil the steaks as indicated above, serve them under a thick blanket of sour cream sauce made as follows:

To a pint of sour cream add ½ cup grated onion, ½ cup chopped fresh mint leaves, salt and fresh ground black pepper to taste. This should cover half a dozen steaks and your guests will love you for feeding them such manna.

STRIPED BASS STEAKS VERONIQUE
(Serves 4)

4 striped bass steaks
1 stick butter

½ lb. seedless grapes, washed
and skinned

Melt ½ stick of butter in a large skillet and saute the bass steaks on both sides until they are done. Place on hot serving plates and keep warm. Add the other ½ stick of butter to the pan. When it melts add the grapes, raise the heat and cook the grapes until they are thoroughly heated through. Pour butter and grapes over the steaks and serve piping hot.

STRIPED BASS AMANDINE-MUSHROOMS
(Serves 4)

4 bass steaks	*1 cup sliced natural almonds*
1½ sticks butter	*½ cup fresh mushrooms,*
juice of 2 lemons	*sliced*

Saute the bass steaks in ½ stick of butter as instructed above. Place the steaks on hot serving plates and keep warm. Melt a stick of butter in the skillet and add the almonds, mushrooms and lemon juice. Raise the heat high and cook until the almonds have turned golden (but not brown), pour over the steaks and serve immediately. Next to haddock amandine, this is the best of all amandines—some folks say it's even better.

PORTUGUESE BAKED BASS STEAKS
(Serves 6)

6 striped bass steaks	*1 cup white wine*
1 16 oz. can tomatoes	*¼ lb. salt pork, diced and fried*
1 large onion, slivered	*brown*
1 diced green pepper	*assorted spices*
1 stalk celery, diced	*Parmesan cheese*

Lay the striper steaks, skin side down, on greased aluminum foil in a large baking pan. Sprinkle over the top the tomatoes and juice (squeeze the tomatoes into segments), the slivered onion, green pepper, celery, white wine, salt pork, a little basil, rosemary, ground cominos, salt and fresh ground black pepper. Preheat the oven to 375 degrees and bake the steaks for 15 minutes; remove the pan from the oven and sprinkle with Parmesan cheese. Return to oven and bake 5 minutes more or until the cheese is brown.

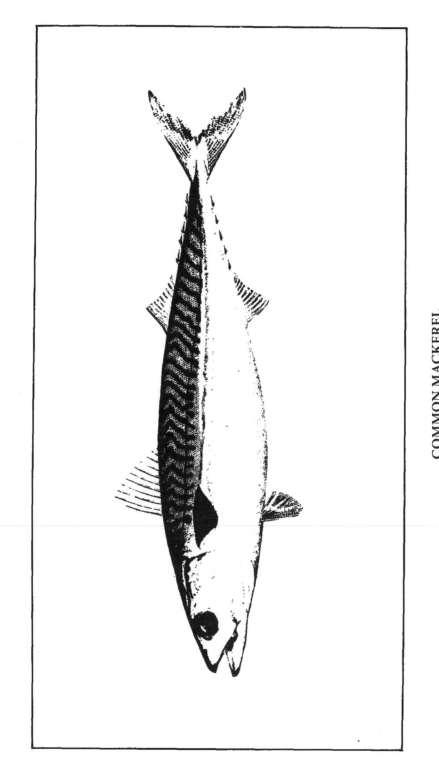

COMMON MACKEREL
(Scomber scombrus)

Holy Mackerel!

As we used to stand on the end of Town Wharf watching the trapboats unload tons of mackerel, John J. Gaspie would exclaim "Holy mackerel! Did you ever see so many good fish?! It makes me hungry; let's galvanize some tinkers and have a feast!" He would disappear inside the fish house with an empty bucket and come back with a pail full of tinkers. Later, as we sat in Cookie's downing the galvanized tinkers and beer, I would say, "Now Father G., Tell me some more things about mackerel." He'd push his schooner toward the barkeep for a refill, cough, light his pipe, and say:

"Man, if you wanta hear some talk about mackerel you oughta come here more in the winter; when this hot stove league starts gamming about mackerel they can shoot more moonshine than about any other fish that swims in the sea. He's got more riddles than all of the others put together." As I finished my second mug I said, "Yeh, where do mackerel go in the winter?" And the fat was on the fire. He lit his pipe again and looked at me squinch-eyed, as if I'd thrown him a hot grounder. Then he laughed:

"Man, I wish I knew! There were people alive in Provincetown when I was young who swore that mackerel spent the winter with their heads buried in the mud off the Newfoundland beaches. That they were there with their tails sticking out, waving back'ards and for'ards with the current like a meadow full of daisies swayin' in the breeze. *Quien sabe*? We useta catch mackerel in the winter by fishing deep.

"Most folks think mackerel go south to Florida in winter like the Provincetown restaurant owners, but I dunno. Away back before the Civil War Provincetown had an old fisherman, Cap'n Nathaniel Atwood; he was just a common fishing cap'n, but he knew his fish so good the scientists took his word for nearly everything he said; every major fishing book ever written in this country says every so often 'Cap'n Atwood says this or Cap'n Atwood says that.' And he wrote a lot of articles for the old fish commission people down in Washington. Well sir, Cap'n Atwood, he had a theory that the mackerel didn't go south at all, he just moved out to the deep water

WINTER
MACKEREL

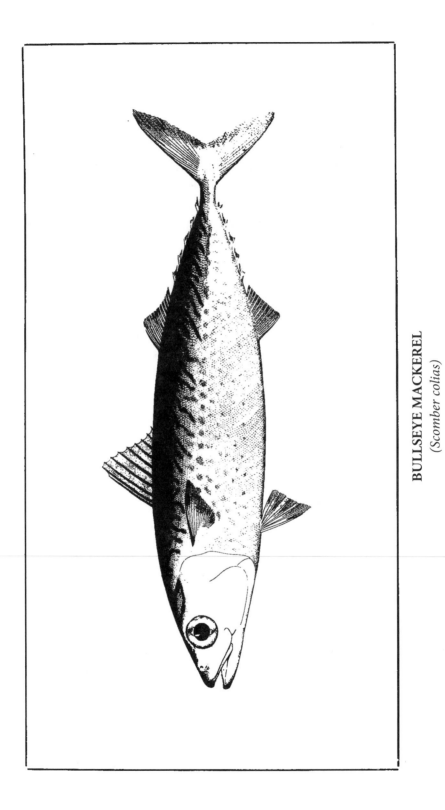

BULLSEYE MACKEREL
(*Scomber colias*)

where he'd lie around on the bottom and sort of cat nap all winter. When the spring weather started warming up the water, the mackerel would start showing first off Cape Hatteras and then on up the coast to Cape Cod. The way they'd come up in a sequence like this led folks to believe they were migratin' north'ard, when it was really just the warm weather which was migratin' up our way. Now I'll tell you this: the people at Woods Hole and down at Fish and Wildlife in Washington, after a hundred years, are saying that probably the ole Provincetown Cap'n was right after all. Maybe they should've carved a mackerel on his headstone, he knew so much about it."

The winter disappearing act wasn't the only trick the mackerel had up his sleeve. Sometimes he wouldn't even show up in the summer. I asked Gaspie about this and he replied:

"Man, there's as many ups and downs in mackerel fishing as there is humps and hollows in a roller coaster. Sometimes they're so thick they glut the market and you can't give them away; and other times they're scarcer'n chicken's teeth and the mackerel price is skyhigh and you can't find a one. I remember as how in 1910 I'd bought a pile of gear and was waiting on them, and not a damn one showed up and I lost my shirt-tail. That's why most fishermen are such good cussers and don't trust nobody, man or fish. The bullseye mackerel got so scarce during the few years after 1910 that the scientists thought he was extinct, like the passenger pigeon. One of them fellers from the Smithsonian, he came up here and begged us to find just one little specimen so he could stuff it to show posterity. Well, we felt really sorry for the guy so we looked and looked, but nary a bullseye could we turn up. Then in a few years they were back here so thick you could walk across their backs in the water almost.

"SPOTTER" ON THE MASTHEAD

"You wouldn't believe it if I told you how thick the schools of mackerel can be sometimes. They feed on the surface and they kick up the awfullest kind of fuss of ripples so you can spot the schools easy. When I used to serve as lookout on the masthead, I could look around and count eight or ten big schools at one time, some of them stretching off as far as your eye could see."

At this point I broke in to ask, "And how about those busted bonanzas, Gaspie?"

"Hmmm, they were sad, weren't they? Sometimes the mackerel would be here by the millions in June or July and we'd be makin' money hand over fist, and what do you think would happen? They'd all disappear at one time like the Lord had snapped his fingers and called them home. We'd be so disgusted we'd beach the boats and stash the gear, then we'd sit back and light our pipes, ready to hibernate and play cribbage and checkers all winter; then durn it! those cussed fish would come back in October, all at one time and in bigger schools than before, and we'd be scrambling all around like a chicken with its head cut off, trying to get back in that water to get 'em."

I felt so sad for the woes of the mackerel fisherman that I busted out into an old fisherman's chantey that Manny Zora had taught me:

ADIPOSE

> *Oh a wet butt*
> *And an empty gut,*
> *The fisherman's life is rosy,*
> *And mackerel are where you find them.*

Being very jealous of Zora and recognizing the song, Gaspie looked askance and said, "you're off key, mate." So I asked him, "Some folks say mackerel go blind in the winter; how 'bout it?" His reply: "Mackerel have funny eyelids, called adipose eyelids. He has two transparent layers of flesh which cover his eyeball except for a little split down the middle. Sometimes in the winter this outer layer turns gray, like a man with cataracts, and I guess that's why some folks say they go blind. But I don't believe it. A fish would starve to death if he couldn't see how to catch his dinner."

"How fast can a mackerel swim, Gaspie?"

"When he is scared or excited he can swim from Town Wharf to Long Point before you can say 'My mammy loves clamburgers.' There's still a lot that people don't know about how a fish swims, but the mackerel swims by vibrating his tail like a dynamo. He burns up oxygen so fast he has to keep a current flowing over his gills or he will smother to death; that's why you can't keep 'em in a tank or aquarium—they need lots of elbow room."

At this point I dropped a little bomb. "Gaspie, what is the difference between a tinker mackerel and a tinker mackerel?"

"Thought you had me, eh? You could sure start an argument asking that. There's two kinds of tinkers: a small baby about six months old and six inches long is called a tinker, and he's just about the best eating you could find anywhere except his cousin, who is small too; he's the true tinker. But he is full grown and a different species. Here in Provincetown he's called the bullseye, or the chub mackerel. He has a bigger eye and finer stripes and blotches on his side than the common mackerel; but the best way to tell is to cut 'em open. The bullseye has an air bladder and the common mackerel doesn't."

(Now just to show you how much disagreement there is about mackerel, one night at Cookie's we were discussing the bullseye mackerel and Johnny Andrews, who worked at the old freezer, said he saw plenty of them every summer, and Captain John Santos, a fisherman, said he hadn't seen one in thirty years. See what the researcher is up agin when he tangles with mackerel?)

Next I asked Gaspie to tell us how Provincetown was big shakes in the old-time mackerel fishery. And he went on and on with his fabulous—and true—story. He told how in days of old, the mackerel fleet of Provincetown and Truro numbered over a hundred vessels, the finest in the land. And how dozens of vessels from other areas would make Provincetown their headquarters during the mackerel season. And how the State of Massachusetts produced over 100 million pounds in 1885, most of it from Cape Cod. Gaspie would end stories like these by exclaiming: "They oughta take that sacred codfish out of the State House in Boston and put a Holy Mackerel in its place."

THE MACKEREL FLEET AT ANCHOR IN THE HARBOR

BROILED MACKEREL

A fresh caught Provincetown mackerel is one of the tastiest of all fish. Its meat is sweet, light and delicate enough to please the palate of the most exacting connoisseur.

Split a mackerel down the back, fold it open, clean out the innards and blood. Brush it with melted butter, place on a buttered sizzle platter or broiling pan skin side down, and broil for 8 or 10 minutes. (Mackerel are so thin you do not have to turn them over.) Garnish with parsley and lemon wedges and serve them on the hot sizzle platter. If a broiler pan is used transfer them to a hot serving plate.

PROVINCETOWN MACKEREL A LA SHOVEL

One of the best old-time Provincetown methods of cooking mackerel was to broil them on a steel shovel (a clean one of course). It worked especially well on the old coal-burning stove or at the fireplace where there were plenty of hot hardwood coals. You took the whole mackerel, head, guts, tail feathers and all, and placed it on the hot shovel resting on the coals; you broiled it on both sides, and the natural oils from the fish and its innards furnished the lubrication necessary. God alone knows why, but the innards gave an inimitable piquancy to the flavor of the fish. Of course it had to be a very fresh fish or you'd be a dead duck.

Cooking things with the stomach left in is a practice of French *haute cuisine*. The red mullet of the Mediterranean is never gutted, nor are those small birds called ortolans, nor woodcocks. Some epicures wouldn't touch a pheasant that wasn't cooked in its feathers; the oils in the feathers produce a distinctive flavor. Oh whatthehell, don't we eat halfshell oysters and quahaugs feathers and all?

MACKEREL A LA ROCK SALT

There's another old-time method of cooking mackerel which must date back to the days when Provincetown was a salt manufacturing center. This requires one of those tin bread loaf pans about 12 inches long by 3 inches wide by 3 inches deep. And you need plenty of rock salt. Use ice cream salt and not that chemical-saturated stuff they throw on icy roads. Wash a nice fat mackerel, leave the guts in and head and tail on. Put ½ inch of salt in the pan and lay the mackerel on it upside down. Fill the pan with rock salt so that the fish is completely encased. Sprinkle water generously over the salt so that it will solidify and harden. Bake in a preheated 400 degree oven for 20-30 minutes or until all the water has evaporated and the salt is as hard as a brick. Turn it out on a platter and deliver it to the table along with a hammer. The diner uses the hammer to bust the block open and get at the beautiful fish inside. Its flavor is out of this world. Contrary to what you'd expect, it is not too salty—it's just right.

A LA ROCK SALT

PORTUGUESE MACKEREL VINHA D'ALHOS

You can't soak a mackerel in a marinade as you would any other fish. His meat would get soggy and fall apart. But you can still jazz him up Portuguese-style. Lay the mackerel on a plate and sprinkle it with onion powder, garlic powder, a little powdered cumin and rosemary, salt and pepper, and rub it in. Then sprinkle on some vinegar and rub that in. Do this 3 or 4 times over a 6-hour period, cutting down on the condiments each time so that at the end you're just using vinegar, and very lightly at that. Fry the cured fish in an iron skillet in bacon grease or lard. Do not use vegetable oil or margarine or butter, as the vinegar and spices would cause it to break down and curdle. Eat enough of these and you'll bust out and sing some Fados.

MACKEREL MOLHO TOMATE

Split a mackerel and broil it on a metal sizzle platter or broiling pan, skin side down. You don't need to turn it over—it's thin and the hot plate will cook the bottom side. When it's done, cover it with a blanket of hot molho tomate (see page 49), and serve it on the hot sizzle platter. If cooked in a pan, remove it to a hot serving plate and put the sauce on top.

This is also a good way to cook small whole bluefish or pollock, or fillets from larger fish. The molho counterbalances the oiliness of these fishes in a truly metaphysical way.

MACKEREL MOLHO TOMATE
A LA CABRAL

Joe Cook's Vo Vo (Portuguese for Grandma) Cabral taught him a slick way of fixing a mackerel. Take a good-size mackerel, leave the head and tail on for good looks, split it down the back, fold open, clean out the entrails and black stomach lining, remove the backbone, rinse well to remove all blood. Dry the fish with paper towels. Lay it on a buttered metal broiling plate and cover with a good blanket of molho tomate; cover the blanket of molho with thin slices of sharp cheese, place 3 or 4 slices of fresh tomato in a row on top of the cheese. Sprinkle it with a few drops of muscatel or sherry, bake for 15 or 20 minutes in a preheated 350 degree oven. Take it out of the oven and slide it under the broiler flame for a moment to give it a glaze. The various elements blend so well together that it's paradisiacal fare. This is also a very good way to cook a freshwater trout.

Hooray for Vo Vo Cabral! She was quite a character. During those gruesome Prohibition days she made an excellent hootch-brandy on her kitchen stove using prunes and raisins as a base. One day, she threw her leftover mash squeezings out the back door to the chickens, about twenty-five of them. Within ten minutes all those chickens were flat on their backs with their feet sticking up in the air. Vo Vo screamed at little Joe, "Run get Friday Cook and tell him all the chickens are dead!" When Friday arrived and surveyed the scene he busted out and almost died a-laughing: "Those chickens aren't dead, they are cold stoned drunk on Vo Vo's brandy squeez-ins'!" Always something exciting going on in Provincetown!

FANNY FIELD'S BAKED MACKEREL

Of course nobody but nobody can equal Provincetown's great Fanny Fields at cooking a fish, but several years ago she taught me how to bake mackerel and it went sort of like this: Spread the split mackerels in a greased baking pan and sprinkle with salt, pepper, shredded onions and canned tomatoes squished up. Bake in a preheated 350 degree oven for 15-20 minutes. Serve at once; this dish loses its taste and attractiveness if allowed to dry out.

BAKED

FRIED MACKEREL FILLETS
BEURRE NOIR

Dip fresh mackerel fillets in milk, then in flour (the yellow dry clam batter used by restaurants is even better); fry in deep fat until browned, set aside and keep hot. Melt ½ stick of butter in a skillet and fry until it is deep brown (*beurre noir*, black butter). Add some chopped capers and a little vinegar to the black butter, place the fillets on hot serving plates; pour the sauce over them and serve immediately.

BAKED MACKEREL WITH
MUSHROOM SAUCE
(Serves 2)

2 mackerels	*1 tbsp. chopped parsley*
¼ cup white wine	*1 clove garlic, finely minced*
2 scallions and 2 inches of their green leaves	*¾ stick butter*
	3 tbsps. flour
6 mushrooms, chopped finely	*1 cup light cream*
	1 cup evaporated milk
1 small onion, chopped	*3 egg yolks, beaten*

Take 2 mackerels, split down the back, and clean. Lay the mackerels in a buttered baking pan. Sprinkle with the white wine, 2 mushrooms finely chopped, and 1 scallion finely minced. Bake for 15 minutes in a preheated 350 degree oven. Place each fish on a warm serving dish and keep it hot while making the sauce.

The Sauce

Add the pan juices to a skillet with ¼ stick of butter; add the onion, scallion, garlic, parsley and mushrooms and saute until the vegetables are soft. Season with salt and fresh ground black pepper. Melt ½ stick of butter in another skillet and add the flour, stirring well to form a roux. Add the cream and evaporated milk and work and stir constantly until the sauce thickens. Beat the egg yolks in a cup and add 2 tablespoons of the hot cream sauce to them slowly. Add them to the main portion of the cream sauce, add the vegetable mix to the cream sauce. Pour the sauce over the mackerel and serve at once, piping hot. Along with this dish you should serve a good Moselle or Rhine wine, well chilled.

MACKEREL WITH MUSSEL SAUCE
(Serves 2)

2 mackerels	½ stick butter
2 doz. mussels	2 cups milk
3 slices American cheese, diced	½ cup fresh mushrooms, chopped
½ tsp. powdered mustard	salt and fresh ground black pepper
3 tbsps. flour	

Steam the mussels and save ½ cup of the broth. Shuck the mussels and beard them; set aside.

Make the sauce thus: Melt the butter in a skillet, remove from the heat and add the flour, stirring to a paste; then add the milk little by little, stirring constantly. Return to the fire. Add the diced cheese and stir until it melts and you have a smooth mix. Add the mustard and mushrooms, white wine and ½ cup of mussel broth; mix well. Add the mussels and stir them in. Season to taste with salt and fresh ground black pepper. Set the sauce aside and keep it hot.

Split two mackerels down the back and clean. Place them skin side up on individual sizzle platters or in a broiler pan. (If sizzle platters are used serve the fish right on the platter. If a broiler pan is used transfer them to hot serving plates.) Broil for 3 minutes, then turn over and broil 3 minutes more. Spread the sauce over the mackerels and serve at once, piping hot.

MACKEREL WITH GOOSEBERRY SAUCE

GOOSEBERRIES

The classical continental way of serving mackerel is with green gooseberry sauce (in France they are called mackerel berries). You can very often find this sauce in gourmet food shops and specialty stores, and most folks can't even guess what its purpose is. It does great things for our beautiful Cape Cod mackerel. Broil the mackerel as instructed above. Heat the sauce and spread over the mackerel and serve at once. Even a full-bodied red wine is good with this. Don't ever let anybody tell you that only white wines go with seafood; if it's a good uncorrupted fish, any good uncorrupted wine will go well with it.

MACKEREL WITH ONIONS
AND OLIVES
(Serves 2)

2 1 lb. fresh whole mackerels	*black Greek olives, radishes,*
1 cup chopped onions	*lemon wedges, capers, onion*
1 cup chopped green olives	*rings, parsley sprigs*

Leave the head and tail on the fish for good looks—it's too beautiful to be mangled. Grasp the fish by the head with one hand, and, taking a sharp knife in the other, split down the back but do not cut all the way through. Spread it open and clean out the innards and the black stomach lining. Insert the knife under the backbone and remove it. Wash well and dry with paper towels. Butter individual metal sizzle platters or a broiling pan and lay the fish in it, skin side down. Brush with melted butter and sprinkle on the chopped onions and olives. Bake in a preheated 350 degree oven for 15-20 minutes. If you're using sizzle platters serve the fish right on the platters; if baked in a pan transfer them to warmed serving plates. Decorate with black Greek olives, radish roses, lemon wedges, capers, onion rings, and parsley sprigs—make it really pretty and voluptuous. Serve piping hot with a bouncing red wine.

MACKEREL WITH TOMATOES AND
GREEN PEPPER
(Serves 2)

2 1 lb. fresh mackerels
1 cup diced green pepper

1 cup canned tomatoes,
  squeezed up

Cook as in the above recipe, sprinkling the tomatoes and green pepper over the fish. Decorate in the same manner and serve some green scallions along with it.

MACKEREL WITH ANCHOVY
AND ROSEMARY
(Serves 2)

The Portuguese and Italians long ago discovered the affinity between rosemary and mackerel. Al Silva, Provincetown's lobster kingpin, dotes on rosemary and mackerel.

Clean the mackerels as indicated above and place on buttered sizzle platters; brush with melted butter. Cut anchovy fillets in ¼-inch pieces and dot the fish with these pieces. Sprinkle with dried rosemary leaves. Broil on one side only for 10 minutes or until the flesh flakes easily when tested with a fork. Garnish with parsley and lemon wedges, and serve piping hot.

MACKEREL WITH GARLIC
(Serves 2)

2 1 lb. whole fresh mackerels   garlic
olive oil   dried rosemary leaves

Dress the mackerels as indicated above. Pound 6 garlic cloves to a paste in a mortar along with 2 tablespoons of olive oil. Brush sizzle platters with olive oil and lay the fish on them. Brush the fish with the garlic-olive oil mixture, sprinkle with dried rosemary leaves and broil as instructed above.

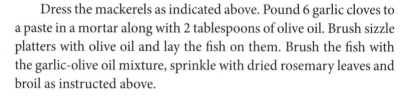

All About Tinker Mackerel

Nature's autumn bounties start showing up on Cape Cod in October, and one of the best of these is the tinker mackerel. A tinker mackerel is a baby mackerel that was hatched the previous summer; by October he has grown to be four to six inches long and he's one of the tenderest, tastiest little morsels that Mother Ocean produces. Like their parents they swim in close-packed schools, and when these schools start coming into the harbor it makes for some lively sport. A kid with a mackerel jig can sit on the end of Town Wharf and catch a bucketful of them in an hour. A jig is a tiny piece of silver-plated lead with a small hook in the tail of it, and when the tinkers are hungry they will fight for the privilege of snapping at it. A fisherman with a cast net can catch a bucketful of tinkers in a few minutes. Seiners using a very small mesh net can catch barrels full of them, and large numbers of them are caught in the trap nets mixed in with the other fish. Since they are surface swimmers, the draggers, which fish on the bottom, do not catch many of them.

JIG

If you are too lazy to catch your own tinkers you can buy them at the fish markets. Or if you're just a plain moocher and have a friend working on one of the trapboats you can ask him to save you a few.

The best of all ways to prepare tinker mackerels is to make molho cru out of them. This Portuguese snack-appetizer is miles ahead of ordinary hors d'ouevres; it approaches the sublime. It's the apotheosis of the tinker. I'd like to sit at a bar and munch them all afternoon, but there never are enough of them for that. When Clara Cook fixes up a batch of them in her kitchen and sends them over to the bar at Cookie's Tap, they disappear so fast you're lucky to get one or two of them.

MOLHO CRU

*24 tinker mackerels batter (see   marinade (vinha d'alhos, see
   below)   below)*

Cut the heads off the tinkers and gut them. Rinse them well and dry with paper towels. Dip them in the batter and fry in deep hot fat until well browned on both sides. Drain on paper towels and cool.

Frying Batter

Take 1½ cups of flour, 1 cup beer, 1 tsp. salt, 1 tsp. baking powder, ¼ tsp. fresh ground black pepper and 2 tbsps. melted butter.

Mix well in a mixing bowl but do not stir too long, or it will make a tough batter. Let rest ½ hour before using. Dip the tinkers in the batter and fry in deep hot fat.

Now I might as well tell you that molho cru is very firm and chewy, and how to get that firm chewy effect into a soft fish like a mackerel was something that puzzled me for years until Victor Pacellini came along and told me. You put the fried fish in a pan or glass dish and leave them in the refrigerator for 24 hours. At the end of that time they will be hard and firm.

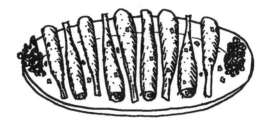

Molho Cru Marinade
(A special type of vinha d'alhos)

12 hot pony or cayenne pickled peppers, chopped
4 cloves garlic, finely minced
½ cup tomato sauce
1 medium onion, chopped
½ cup vinegar

½ cup water
¼ cup olive oil
2 tbsps. mixed pickling spices
½ tsp. ground cumin
salt and fresh ground black pepper
pinch of sugar

After making the vinha d'alhos marinade by combining the above ingredients, place the fish in a flat glass dish or enamel pan and pour the marinade over them. Let them soak for an hour or two, turning them over now and then. Do not marinate them too long or they will get soft again. Remove from the marinade and serve them only to your best friends—they're too damn good for casual acquaintances! They should be hot from the peppers: spicy, garlicky, and pickle-ish—a whole symphony of tastes; serve them with beer or chilled wine.

The Joy of Smoked Mackerel

Smoked mackerel is a delicious treat that used to be very common in Provincetown, but since it requires a little work it has gone out of style. Why bother, when you can buy lox or smoked whitefish at the delicatessen for only three dollars a pound? Fish that you struggle over and smoke yourself, however, has a much better flavor; it's the savor of sweat.

It's a very simple matter to build a small back yard smokehouse out of an old barrel or an old refrigerator. Or if you have a brick barbecue pit you can easily build a plywood smoking box to fit on top of it. In addition to mackerel you can also smoke thinly sliced bluefin tuna, alewives, herrings, pollocks, bluefish, butterfish and other of the oily fleshed fishes. Or you can smoke haddock lightly and call it "finnan haddie." With the price of smoked fish as high as it is, I've often daydreamed of building a nice commercial fish smokehouse, but like my other pipe dreams the idea always goes up in smoke. If you'd like to tinker with the idea yourself here's how to go about it:

HOW TO SMOKE MACKEREL

Cut off their heads, but leave on the hard bony plate just below the gills, the "collarbone" it's called. Clean stomachs of all intestines, membranes, black skin and the like, wash the fish thoroughly under a running faucet and put them in a container of clean water and let soak ½ hour to leach out all remaining blood. Next make a solution of brine in the proportion 1 pound of salt to 1 quart of water. Let them soak in the brine for 1-3 hours, depending on how fat the fish are; this "conditions" them. Next remove them from the brine and rinse them thoroughly. Lay them on chicken wire mesh drying racks in a breezy, fly-free location for an hour or two until both sides are dry (a wet soggy fish does not smoke well, and it gets a grayish color instead of the rich brown that is desired).

Start the fire under the smoking barrel an hour before beginning to smoke so that moisture present in the tunnel and barrel will evaporate. Mount the fish on the smoking sticks or rods, or lay them

on the wire-mesh smoking trays (make sure that no two fish are touching each other); place in position inside the barrel.

For smoking fish hardwood is always the best wood—the nut woods such as oak, hickory and beech. Hardwood sawdust is required to keep the fire "smothered" and produce smoke. If you can't get suitable wood, an excellent shortcut is to use charcoal and keep it covered with sawdust. Never use pine wood or sawdust; it gives a resinous flavor to the fish. Keep a close watch on the fire and never let it go out. Six hours is usually sufficient smoking if the fire is not too hot. An 8- or 12-hour slow smoke is even better. Time adjustments come with practice. The fish are done when they have a rich brown color; they shouldn't be allowed to blacken like charcoal-broiled steer.

If smoked properly, the fish should keep about 10 days at room temperature. However it's safer to keep them in the refrigerator, wrapped in wax paper or aluminum foil to prevent drying out. When ready to eat, brush them with the sauce given below, then brown them a little under the broiler. As is the case with most other seafood dishes, smoked mackerel should be washed down with something dry, cool and pungent—wine or beer.

SAUCE FOR SMOKED MACKEREL

1 8 oz. can tomato sauce   *dash of Tabasco*
1 clove garlic, minced   *fresh ground black pepper*
1 tbsp. lemon juice

The fish is already salty from the brine. Mix the sauce ingredients well and brush lightly on the smoked mackerel; brown lightly under the broiler. Serve as a snack with cold beer.

An Old Fashioned Treat
Brine Salt Mackerel

John Gaspie was a past master at making brine-salt mackerel which, as every gourmet knows, is delicious fare. By standing at his elbow I was able to steal his technique verbatim.

Wear a cotton or canvas glove on one hand to keep the fish from slipping. Grab the fish by the head and take a sharp knife and start cutting right at the front of the head, cut straight down the back, staying close to the backbone but not cutting through it (and not cutting deep enough to go through the whole stomach). Stop cutting just before you get to the tail; pick the fish up one half in each hand and flip it open like the covers of a book. Clean out the stomach and the black stomach lining, the gills and all the blood—especially around the backbone. Wash the fish well under a running faucet, soak them for ½ hour in a tub of mildly salted water so that all the remaining blood will leach out, then rinse them under the faucet again. (Note: This procedure is for small fish under 1½ pounds. Larger fish should be filleted and these do not require as much cleaning and rinsing.)

To cure the mackerel they should be salted away in a watertight keg or earthenware crock or even an old churn will do. The first stage of the cure is to take each fish and rub it thoroughly on both sides with dry salt; then pick it up with as much salt clinging to it as it will hold. Sprinkle a thin layer of salt on the bottom of the container. Pack the first layer of fish on the bottom with the skin side down, then sprinkle a thin layer of salt over the layer of fish. Keep stacking them in this manner, with salt covering each layer, until the container lacks only 2 or 3 inches being full.

Next, mix a supply of brine in the proportion 1 pound of salt to 1 quart of water (a good brine is strong enough to float a potato) and pour the brine over the fish until it covers them. Cover the container and let it sit in a cool dark place for 12 days. At the end of this period the salt and brine will have "cut through" the fish, dissolving their oils and enzymes, firming up the flesh and pre-

serving it. Take them out and wash off all salt and brine carefully. Clean out the container also. Next sprinkle a layer of salt on the bottom of the container, pack in the layers of fish and salt as before and at the end cover with brine as before. In the future, check the container now and then to replace any brine that may have evaporated; the fish should never be allowed to show above the top of the brine. They will keep for several months if stored in a cool place.

To freshen salt mackerel you should soak the fish for 12 hours or more in a big pan of fresh water. A little practice will teach you just how long you like your fish soaked. Soaking it in milk for a little while at the end will improve the flavor.

BROILED SALT MACKEREL

Freshen the fish, wipe it dry, pepper it, squeeze a little lemon juice over it, dot with butter and place it in a sizzle platter or broiler pan. Put it under the flame and broil it to a rich brown on the flesh side, then turn over and broil on the other side, which will not take as long. Serve flesh side up, garnished with lemon slices, watercress, parsley, etc., and new boiled potatoes. This makes one of the best of all New England breakfasts.

BAKED SALT MACKEREL

9 salt mackerel fillets	milk
4 onions	Tabasco
4 potatoes, parboiled, peeled and sliced	fresh ground black pepper
3 tbsps. grated American cheese	chopped fresh parsley
	Parmesan cheese, bread crumbs
sour cream	and paprika

Gaspie had a baked salt mackerel dish that was really out of this world. His gourmet friends were always badgering him to make it. Here's how he did it:

Place a tablespoon of olive oil in a casserole or pot and oil the sides with it; place a layer of sliced onions on the bottom, then a layer of sliced potatoes, then sour cream; sprinkle on grated American cheese, parsley, Tabasco and black pepper. Put a layer of fillets on top of it all, then start with another layer of onions, potatoes, etc. Keep stratifying until all the materials are exhausted. Pour in milk until it just reaches the top of the geological formation. Have the oven preheated to 350 degrees, and bake the fish for 25 minutes. At the end sprinkle with mixed bread crumbs, Parmesan cheese and paprika and brown under the broiler. Bring with you a healthy, husky appetite and a bottle of good wine, and dive into it.

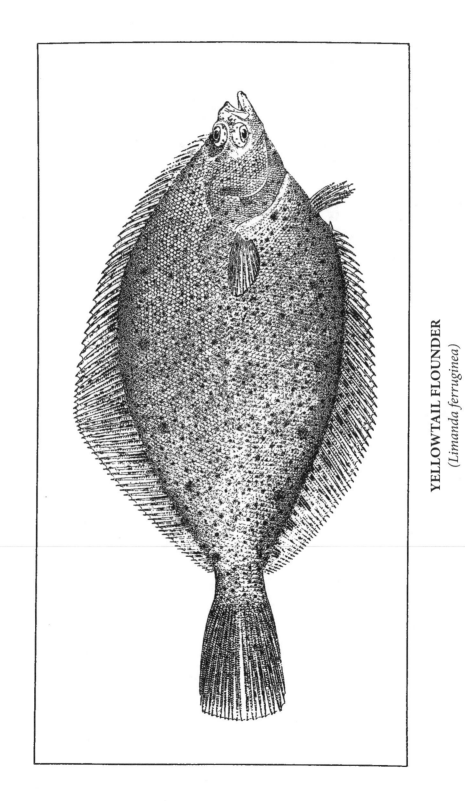

YELLOWTAIL FLOUNDER
(*Limanda ferruginea*)

Floundering Among the Flounders

We have a dozen species of flounders in the waters around Cape Cod but only five of these are plentiful enough to make them economically important. These are yellowtail, gray sole, fluke, blackback and dab. We have listed them in their order of popularity as eating fish. Cape Codders are probably the greatest conoisseurs of flounder eating in the world, and I have taken a poll among my friends to establish this gastronomic rating table. It's just a consensus, mind you, and some have different rating schemes.

Make no bones about it, most of our flounders are just as good as the famous Dover sole and plaice of Europe. All the species are very closely related and their flavor is universally superb. The source of our trouble is our cooks. Most of them haven't passed beyond the fry and broil stage. This is like dropping out of school at the eighth grade. Flounder has such a distinctive built-in flavor that a cook can try all sorts of high-class gourmet tricks with it without damaging its character.

On a low-class tugboat or tramp steamer, the captain has a unique way of choosing a cook for the day. He spots a group of idle deckhands standing around and he throws a skillet at them. The one that catches it is cook.

Provincetown's fishermen are a lot smarter than that. They can recognize talent. On every fishing boat, there's at least one crew member who has a flair with the vittles. The job usually devolves upon him, with lifetime tenure, and next to the captain, he's the most important man on the boat.

Just such a "genius of the galley" is Victor Pacellini, the Provincetown Portuguese with an Italian name whom I've referred to before; you can name any fish that swims and Victor will reel off the twenty best ways of cooking him. Victor is crewman-cook on Captain Seraphine Codinha's *Peter and Linda*. Captain Codinha, a bon vivant and gourmet himself, weighs in at a scant 320 pounds. When he gleefully jumped overboard at the Blessing of the Fleet

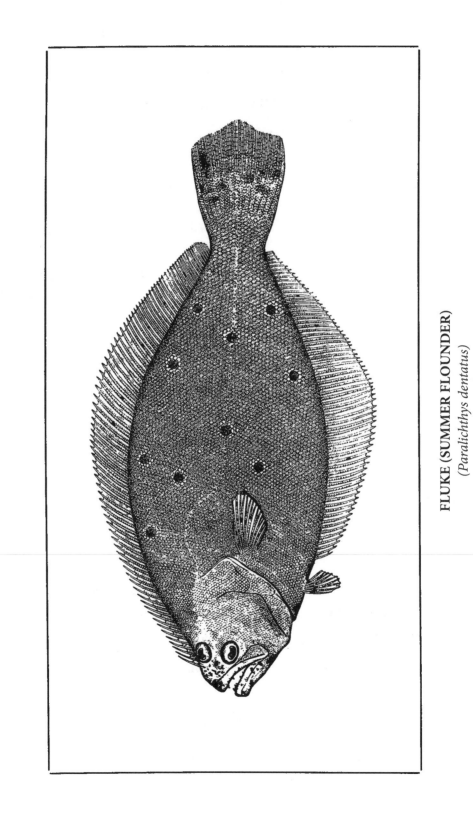

FLUKE (SUMMER FLOUNDER)
(Paralichthys dentatus)

a couple of years ago, it took six strong men to drag him up out of the water and over the gunwale. I have often wondered whether it was Victor's shipboard cookery that gave the captain his expanded midriff.

So if you'd like to see what Provincetown fishermen on a good high-line vessel have for lunch, here are three flounder recipes that Victor flipped off for me in rapid succession. He invariably begins his recipes, "Take some live, flipping flounders out of the trawl . . ."; readers will have to get them at the fish market.

BAKED FLOUNDER ROLLS A LA VICTOR

Scale the flounders but don't skin them. Cut off the fillets; cut each fillet lengthwise down the middle into 2 pieces. Starting with the small end, roll them loosely around the index finger and pin the roll together with a toothpick. Fill the center holes with a bread stuffing of your own invention (using fried onions and scallops? shrimp? crumbled bacon? diced fried salt pork?). Line a baking pan with aluminum foil, grease it with butter and lay the flounder rolls on it. Brush them generously with a lemon-butter sauce. Cover them with another sheet of aluminum foil and bake in a preheated 350 degree oven for 15-20 minutes. Tip from Victor: The bottom sheet of aluminum foil should always be made kind of crinkly and not smoothed out completely. If it's smooth and slick, the fish will stick to it.

FLOUNDERS A LA BUTTERMILK

Cover the bottom of a baking pan with foil; butter the foil, lay flounder fillets skin side down on the foil. Take a brush and slosh salted buttermilk generously on top. Sprinkle with chopped chives, salt and fresh ground black pepper. Cook in a preheated 350 degree oven for 10 or 15 minutes, basting now and then with the pan juices. Serve on hot plates with the juice spooned over the fillets.

The Yellowtail

The yellowtail is almost unanimously the most popular eating fish among the flounders, and this in spite of the fact that his body is extremely thin. His fillets are sometimes not much thicker than a piece of cardboard. A fish twelve inches long weighs only half a pound; a fifteen-inch fish weighs one pound. Their long thin fillets have to be handled very carefully or they will crumble and fall apart while being cooked.

YELLOWTAIL FLOUNDER FILLETS
PAN FRIED IN BATTER

The best batter for frying flounders is the yellow flour-type breader used for frying clams. Its market names are "Supreme Clam Breader" or "Red-I-Breader." It gives the fish a beautiful golden brown color. If there's a sacrilege in the world of cookery, it is to drop a beautiful flounder fillet in a fryolater; the deep hot grease will destroy the fish's delicate flavor in just a few seconds flat. Here's the way really to do it:

Heat clarified butter over a low fire in a skillet; dip the flounder fillet in milk, then in the dry breader, shake off the surplus flour and lay it in the butter in the skillet. Saute gently (a saute is a very slow fry, remember). You should shake the skillet now and then to keep the fillet loose and prevent it from sticking to the bottom; if it does stick it will nearly always fall apart when you try to flip it over. After it has browned on the first side take a large spatula and carefully lift it up and flip it and brown the other side; the proper color is a light golden brown and never a dark burned look.

Place the fillet on a heated serving plate, sprinkle with melted butter, paprika and chopped parsley. Provide lemon wedges. It's one of the best pieces of fish you'll ever eat. It requires no sauces except the butter and lemon juice. (Anybody who would put ketchup or cheap tartar sauce on a beautiful flounder fillet should be burned at the stake.) Serve a good dry white wine along with it.

Of course, if you can't get yellowtails you can substitute the fillets of any of the other flounders and get good results.

SPICY YELLOWTAIL FLOUNDER FILLETS

BAR-B-Q
GRILL

2 lbs. fresh yellowtail flounder fillets	*¼ cup grated onion*
	2 tbsps. brown sugar
½ cup vegetable oil	*2 tsps. salt*
½ cup water	*1 tsp. powdered mustard*
1/3 cup lemon juice	*1 clove garlic, finely chopped*
1/3 cup Worcestershire sauce	*1 tsp. Tabasco sauce*
	paprika

This recipe calls for a barbecue grill or hot coals or an open hearth or campfire, but if none of these is handy, you can do it almost as well in the broiler of your oven.

Have the fillets cleaned and ready. Combine the sauce ingredients except paprika and simmer for 5 minutes, stirring occasionally. Cool. Place the fillets in a single layer in a shallow baking dish. Pour the sauce over the fish and let it marinate for 30 minutes, turning once. Remove fish, reserving sauce for basting. Place fish in well-greased, hinged wire grills. Sprinkle with paprika. Cook about 4 inches from moderately hot coals for 5 minutes. Baste with sauce and sprinkle with paprika. Turn and cook for 5 to 8 minutes longer. If the fillets are very thin reduce your cooking time accordingly. Our yellowtail flounders are one of the tastiest little dabs on the market, and this recipe makes them skyrocket!

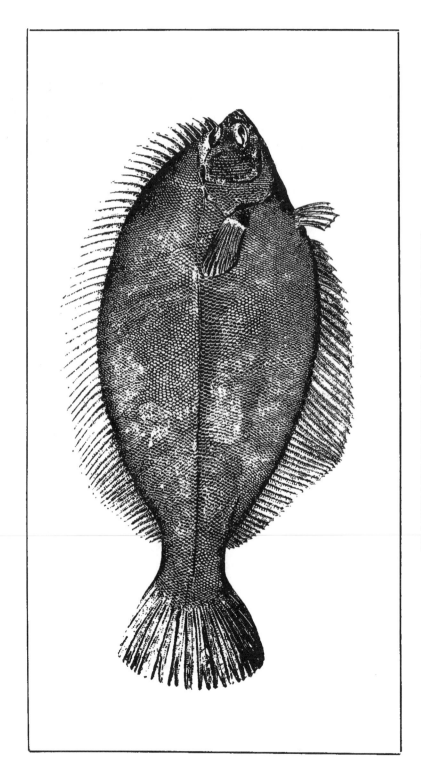

BLACKBACK FLOUNDER (WINTER FLOUNDER)
(Pseudopleuronectes americanus)

VICTOR PACELLINI

**Hoisting a box of flounders from the hold of the
"Peter and Linda"**

BLACKBACK FLOUNDERS WITH SALT PORK

Rub some thick blackback flounder fillets with a layer of salt and let them sit in the refrigerator overnight. Wash them well the next day, then dry them with paper towels and sprinkle moderately with salt and fresh ground black pepper. Melt some margarine and chop some onions and brown them in the skillet on a fast hot fire. (Margarine works best here because it has a high smoke point and will not burn or scorch.)

Set the onions aside and fry some diced salt pork cubes until they are ¾ done. Cover the bottom of a baking pan with foil, grease it and lay the fillets on it, skin side down. Sprinkle with onions and pork cubes. Preheat the oven to 350 degrees and bake the fillets for 10 minutes. Remove the pan from the oven and sprinkle the fillets with Parmesan cheese. Cook for 5 minutes more, or until the cheese and pork cubes become brown. Place fillets on hot plates and serve immediately.

SALT PORK LOVES SEAFOOD!

About Stuffing Flounders

I stake my claim to being the first chef to introduce New Orleans–style stuffed whole flounder to Cape Cod. I cooked it in the kitchen of the late Al Graham's restaurant down on Wellfleet Harbor more than ten years ago, and the idea has spread around a good bit since then. It's always one of the most popular items on any menu. I learned the recipe from the late great Joe Astorias, a Creole, who was head chef at the Roosevelt Hotel in New Orleans. When you use fresh-caught Provincetown flounders with this system, you can achieve heights of gastronomic glory.

WHOLE STUFFED FLOUNDERS

6 whole 1½-2 lb. flounders
1 cup chopped boiled
    shrimps
1 cup chopped scallops, lightly
    poached
1 large onion, chopped
4 cloves garlic, minced
½ sweet pepper, finely
    diced
1 piece celery, minced
2 tbsps. chopped parsley

1 cup fresh mushrooms,
    chopped
1 tsp. prepared mustard
1 tbsp. Worcestershire sauce
dash Tabasco
4 eggs
¼ loaf French bread
1 tbsp. butter
½ cup sauterne
salt and fresh ground black
    pepper

Keep the heads and tails on the flounders for good looks. Scale them and gut them and rinse out the body cavities thoroughly. Lay the flounders flat and cut an "X" lengthwise on the body (see drawing). Fold back the corners of the cut and lift out the backbone.

Saute the celery, onion, garlic, green pepper, parsley and mushrooms until soft and golden. Add the shrimp and scallops. Moisten the bread until workable with the fingers; make a paste of it. Beat the Worcestershire sauce, Tabasco, sauterne and mustard into the eggs until thoroughly mixed. Pour this mixture over the bread, adding the sauteed vegetables, shrimp and scallops; mix well. Divide the mixture into 6 parts and stuff lightly into the cavities of the flounders. Sprinkle the fish with melted butter, salt and pepper and finely minced garlic.

Bake at 400 degrees until nicely done and golden brown, about 25 minutes. Or you can broil them in butter about 4 inches from the flame, 6 or 8 minutes on each side. Place them on hot serving plates and sprinkle with a teaspoon of sherry and chopped parsley. Serve at once, piping hot.

"WEIGHING IN"

It's in the Bag

1.

After doodling around in the kitchen I have developed a Flounder Fillets *en Papillote* which I wouldn't be ashamed to serve to Craig Claiborne or James Beard, should they ask. *En papillote* means "in the bag." Wrapping up food to preserve its juices has been practiced with such materials as palm leaves, grape leaves and cabbage since ancient times. Cooking fine fish in parchment bags reached its heyday in France with such razzle-dazzle practitioners as Escoffier, Brillat-Savarin, *et al.* It's a high-toned practice, but there's no reason to be afraid of it; it's nothing but seafood sandwiched between slabs of seafood. Our modern aluminum foil is an improvement over parchment.

FLOUNDER FILLETS EN PAPILLOTE

2.

6 large flounder fillets
    (or 12 small ones)
4 chopped scallions and 2
    inches of their green
    leaves
6 fresh mushrooms,
    chopped
¼ cup sherry
2 egg yolks, beaten
1 cup chopped shrimp
    meats

1 cup chopped scallop meats
    (or crabmeat)
1 clove garlic, minced
2 cups fish stock or bouillon
½ cup butter
2 tbsps. flour
pinch of cayenne
pinch of nutmeg
salt and fresh ground black
    pepper

3.

Heat the fish stock and poach the fillets in it until they are ¾ done. Remove carefully, reserve the stock. Melt the butter in a skillet and saute the scallions until they are transparent, add the garlic and mushrooms, add the flour and blend it in. Add the 2 cups of fish stock and simmer until it thickens a little, stirring constantly. Add the seasonings, the sherry, the shrimp, scallops (or crabmeat) and cook gently for 5 minutes longer. Remove from the fire and stir in the egg yolks. There's your sauce.

Place a fillet in the center of a piece of buttered aluminum foil, lay on it a good layer of the sauce and place another fillet on top of it. Lift up the edges of the foil and crimp them and roll them down, crimp and roll up the ends, producing a hermetic seal. Bake in a preheated 400 degree oven for 15-20 minutes. Serve them in the sacks and let your guests have the fun of opening them. Of course this calls for a very good white wine, or even Champagne.

Blue Murder

The bluefish, *Pomatomus saltatrix*, is really the bully of the town, the meanest fish that swims in the sea. He is found all over the world: Pacific Ocean, Atlantic Ocean, Australia, Good Hope, Brazil, Cape Cod—you name it, he'll be there leaving his bloody trail of murder. He is one of the most carnivorous, omnivorous creatures in nature, greedy beyond belief. Brutal and full of blood lust, he kills many more times his own weight in fish each day but eats only a portion of it, and when he is gorged he vomits it up like an ancient Roman and starts eating again.

Some scientists have estimated that each bluefish will kill 1,000 other fish each day of his life. This must put a heavy load on the ecological balance of the ocean. They travel in large schools like wolf packs, destroying everything that falls in their path. Striped bass and other larger fish get the hell out of the way fast when they see bluefish coming. If you see the carcass of a striped bass washed up on the beach with a big chunk bitten out of its belly, it was probably a bluefish that did it, just for spite.

Back in the Gay Nineties, trolling for blues from a sail-boat was considered one of the great sports. I have an old Cozzen's print showing how they did it. A guy sat in the stern close to the tiller, constantly feeding a chumming machine with menhaden and mackerel and dumping the ground-up fish into the water to attract the blues. This machine was an enlarged version of a standard sausage grinder with a coarse blade; it had a wooden chute attached to channel the grindings overboard. (Joe Perry of the Fo'c'sle has one

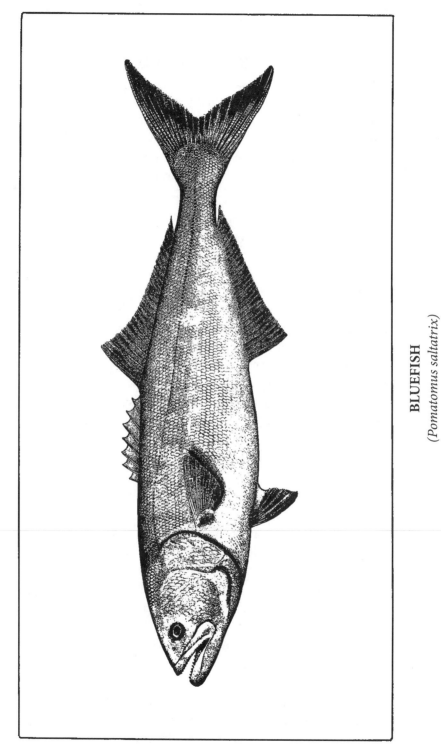

BLUEFISH
(*Pomatomus saltatrix*)

of these chummers that was used by his grandfather. He let me use it to grind sea clams and scallops a few years ago when I was the stuffed shellfish kingpin of Provincetown. I've been trying to get Joe to give that machine to a good fisheries museum, but Joe says "I'm the museum," and he may be right at that.)

BROIL IT

Bluefish should be gutted and cleaned out as soon as they are caught to avoid their acquiring a flavor of tennis shoes. And they should be cooked and eaten as soon after catching as possible. I, for one, would not eat a bluefish in an inland town, a hundred miles from the seacoast, unless it had been flown there by helicopter. Like mackerel, salmon, bonito and albacore, the bluefish is very oily and should never be fried. The only way to cook it is to broil or bake it. The cream and white sauces are much too rich for it; the light and acid Portuguese molho tomate is ideal. A fish weighing four or five pounds is the best for eating.

BROILED BLUEFISH

Brush a bluefish fillet lightly with butter, sprinkle with salt and pepper, and place it on a broiling plate, skin side up, 4 inches below the flame. After the skin has browned, turn the fillet over and broil the other side; the second phase does not take as long because the fish is already hot and partially cooked by the broiler plate. Garnish with parsley and serve with lemon wedges. The flesh of the bluefish is more moist than striped bass and for this reason many gourmets consider it superior.

Another version: Cover the broiled fillet with a blanket of Portuguese molho wine-tomato sauce (see page 49).

STUFF IT

BAKED BLUEFISH STUFFED WITH
WELLFLEET OYSTERS

Take a whole 5-pound bluefish and stuff it with a Wellfleet oyster dressing made as follows: Place 3 dozen oysters and their liquor and a cup of white wine in a pan, add a little fresh ground black pepper (the liquor furnishes the salt), poach the oysters gently until their edges curl; drain off the broth and use it to wet down

and knead 3 or 4 slices of French bread into a paste. Mix this paste with the oysters and stuff the bluefish with it. Sew the fish up, lay it on greased aluminum foil in a baking pan and bake in a preheated oven at 350 degrees for 30 minutes or until it is browned and cooked through. Brush it a couple of times with melted butter during the baking to keep it from drying out. Lay the whole fish out on a platter on a bed of lettuce leaves. Serve a tomato sauce on the side and a bottle of white wine moderately chilled.

The Story of Swordfish

Swordfish has become one of the most popular fish in seafood restaurants today. It is right up there on top with haddock, flounder, and striped bass; it's a Cinderella success story without parallel. Before the Civil War there was no market for it in this country and the fishermen could not give it away free. But in the latter half of the nineteenth century it began to catch on with epicures in Boston, New York, and on the West Coast, and it has been rising in popularity ever since.

During the Depression it sold for 19 cents a pound, by 1947 it had climbed to 40 cents, and it pains me to have to tell you this, but at the time of this writing it was selling for $3 a pound wholesale—more than lobsters. Its price on the menus is astronomical, yet the public wants it, demands it, and pays cash for it. So you won't find the restaurants or the fishermen complaining.

The broadbill swordfish, *Xiphias gladius*, is one of the strangest, weirdest, spookiest of all the fishes. Nobody knows where he comes from in the summer or where he goes in the winter.  Nobody has ever caught a swordfish with fertilized spawn in it; nobody has ever seen them pitching woo or building a nest. They are scattered all over the world. They can grow to a weight of over 1,000 pounds, and a fish that big can be fifty to a hundred years old. The average fish caught today is around 200 pounds. A swordfish is round-bodied, like a torpedo, and he can swim faster than greased lightning. He can dive as deep as any known fish: out beyond the continental shelf he can dive to the bottom of the Atlantic in the regions of perpetual darkness and feed on blind sea creatures which never see the light of day, and where pressures are so intense they would explode a submarine.

His sword is always about half the length of his body and it's not just for looks, either. He keeps it sharpened and well-honed and when he's mad he can ram it through the belly of a great sperm whale or a giant squid or the planking of a dory or light schooner. Swordfish have a horrible temper and old-timers thought they went crazy at times. In the old days when a dory fisherman was handline-fishing for halibut and caught a big swordfish by mistake, if he were smart he grabbed a hatchet and cut the line, then grabbed the oars and got out of there fast: if the fish got mad he could ram through the bottom of the dory like it was kindling wood, sometimes impaling the fisherman himself, but most times simply drowning him by destroying his boat.

Swordfish also use their sword as a good harvesting weapon. Swimming through a school of mackerel or menhaden they thresh their sword rapidly from side to side, slaughtering hundreds of fish; after the killing spree they turn around and come back and devour their victims at leisure.

SWORDFISH

SHARK

Swordfish love to bask in the sunshine by floating on the surface of the sea, and this habit leads to their downfall. The lookouts on the mastheads of the fishing boats can spot them by their dorsal fins sticking out the water; they can be distinguished from sharks because their fins are sharper than the squat triangular fins of a shark. They are caught by being harpooned from the "pulpit," the light chairlike apparatus located out close to the end of the bowsprit. Next time you see a painting of an old-time Provincetown fishing schooner, take a close look and you will see the flimsy pulpit away out there over the water, a lonely and dangerous location for the harpooners to while away their time and sometimes work.

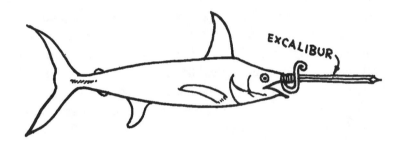

EXCALIBUR

The best fishing grounds for swordfish are right here in New England. They stretch from Block Island and Nantucket shoals out to Georges Bank and up to Cape Breton Island, Nova Scotia. Over 6 million pounds a year have been harvested from these fields. When you see a Japanese fishing vessel out on our grounds you can pretty well guess what it is looking for; swordfish is regarded as a treasure in Japan. The skyhigh price has led to overfishing which has greatly limited the supply (or maybe vice versa), and when you eat swordfish today you should savor it carefully and remember that it is more costly and more tasty than lobster.

PULPIT

But dammit, most cooks in modern automated restaurants do not know how to cook it; at those roadside castles along the superhighways your swordfish steak can be hard and dry as a bone, unchewable, unpalatable and difficult to digest. Like haddock, the swordfish's flavor is actually improved by freezing, but it has to be thawed carefully and cooked properly or you're out of luck.

It's almost sacrilegious to shove a swordfish steak into a damnable microwave oven and thaw it and cook it in four minutes flat. The best swordfish steaks are one inch to one and a half inches thick, and although it's an oily fish, they need a long, slow broil with plenty of butter and frequent basting to keep them moist. Or they should be gently sauteed in butter, or baked in a casserole with plenty of oil, wine, etc., to keep them wet.

SWORDFISH STEAK

Some of the best swordfish I ever ate was partaken of with Manny Zora in a small waterfront restaurant in Olhao, Portugal. The place had only three tables and seated twelve people, and if you wanted something special you had to ask for it in advance. So at about 10 A.M. one day we passed by and Manny spoke to the proprietress, Signora Henrique, in Portuguese: "Mamma, we're hungry for swordfish!" And she replied, "Boas (okay), be here at noon sharp." After we left she ran across the street to the fish market and bought the fresh fish, and when we arrived for lunch she placed before us a steaming platter of swordfish steaks smothered with onion, flavored with wine and a touch of garlic. It was one of the best dishes I ever ate, and all I could do was keep saying over and over the only Portuguese word I know: "Wow! Wow! Wow!" Including the beautiful quart of potent homemade wine, the check was only $3, and again I said "W—W—W." Gad! We Americans sure have a lot to learn about enjoying life.

DORY FISHERMAN
CATCHING SWORDFISH

BAKED PORTUGUESE SWORDFISH

The Portuguese like their swordfish steaks much thinner than we do, and they cook them well done. Pour a cup of olive oil into a baking pan, slice 2 or 3 onions and lay onion rings in the pan. Add 2 garlic cloves, finely minced. The thin steaks should be ¼ to ½ inch in thickness. Rub the steaks with lemon or lime juice and salt and pepper, and lay them on top of the onions; sprinkle a cup of dry white wine over them. Bake in a preheated 350 degree oven for 25 minutes or until the fish is tender and flakes easily with a fork. Baste it frequently while baking to keep it from drying out. Place the fish on a hot serving platter and cover with the onion rings and pan juices; decorate with parsley and lemon wedges. Serve with a good red Portuguese or Spanish wine, or an Italian Valpolicella.

BROILED SWORDFISH STEAKS

This is the classical American way of cooking swordfish. The steaks should be 1-1½ inches thick. Rub them well with melted butter, lemon juice and salt and fresh ground black pepper. Place them on sizzle platters or broiler pans with a generous amount of melted butter. Broil 4 inches from the flame for 6-8 minutes on each side, depending on the thickness of the steaks; baste frequently to keep

CUTTING STEAKS

them from drying out. The fish is done when it is lightly browned and flakes easily and is opaque white clear through. Serve with maitre d'hotel butter; either pour it over the fish or serve it in a small side dish so that the guests can dip each bite of fish into the sauce. (Despite its fancy name, maitre d'hotel butter is nothing but parsley, butter and lemon juice with perhaps a few chopped chives: melt a stick of butter and add the juice of 2 lemons and 2 tablespoons of chopped parsley and thar y'are.)

THE PERFECT
SAUCE

CHARCOAL BROILED SWORDFISH

Swordfish is very tasty when broiled over charcoal. Baste frequently with butter and lemon juice to keep it moist.

SWORDFISH WITH ROSEMARY

Another Portuguese trick. Rub the steak with butter, lemon juice, salt, pepper and dried rosemary leaves. Broil as instructed above.

PEPPERED SWORDFISH STEAK

Rub the steak with butter and lemon juice and salt. Crack peppercorns with a pestle and mortar and press this coarse pepper into the flesh of the steak. Broil as instructed above.

SWORDFISH BOILED IN BEER

BOIL HIM IN BEER!

Heat enough beer in a pan to cover your steaks, add salt, a bay leaf, several cracked peppercorns and 2 cloves of garlic, crushed. Place the steaks in the pan and boil gently for 15 minutes or until the flesh flakes easily and is opaque white clear through. Drain the steaks and place on a hot serving platter. Pour maitre d'hotel butter over them and garnish generously with watercress and lemon wedges. Watercress is not just a decoration; I love to eat every bite of it.

POACHED SWORDFISH HOLLANDAISE

Poach swordfish steaks as instructed in the above recipe, but use a good rich fish stock instead of beer. When ready to serve cover the steaks with a blanket of Hollandaise sauce.

SWORDFISH IN MUSHROOM SAUCE
(Serves 2 to 4)

2 lbs. swordfish
½ cup American cheese,
   diced
½ tsp. powdered
   mustard
1 cup sliced fresh
   mushrooms

2 tbsps. flour
½ stick butter
2 cups milk
½ cup dry white wine
salt and fresh ground black
   pepper

Boil the swordfish for 10 minutes in salted water. Remove the skin and the layer of fat underneath and break the meat up into chunks. Melt the butter in a skillet, remove from the heat and add the flour, mixing well, then add the milk little by little, stirring constantly. Add the white wine and mustard. Return to the fire and add the cheese cubes, stirring until they melt and the mixture is smooth. Add the mushrooms and swordfish chunks. Season to taste with salt and fresh ground black pepper. Cook for a few minutes longer until the flavors are blended and the mushrooms become limp. Serve white wine with this.

Renaissance of the Atlantic Salmon

Joy to the world, the Atlantic salmon has returned! This fine fish, once plentiful in New England, was only a few years ago thought to be headed for extinction, and ecologists, biologists, zoologists, ichthyologists and sportsmen were very unhappy about it. He was a victim of civilization and "progress" and mankind's don't-give-a-damn attitude regarding the flora and fauna of this planet. The beautiful Atlantic salmon (*Salmo salar*) spends most of his life in the broad wide ocean, but like the alewife he swims up into rivers and creeks to spawn and the young ones stay there about a year until they are big enough to swim down to the sea and fend for themselves.

Every decent river in New England from the Hudson on up through Maine and then to Labrador used to have its salmon run in June and July, and the catches were tremendous for both commercial fishermen and sportsmen. (For a sportsfisherman the hooking of a ten- or twenty-pound salmon on a light flyrod can be the battle of a lifetime.) But then we began to build dams which blocked off the rivers, and mills and factories began to spew their excretions into them and they became so polluted that not even a mud turtle could live in them. The Atlantic salmon—can you blame him?—was so disgusted that he turned around and swam back out into the ocean and died. For many years there have been no Atlantic salmon in New England, not even northern Maine. The paper mills and sawmills polluted even those remote waters.

By ecological wisdom and sensible conservation measures such as fish ladders over dams, the Canadian government began to protect the salmon, and it was in New Brunswick, Nova Scotia, and other maritime provinces that the harassed fish made his last stand, defeated extinction, and now is staging a comeback. Most of the salmon steaks and whole fish that we are lucky to purchase in the fish markets today are from Canada. If you can find them, the whole

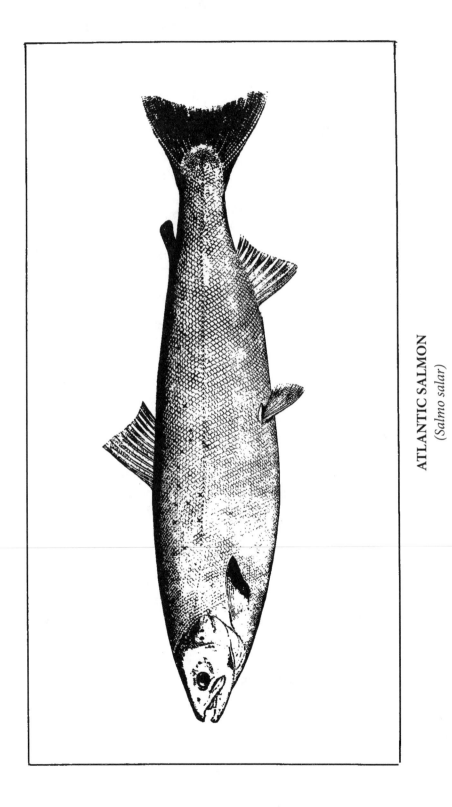

ATLANTIC SALMON
(Salmo salar)

fish are the best buy; they weigh eight or ten pounds and you can cook them whole or cut them up into steaks yourself as follows:

Cut off the head just above the "collarbone," then cut off the collarbone. Cut off the tail. Cut off the side fins and belly fins. And here's the trick for removing the large dorsal (top) fin and the bones that are attached to it: Cut a slot in the body about 1½ inches deep on each side of the fin and lift it up at the back extremity; the whole fin and its bones will lift right out in one piece.

You're now ready to cut the fish into steaks. Lay it on a board and start cutting crosswise. You use a heavy sharp cutting knife, cut down to the backbone and then take a wooden mallet or rolling pin and whack the back of your knife to make it cut through the backbone. The steaks should be about 1-1½ inches thick and should weigh a half pound each. Other fish steaks usually weigh ¾ to 1 pound each, but salmon meat is so rich that a half pound of it can fill any normal person.

NEW ENGLAND SALMON WITH EGG SAUCE

Make enough liquor to cover your steaks in a poaching pan with salted water, 2 tbsps. mixed pickling spices, 2 bay leaves, 1 lemon, sliced, and fresh ground black pepper. Boil vigorously for 15 minutes to give it "punch." Lower the heat and place the salmon steaks in the water and poach gently for about 10 minutes or until the flesh flakes when tested with a fork. Another test for doneness is when the backbone segment will lift out easily without any meat clinging to it.

Drain the steaks and place them on heated serving plates; cover with egg sauce, sprinkle with paprika and chopped parsley, and serve at once. On the side serve green peas and new boiled potatoes.

Egg Sauce

Melt ½ stick of butter in a skillet and remove from fire; add 3 tablespoons of flour and stir well. Add a cup of milk a little at a time, stirring constantly, add a cup of fish broth (or a cup of cream). Add 1 tablespoon prepared mustard and 1 teaspoon powdered mustard.

Mix well, return to fire and cook slowly until it thickens; then add 5 hard-boiled eggs, chopped up, and stir them in. Season with salt and fresh ground black pepper—be generous with the pepper. Pour the hot sauce over the salmon steaks.

WHOLE BOILED SALMON

Old-time Provincetowners had a unique method of boiling whole haddock that is applicable to salmon. Take a whole fish of 5 or 6 pounds, leave the head and tail on for aesthetic reasons. Sew it up in a piece of clean linen with straps at each end for lifting. (If you don't have any linen you can just use cheesecloth with flaps at each end for handles.) In a turkey roasting pan or large dish pan, boil up a spicy liquor, sufficient to cover the fish, as instructed above. Place the fish in its shroud in the liquor and boil gently for 25 to 30 minutes, or 5 minutes for each pound of fish.

Be careful not to break the fish up. Lift it out carefully, remove the shroud, place the fish on a platter. Carefully remove the skin, revealing the beautiful pink flesh beneath. Decorate it tastefully and with restraint with sliced truffles or slices of olives, green and black. Cool it, chill it in the refrigerator and serve cold, decorating the platter profusely with parsley, watercress, olives, or boiled eggs, quartered. If you want to be really fancy about it, you can cover the fish with several layers of good tart salty aspic; then it will be a real showpiece, almost too pretty to eat. Cold salmon should be accompanied by tart homemade mayonnaise or white remoulade sauce with chopped eggs in it.

POACHED SALMON STEAKS HOLLANDAISE

Poach the steaks as instructed above in the egg sauce recipe. Place the steaks on a heated serving plate and cover with a blanket of Hollandaise sauce.

BROILED SALMON STEAKS

Place the steaks on individual buttered sizzle platters or in a broiler pan. Brush with butter and lemon juice, sprinkle on salt and pepper. Place it 4 inches below the flame and broil for 6 minutes on each side, basting frequently with butter and lemon juice. Serve with a stuffed tomato between the "wings" of each steak. Tomato stuffing: cottage cheese, chopped scallions or onions, lemon juice, salt and pepper. The egg sauce and the Hollandaise sauce both go well with broiled steaks.

STUFFED TOMATO

BROILED STEAK

FRANK COOK WITH HIS 270 POUND HALIBUT

He caught it with his bare hands with the line shown in the photograph.

Halibut, King of the Flatfish

Old man Frank Cook, of Provincetown, eked out a living by fishing from a dory with a hand line. Dory fishing was a dull monotonous life fraught with danger; it was hard work and low pay, but a few stubborn individuals kept the profession alive and Provincetown always had its solitary dory fishermen, as crusty and weather-beaten a group as you could find anywhere in New England. They would row or sail their dories out to Long Point and around to Wood End; the usual catch was flounder, cod and haddock.

But on a fine summer day about eighty-five years ago, old man Frank Cook, while fishing from his dory off Wood End, snagged a lunker of a fish that was to gain him immortality and a permanent place in Provincetown's piscatorial Hall of Fame. The fish was a halibut and it tipped the scales at 270 pounds; this must have been pretty close to the world's record at that time (1890). What a battle it must have been! Picture the old man alone in his dory, clinging to his line, Nantucket sleigh-riding all over the place, battling against the leviathan for hours. And, when both were exhausted, how did the old man ever get his catch into the boat and back to the wharf? My idea is that he must have conked the fish with an oar, attached a line to him, and towed him in like a barge—another difficult job, especially if the weather happened to be a little rough. The details are lost but the faded photograph on the opposite page tells the fish story. Ernest Hemingway wrote fiction. But this was the naked truth. The photo was reproduced in newspapers all over the country, and tens of thousands of postcard reproductions were sold in  gift shops. For several years afterward the first thing a new visitor to Provincetown would ask is "where's Mr. Cook who caught THE FISH?" Like the old town crier George Washington Ready, who saw a real sea serpent, Mr. Cook has a permanent niche in the town's salty folklore.

And of course halibut still ranks as a major market fish and great gourmet fare. Manny Zora used to chase halibut in his *Sea Fox*, and even today Stuart Phelps is going out after them in his *Willet*. If you can get ahold of some halibut from Stu or the local fish markets,

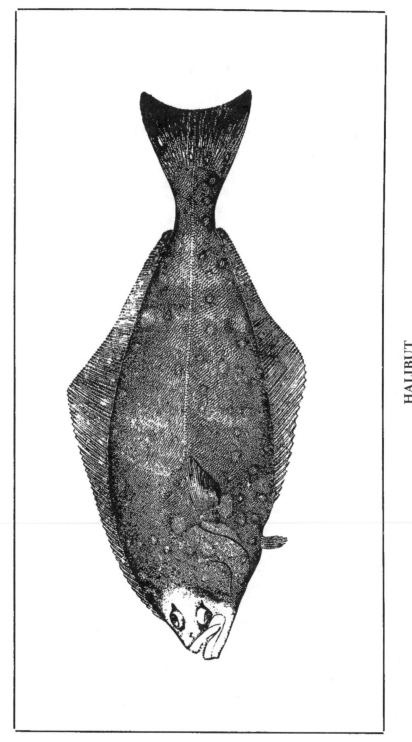

HALIBUT
(*Hippoglossus hippoglossus*)

you should try some of the following old-fashioned recipes in your kitchen.

BROILED HALIBUT STEAKS

Take some halibut steaks about 1 inch thick and rub them with a thick layer of salt; place them in the refrigerator overnight, next day rinse the salt off and dry them. Coat them with melted butter and broil on each side for 8 or 10 minutes. To serve, pour lemon-butter sauce over it and sprinkle with chopped parsley. This is the simple, classic way of cooking halibut without frills. Now for some frills:

BROILED HALIBUT WITH FRESH MAYONNAISE

Cure with salt and broil as above; at the end cover with fresh homemade mayonnaise and put back under the broiler for a minute or two. Now listen: when I say fresh homemade mayonnaise I mean exactly that. If you try to sneak by with that cheap commercial mayonnaise then you will have defiled a fine fish who sacrificed his life for your enjoyment.

BAKED HALIBUT WITH SALT PORK

Salt pork and halibut go beautifully together. Lay some steaks in a greased baking pan and cover them with thin slices of salt pork (or diced pork). Bake it until the fish and the pork are done.

OLD PROVINCETOWN CREAMED HALIBUT

One of the favorite old-time Yankee ways of cooking halibut was to cream it. Those old-timers used butter and eggs and cream like they grew on trees. Boil 2 pounds of halibut and flake it into small pieces; put it in a saucepan and add a dozen well-beaten eggs, a cup of cream, a stick of melted butter, a pinch of nutmeg and salt and fresh ground black pepper to taste. Cook it very gently, stirring constantly until it is well blended and the eggs are cooked. Serve very hot in big piles on top of toast. This makes a helluva hearty breakfast.

POACHED HALIBUT WITH
HOLLANDAISE SAUCE

In a pan of salted water place several peppercorns, 3 or 4 cloves, a few allspice and a couple of lemon slices. Boil the water for a few minutes; lower the heat and place the fish in the water and poach until done. The meat should be white and firm and flake easily with a fork. Place the fish on hot plates and cover with a layer of good fresh-made Hollandaise sauce.

PORTUGUESE VINHA D'ALHOS HALIBUT

Salt cure the steaks as above, rinse and dry. Maké a marinade of ½ vinegar, ½ water, some olive oil, chopped onion, minced garlic, a few whole peppercorns, crushed black pepper, crushed cumin seeds, thyme, basil, a few cloves and allspice. Place the steaks in this marinade for 2 or 3 hours, turning them over frequently. At the end, dry them off and broil them with butter, or dip them in milk or egg batter and fry in deep hot fat.

PORTUGUESE BAKED HALIBUT
WITH MOLHO SAUCE

Salt cure the steaks as above, rinse and cut them up into 1 inch chunks. Make a molho sauce (see page 49.) Put the halibut chunks and some chunks of boiled potatoes in a baking pan and cover with the molho sauce; bake in a moderate oven for 15-20 minutes. Decorate with parsley and serve the fish in the pan it's cooked in.

How to Grill a Fresh Sardine

The fresh herring sardine is one of the most delicious of fishes and sometimes it is very plentiful right here in Provincetown. But the fishermen regard it as a "trash fish" and most of them are thrown back to the seagulls. If you're lucky you may find some on sale in the fish markets. These sardines are 6 to 8 inches long and the flavor of the fresh fish is completely different from that of canned sardines.

The best way to cook them is to charcoal broil them; I had to go all the way across the Atlantic to Portugal to find out about this process. In the fishing town of Portimao, on Portugal's Algarve coast, there is a small nameless restaurant right on the docks, with a charcoal grill in the front yard, and the only thing it serves is grilled sardines and homemade red wine. It's a real epicurean feast, and this frowzy little restaurant is famous all over Europe; it's written up in all the guide books.

CHARCOAL BROILED SARDINES

Provide about 6 or 8 sardines for each person. Leave the heads and tails on, gut them, rinse well and dry with paper towels. Bury them in coarse salt and let them cure for an hour. Dig them out and brush off most of the salt, but not all of it. Rub with olive oil. Place on the grill about 3 inches above the hot coals and brown lightly on both sides.

You eat these bare-handed as follows: Split a Portuguese roll and lay the broiled fish on the bottom half. Tap the fish gently with the other half of the roll to break the skin, then peel it off. Pick the layer of fish off the bones with your fingers and happily devour it, then turn the fish over and do likewise to the other side. Keep using the same half of roll to hold each new fish, and by the time you have eaten 6 or 8 fish, the roll will be nicely soggy and saturated with sardine oil. Then you should eat it too. Wash it down with a good red *vin du pays*.

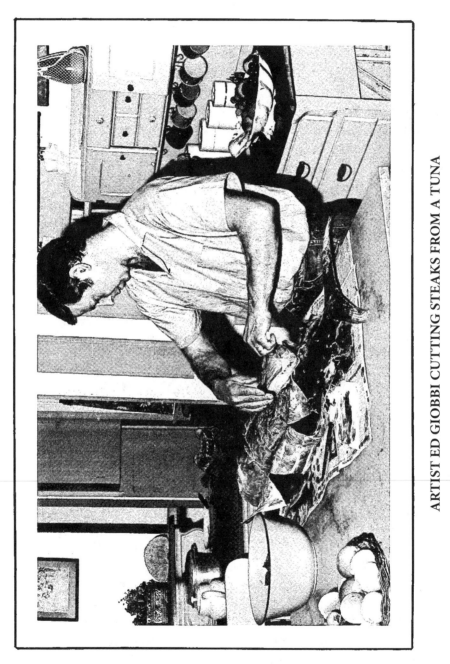

ARTIST ED GIOBBI CUTTING STEAKS FROM A TUNA

A well known gourmet, he has written several cookbooks.

The Haughty "Horse Mackerel"

When the giant bluefin tuna are running, you can sometimes find some delicious fresh or "galvanized" tuna dishes on the menu in Provincetown restaurants, and what glorious fare it can be! It's a cinch that very few people in this country ever ate a fresh tuna steak. Most TV watchers think tuna just comes out of cans, and most of it is just dog and catfood, with some for people. But in Japan fresh tuna sells for $10 a pound and Japanese buyers hang around on New England fish wharves buying up all they can, putting it on board transport planes, and flying it to Japan. Hence it's getting pretty scarce and you'll be lucky to find a fresh tuna steak in a fish market or restaurant.

Good tuna steaks should be about 1½ inches thick; they should be soaked in salty water for a couple of hours to leach out their blood. Then they should be dried with paper towels and coated with a ¼ inch thick layer of salt and allowed to "cure" for 2 or 3 days in the refrigerator. At the end of this time, take the steaks and rinse off all the salt, "galvanize" them overnight in a good vinha d'alhos marinade. Next day, take the tuna out of the marinade, brush off all the herbs and spices and dry them well.

Make a good molho tomate (page 49). Peel and halve or quarter some Irish potatoes, boil them until they are done, and place them in your molho tomate. Now here's where you can make a choice and it's good either way: slowly saute, or broil, or bake the thick tuna steaks, then put them on preheated serving plates and cover them with a blanket of molho sauce, and surround with potatoes. After eating this, you'll never enjoy your drug store tuna salad sandwich again!

Pollock, A Neglected Fish

Pollock has never become popular in America because of its wild, gamey, fishy taste. So wot?? Ain't a fish spose to taste like a fish? This makes him ideally suited to the methods of Provincetown Portuguese cuisine: marination, salt soaking, cooking with bouncy sauces, and even drying. (Small pollock make good Skully Joes.) If our Portuguese seafood cooking methods were known all over the country, it's a safe bet that national seafood consumption would double. Neglected species like pollock, giant tuna, mackerel, catfish (wolffish) would find their legitimate place on the market. Get ahold of some good pollocks and test your skill with the following basic methods.

POLLOCK MOLHO TOMATE

Salt does magic things to pollock just as it does to fresh tuna. It takes away the gamey flavor. Take some pollock fillets and coat them with heavy layers of salt, place in a glass dish or earthenware crock and store in the refrigerator for a day or two. Remove fillets, wash off the salt, dry them with paper towels and poach, fry, or broil them with bacon drippings. Place them on a hot serving plate and cover with a blanket of molho tomate (see page 49). Serve with boiled, sliced potatoes.

ARROZ NU CAL

John Santos, who fishes on the *Peter and Linda*, told me this old Portuguese trick. You rub a whole pollock inside and out with salt and garlic. Put it in a greased baking pan and sprinkle it with slivered onions and tomatoes and bake it. Meanwhile, take the head of the fish, removing the gills, and boil it with salted water and rice until it becomes a stew. Serve the baked fish and the stew together. If you'd rather skip the rice stew, serve it with John's "noodles amandine," buttered noodles mixed with almonds that have been sauteed golden brown in butter.

"BOSTON BLUE"

This is how the pollock sneaks into high-class Boston restaurants. (Why can't we stop this hypocrisy?)

Take a whole pollock, remove the gills, rub it inside and out with salt, pepper and butter. Stuff it with a dressing made of bread, onions, brown fried pork cubes, herbs and perhaps a few chopped fresh mushrooms (even Provincetown wild mushrooms, if you happen to have some). Place the fish in an oiled baking pan, cover with a few strips of bacon and bake in a slow oven until done.

SPAGHETTI WITH POLLOCK FISH BALLS

2 1½ lb. pollocks	*1 cup olive oil*
2 cloves garlic, minced	*1 tsp. basil*
2 tbsps. chopped parsley	*pinch crushed red pepper*
1 egg	*seeds*
½ cup Parmesan cheese	*1 lb. spaghetti*
1 32 oz. can plum tomatoes	

Fillet the pollocks and save the heads and bones. Chop the fish fillets as finely as possible. Add ½ the garlic and ½ the parsley and continue chopping until well blended. Place the mixture in a mixing bowl and add the egg, salt, pepper and cheese and mix well. Shape mixture with hands into balls 1-1½ inches in diameter.

In a skillet, combine the remaining garlic, parsley, tomatoes, oil, basil and hot pepper seeds; simmer for 10 minutes, then add the reserved fish bones and heads (from which the gills have been removed). Cook over high heat for 5 minutes, lower heat and simmer 10 minutes longer. Add the fish balls and simmer slowly for ½ hour. Remove and discard fish heads and bones. Remove the fish balls and set them aside, keeping them warm.

Cook the spaghetti in boiling salted water until "*al dente*" (firm to the tooth); drain it quickly, add it to the sauce in the skillet and toss well. Add the fish balls and heat through, but be careful not to overcook. Serve on heated dishes. Note: If pollock is not available use whiting, haddock or cod.

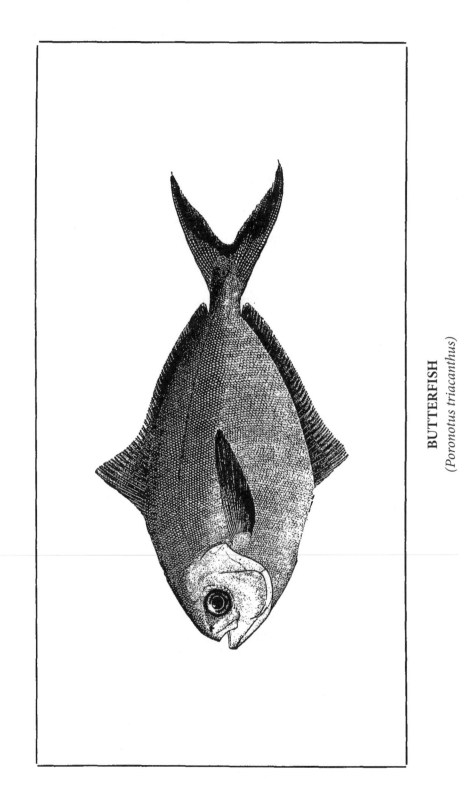

BUTTERFISH
(Poronotus triacanthus)

The Beautiful Butterfish

Without the slightest doubt, October is Cape Cod's best month. On a good day the air is crisp and cool, and the light is bright and sharp as a razor; the pale blue sea and the aquamarine sky sparkle and compete for the eye's attention, the atmosphere is so clear and devoid of haze that you can stare off across the sea into the far heart of infinity. Between sunset and darkness the waters of the harbor can pass through a whole unbelievable cycle of color changes, and this cycle itself can change completely from day to day. At sunset it might be a bright light, blue-tinged with rose, and a few minutes later it will become like polished silver, then like burnished pewter, and next it will be a gun metal blue like a polished Toledo blade. And if there happen to be dark clouds in the background across the harbor, the water will turn into the richest tone of indigo you could imagine; the white boats bobbing in the harbor will become whiter than white, something outside the spectrum, a luminescent trick played on the retina by a never-never landscape.

The little old white lighthouse sitting out on Long Point is the constant gauge, like an optical metronome, to which the eye always returns to discover the beat, the vibrations of each day's visual symphony. As William Butler Yeats said, "Lulled by this sensuous music one neglects monuments of unageing intellect." October fever makes you much lazier than spring fever. One almost forgets the hungers of the flesh—food, drink, sex, and the old agonbite of inwit, as Joyce called that indefinable gnawing in our viscera.

One of the blessings of October is that it signals the opening of the shellfish beds. The quahaugs, steamers, mussels, sea clams and bay scallops are plump, sassy, tasty, ready to be exploited and cooked into all sorts of fabulous dishes. In inland areas they harvest the fruit and grains of orchard, field and meadow, but here on Cape Cod we are blessed with the bounties of the sea, salt marsh and the intertidal stretches of beach. "*Frutto misto del mar*" mixed fruit of the sea—that's the poetic title which Sal del Deo gives to his mixed shellfish appetizer, and it has deep spiritual meanings, it's not just grub to gorge on.

And October begins some great offbeat fish-eating that you'll never encounter in a big restaurant, or read about in a cookbook, or see on a TV cooking program: small whitings, baby butterfish, and as the weather gets cold, codfish cheeks and tongues. Baby butterfish are one of the most delicious treats that Mother Ocean provides, and one of the rarest. They are only here during October, and sometimes many Octobers can pass when you'll never see a one of them. Then when they are plentiful, you can sit on the end of Town Wharf and, using the very smallest hook available, baited with a tiny piece of squid, you can snatch them in fast and fill a 10-quart bucket in a couple of hours. Large numbers of them get tangled up with the bigger fish in the fish traps or in the draggers' trawls, and this is one "trash" fish that the fishermen do not throw back. They save every one of them and pass them out to their relatives and friends. Sometimes a fisherman will bring a bucket of baby butterfish into Cookie's, and Joe and Wilbur will put on a fish fry. They'll fry these babies and the customers will sit there all afternoon nibbling the fish and washing them down with beer.

BABY BUTTERFISH FRIED

Baby butterfish are about the size of your little finger. You don't have to clean them. You just drop them whole in flour, then fry in deep hot fat until they are crisp, and drain on paper towels.

Serve them up piping hot. Sprinkle the little jewel with salt and pepper and a few drops of vinegar and plop it into your mouth and devour it, head, tail feathers and all. It's truly a one-bite fish. I hope that millionaire hostesses in Park Avenue penthouses never find out about baby butterfish. They're such a good hors d'ouevre that their price would rise as high as caviar and then us homefolks wouldn't get any.

He's a Good Skate

Another much maligned and neglected fish is the barn-door skate, and when you take one look at him you can see why. He'd never win a piscatorial beauty contest, yet, believe it or not, skate wings are one of the greatest of seafood delicacies. A high-class restaurant in France will murder your pocket book for a dish of *Raie au beurre noir* (skate with black butter).

RAIE (SKATE) AU BEURRE NOIR

Cut off the skate's wings and parboil them enough to remove the tough thick skin. Cut them up into bite-size scallops. Dip them in flour and fry them lightly. To make the black butter sauce, scorch a stick of butter in a skillet until it's a rich brown, add a clove of garlic, minced, the juice of ½ a lemon, salt and fresh ground black pepper. It gets poured over the finished product. But first take 3 tablespoons butter, 2 strips anchovy (or anchovy paste), a good dash of Tabasco, a generous sprinkling of paprika and scrunch it all up together until it is creamed. Smear it on slices of toast, lay the skate scallops on top and cover with the beurre noir. You don't have to go to Paris to eat well.

SKATE

PORTUGUESE SKATE STEW (ARRIAH)

Cook up a batch of molho tomate (page 49) and add a batch of skate wing scallops to it, simmer for 30 minutes, and there's your delicious "*arriah*." It's as simple as that.

An Ugly Specimen
But Delicious Dining

The goosefish is without a doubt the ugliest thing that swims in the sea. You won't find it on any restaurant menu or in the fresh fish markets. And this is a damn shame because it is one of the most delicious of fishes. Although it brings only about 10 cents a pound, Provincetown fishermen save all their goosefish tails. They are shipped to New York and there they are frozen and shipped to Spain and Portugal, where they are held in high esteem. So there we go, feeding other epicureans when we should be feeding ourselves.

A goosefish is a mouth with a tail attached. His mouth is so big he can swim up under an unsuspecting goose, or duck, or seagull and swallow him whole before the poor bird even knows what's happening to him. A few years back a group of boys were sitting around on the end of Town Wharf watching an old seagull paddling around in the water, when suddenly the gull just disappeared. A boy grabbed a knife and dove into the water; a few seconds later that badly frightened seagull rose to the surface and took off like a bat out of hell for Cuttyhunk Island. The kid had slashed a goosefish open and set the seagull free. There are many apocryphal tales of the things that have been found inside a goosefish's stomach.

To dress a goosefish you simply cut off the tail and throw the body away. The tail can be filleted horizontally, or cut crosswise into steaks and cutlets. The meat is very sweet and delicate in fla-vor, making it a favored choice for bouillabaisse and other stews.  It calls for good strong sauces with plenty of onions, tomatoes, garlic and things like that. It's great to dip the cutlets in flour and fry them in deep hot fat; although I usually look down on frying seafood, I make an exception for the goosefish. Captain Seraphine Codinha really dotes on boiled goosefish tails. Not just for dining pleasure but for very practical reasons. He has invented the "Cod-inha Crash Goosefish Diet," which is something that the dieting specialists all over the country should sit up and notice. By eating nothing but boiled goosefish tails for several months, he shed 120 pounds of fat, whittling himself down from 320 pounds to 200. We now call him Captain "Skinny" Codinha.

BOILED GOOSEFISH

Slice a head of cabbage into a good-sized pot. Slice ½ dozen large onions and add them to the pot. Cover with fish stock and boil until the vegetables are almost done. Add 2 or 3 pounds of goosefish slices and enough fish stock to cover. When it returns to a boil cook for 15 or 20 minutes more. Serve in large soup bowls. The broth is as good as the solid parts.

How to Cook a Sea Serpent

Some gourmets can't work up much enthusiasm for sea serpent, but other aficionados of the skillet will swoon with rapture at the mere mention of this seafood delicacy. True, it is rare, and hard to come by. And if you don't follow the proper procedures in preparing it, then its flavor is as rank as a dead jellyfish and as tough as petrified mammoth skin.

The only really good part to eat is the tail, starting just below the 132nd cervical vertebra and moving outward So you make like a chiropractor and count down to the 132nd knuckle of the backbone and cut off the tail and throw the front part away, or feed it to the cat. Cut off as many 1½ inch thick steaks from the tail as you and your family and neighbors can eat the first day, and put the rest of it in the deep freeze. It improves when aged about six months in the freezer. To tenderize each steak lay it on a thick block of wood and pound it for 15 minutes with a baseball bat, turning it over now and then.

Now to get rid of that high snakey flavor you coat each steak with ½ inch of salt on each side, and put them in the refrigerator to leach all night. Next day rinse off all the salt and put the steaks in a good Portuguese vinha d'alhos marinade for 2 or 3 hours, turning frequently. Take out of the marinade and wipe dry. Now you have two choices. Either broil the steaks in butter and serve with maitre d'hotel butter sauce, or dip them in batter and fry them in deep hot fat, and when done, cover with a good Portuguese molho tomato-wine sauce. Since serving sea serpent is a festive occasion you should provide a good Pol Roger or Piper Heidsieck so that everybody will be suitably anaesthetized.

Most of our local restaurateurs are too busy to get involved with the technicalities of preparing sea serpent, and the public is a little too squeamish about it anyhow, but if you are lucky enough to obtain a serpent who is neither too old and tough, nor too young and squishy, then I will be glad to come over to your house and cook him for you.

Provincetown's most famous sea serpent was the one seen around 1886 by town crier George Washington Ready, out at Herring

Cove, that body of water just this side of Race Point Light. Before the dike and the airport were built, there was a deep-water harbor out there, an ideal spawning ground for sea serpents. Mr. Ready said: "I was walking along the beach at Herring Cove when I saw a monster 300 feet long colored like a rainbow and with sharp bony scales like the teeth of a mowing machine. It scorched a path over the dunes, cutting down with its huge tail trees over a foot in diameter, and then disappeared in Pasture Pond. As it slid in, the water gradually receded until the pond was drained completely. Only a great hole remained in the center of the pond bed. I ran to town to get a 250 fathom sounding line but couldn't reach the bottom of the hole." That was the last anyone ever saw of the serpent.

According to Mr. Ready's description, this giant reptile looked very much like the one in our illustration. Since his name was G. W., there were few who doubted his veracity. The story was printed in newspapers all over the country, and Provincetown was pushing Loch Ness off the front pages. However, among gourmets who know, it is the smaller and less publicized serpents which make the best eating.

SEA SERPENT

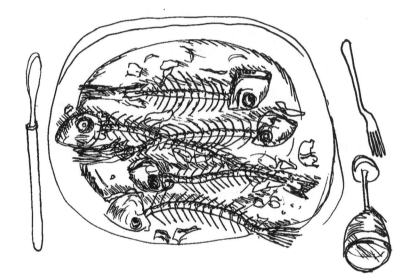

Index